The Ps...

Also by John L. Smith and published by Palgrave

The Psychology of Action

The Psychology of Food and Eating

A Fresh Approach to Theory and Method

John L. Smith

palgrave

First published 2002 by
PALGRAVE
Houndmills, Basingstoke, Hampshire RG21 6XS and
175 Fifth Avenue, New York, N.Y. 10010
Companies and representatives throughout the world

PALGRAVE is the new global academic imprint of
St. Martin's Press LLC Scholarly and Reference Division and
Palgrave Publishers Ltd (formerly Macmillan Press Ltd).

ISBN 0–333–80020–6 hardback
ISBN 0–333–80021–4 paperback

This book is printed on paper suitable for recycling and
made from fully managed and sustained forest sources.

A catalogue record for this book is available
from the British Library.

Library of Congress Cataloging-in-Publication Data

Smith, John L., 1945–
    The psychology of food and eating : a fresh approach to theory
and method / John L. Smith.
        p. cm
    Includes bibliographical references and index.
    ISBN 0–333–80020–6 (cloth)
        1. Food–Psychological aspects. I. Title.

    TX357 .S5584 2001
    641.3′01′9–dc21   2001045146

10   9   8   7   6   5   4   3   2   1
11   10   09   08   07   06   05   04   03   02

Typeset in Great Britain by
Aarontype Ltd, Easton, Bristol

Printed in China

To *AB*

Contents

List of Tables and Figures   x

Preface   xi

Acknowledgements   xviii

1 Introduction   1
Babies and Mother's Milk   2
Children and Food   6
Attitudinal and Cognitive Basis in Choice of Dish
    and/or Menu   10
Famine   13
Poverty and Malnutrition   17
Plan of the Book   21

PART ONE: FOCUS ON THEORY

2 Non-Biological Perspectives   27
Psychoanalytic Theory and the Good Breast (Freud
    and Klein)   28
Structuralism and the Culinary Triangle (Lévi-Strauss)   31
Food Codes and the Grammar of Eating (Douglas)   34
The Semiology of Food and Cooking (Barthes)   37
The Sociology of Contemporary Food Consumption
    (Warde)   40
Food Consumption, Class, and Cultural Capital
    (Bourdieu)   42
Conclusion   46

3 Hunger, Flavour, Digestion and Kitchen Chemistry   48
Hunger   49
  Stomach distension   49
  Homeostatic mechanism in the blood   50
  Hypothalamus as centre for control   51
  Neuropeptide Y and obese gene product   53
  Satiety signals   53

The Biochemistry of Flavour   54
  Taste   54
  Smell   57
Digestion   60
Kitchen Chemistry   63
Case Study: A Simple Lunch at Home   66
Concluding Discussion   71

**4 Eating Disorders: The Feminist, Control and
   Biomedical Discourses   74**
Anorexia Nervosa   75
The Feminist Discourse   76
  Post-structuralist, Lacanian discourse   76
  Conversations with anorexic women: Malson's analysis   82
  Orbach on female fatness   84
The Discourse of Control   89
The Biomedical Discourse   98
Concluding Remarks   101

PART TWO: POST-POSITIVIST RESEARCH REPORTS

5 Dinner Party (Agentic Participant Observation Case Study)   107
A-priori Hierarchical Analysis of the Dinner Party
  Episode   108
  Task and critical path analysis   109
Dramatis Personae   110
Episode A: Conception   112
Episode B: Advanced Preparation   120
Episode C: Penultimate Chores   123
Episode D: The Home Stretch   127
Episode E: Main Dinner   132
Episode F: End Game   138
Planning and Scheduling Issues   140
Conclusion   145

6 Eating Out in a Small Way (Idiographic Observation)   147
EO1: Self-Service Lunch at a Vegetarian Restaurant in
  Central London   149
EO2: Afternoon Snack in the Food Court of a Small
  Shopping Mall in Central London   154
EO3: English Breakfast in a Central London Hotel   160

EO4: Lunchtime Sandwich at a Riverside Pub in
Sunderland 163
EO5: Lunch at an In-Store Cafeteria in Sunderland
City Centre 166
Conclusion 170

7 Food Discourse (Magazines and Cook Books) **173**
Introduction 173
Women's Magazines 174
Elle (September 2000) 174
Cosmopolitan (September 2000) 180
Good Housekeeping (September 2000) 181
Cook Books 186
Concluding Comments 192

8 Conclusion **194**
Discourse Matrix 195
Preliminary Introduction to Hermeneutics 200
Food Texts and Hermeneutics 202
Future Directions 208

Appendix 1: Recipe for Potage au Potiron (Pumpkin Soup)
(Grigson, 1980) 214
Appendix 2: Recipe for Gorgonzola Cheese and Apple Strudel
with Spiced Pickled Pears (D. Smith, 1995) 214
Appendix 3: Recipes for Chocolate Chestnut Pavé and Chantilly
Cream (Willan, 1989) 217
Appendix 4: Costings for Dinner Party 219

Bibliography 221

Name Index 230

Subject Index 234

List of Tables and Figures

Tables

1.1   Table manners: comparison between 1701 English
       etiquette and 1997 Australian families   8
8.1   The location of discourses within the text   196

Figures

2.1   The culinary triangle   32
3.1   Conventional taste map for the tongue   55
3.2   Odour prism   58
4.1   Flow diagram for ordinary daily dieting   91
4.2   Flow diagram for weekly diet plan check   93
4.3   Self-control (dieting) feedback loop   95
5.1   Dinner party vertical timeline chart   111
5.2   Network diagram for dinner party sub-episode A
       (Conception)   113
5.3   Network diagram for dinner party sub-episode A^5
       (Define menu)   117
5.4   Network diagram for dinner party sub-episode B
       (Advanced preparation)   120
5.5   Network diagram for dinner party sub-episode C
       (Penultimate chores)   124
5.6   Sub-episode D (The home stretch): vertical timeline chart   128
5.7   Network diagram for dinner party sub-episode E
       (Main dinner)   133
5.8   Dinner party seating arrangements   137
5.9   Network diagram for dinner party sub-episode F
       (End game)   139
6.1   Hand-written field notes for Episode EO1   150
8.1   The textual world of food psychology   203

Preface

I've just been to the shops to get a loaf of bread. I can feel that it is still warm from the baker's oven as I take it into the kitchen. The crust smells fresh and yeasty. I start to make a sandwich for my lunch. I cut the bread, slice a tomato, and pick some basil leaves from a plant pot by the window; it's all done in a couple of minutes. I take a bite and start to chew. The aroma of the basil hits me, followed seconds later by the taste of the tomato. The texture and flavour of the bread runs through the whole experience, as one delicious mouthful follows another.

In describing my lunch I make the point that it is not always necessary to engage in elaborate preparation in order to produce a tasty snack, although I acknowledge that a diet based solely on tomato sandwiches might pall in times of plenty. I enjoy food, I like cooking, and I don't mind shopping for ingredients. I realise that this may be unusual for a man, since recent studies have confirmed the persistence of marked gender differentiation within family households along the traditional lines. Beardsworth and Keil (1997) in their review found the incidence of families where men break this norm to be as low as 1 per cent in some cases, and Gregory (1999), in her own study, could find only one family among 75 where this happened. In Warde and Hetherington's (1994) Greater Manchester survey, men prepared the meal in only 11 per cent of the households and shared in the preparation in only 5 per cent. The less extreme figures in this survey may have been due to the fact that there was a relatively high proportion of professional and managerial men in the sample.

It is not the case that all studies indicate a lack of change. Sullivan (2000), in her analysis of time-use diary data, has found some evidence for a drift towards equality. She examined data from surveys conducted across a twenty-year span from 1977 to 1997, in the UK. She was concerned with contribution to household domestic work, in general, rather than with food-related tasks in particular. She reported a modest increase in men's participation (in terms of time contributed) and a more substantial increase among 'egalitarian' couples who were full-time employed (see Sullivan, 2000, p. 453). However, with regard to food work, Warde and Martens (2000) report that, in a sample of 599 couple households, most tasks, with the exception of table clearing and dish-washing, were done predominantly by women alone. Even though the situation is less extreme than it was in the 1970s, male activity in the kitchen is not the norm. In view of this, it may be helpful to summarise those aspects of my biography which may throw some light on my situation, if not actually explain it.

My Culinary Background

My father died when I was a baby and I grew up in an extended family household. The majority of people living in the house were female, although I do have an elder brother. My mother went out to work and my great-aunt stayed at home to look after me when I was young. My aunt also did the cooking and she produced extremely tasty food, cooked in a conventionally English style. I believe she had done some cooking in the hotel trade when younger. As a psychologist looking back, I am sensitive to the fact that there were no obvious male role models in the house, excepting my elder brother. Both my grand-fathers died when I was fairly young. Of my two uncles, one emigrated to Australia and the other I seldom saw. Lest this picture appear too gloomy, I should add that there was lots of love within the household and, by and large, plenty of laughter.

My mother was the breadwinner, in the old-fashioned sense, and earned the family income from working as a secretary in the local government offices. My upbringing was conventional in terms of what was expected of boys and girls and I am not trying to give the impression that I was brought up in a family with progressive liberal ideas. At school, too, the prevailing gender stereotypes were endorsed. In fact the first time I seriously considered that gender roles might be anything other than what I had always assumed them to be would have been when I read Oakley's (1972) *Sex, Gender and Society* as an undergraduate. At the time, I felt that if men were ever to progress beyond merely being helpers in the kitchen, they needed to be given responsibility for the whole process of food preparation, at least for the meals they agreed or contracted to provide. I understood this process to include shopping for ingredients as well as finding recipes and doing the cooking. Apparently, it is still the case that many men find food shopping and other aspects of kitchen life to be a problem (see Gregory, 1999). Food shopping is something that I have always taken in my stride.

Back in the 1950s, I remember in the school holidays going to the shops at the end of the road to buy the family food supplies. This happened more or less on a daily basis. Working from a list, I would make separate calls to the baker's, the butcher's, the grocer's and the greengrocer's shops. Sometimes I would also call at the newsagent's and the ironmonger's (for paraffin or kindling wood). Usually, I made these trips on my bicycle. Of course, the days of local shopping are long since gone (at least for those of us gainfully employed in the Western industrialised nations) and I now make the weekly trip to the supermarket instead. I found the transition from local shopping to supermarket shopping reasonably straightforward.

Moving on from the acquisition of ingredients to their preparation, I was able to learn a few basic cooking skills at home while I was growing up. Some of these were acquired by hanging round the kitchen watching or helping my great-aunt as she made her pastry, baked her cakes, tended her roasts, or whatever. Then at a later stage, when I was a teenager, my mother made sure that I knew how to cook my own tea so that I could cope with things for myself on those occasions when my aunt was ill in bed and my Mum was at work.

When I married in the 1960s I took some interest in cooking but my wife was mainly in control of the kitchen. In fact I can remember it was she who made the tomato sandwiches I took to work for my lunch most days. At best, I played a rather subsidiary role as a willing helper when we were cooking for guests. After I divorced, in the 1970s, I shared a house with two of my fellow research students at Sheffield University. They later married one another and both became my life-long friends. In our shared house, we cooked in strict rotation. The rule we operated allowed the person whose turn it next was to cook, to decide precisely when he or she would cook and so we did not always eat together every evening. When convenient, the duty cook would announce his or her intention to provide a meal on a particular evening and check that everyone else would be home to eat it. Whoever cooked took responsibility for choosing what to do for the meal, buying the ingredients, and washing up the pots, pans and dishes afterwards. We felt that if the washing-up was delegated to someone else, this could have the effect of encouraging the cook to be unnecessarily extravagant in the use of utensils. Needless to say, we had no dishwasher (an inside toilet would have been a luxury).

Around this time I decided that I would try to improve my cooking skills. This was partly because I wanted my contribution to communal meals in the household to be more than just edible and partly because I was determined not to become over-dependent on the student union cafeteria. I worked autodidactically from a very helpful cookbook (Patten, 1972) and started to feel more at home in the kitchen. I remember that I began to make things like jam and bread, even though they were not especially relevant to the production of the evening meal. Over the years I bought more cook books (perhaps a few too many) and started to watch some of the food and cookery programmes on TV. I have maintained an active interest in cooking ever since.

Currently, I regard myself as a competent all-round home cook but by no means do I aspire to gourmet cooking. Compared to others, I think my interests may be a little narrow. For example, I have not taken the trouble to learn about many of the cuisines that are foreign relative to my own (Thai, Chinese, and so forth). Having said that, I regularly cook pasta and curry dishes but do so without going to any great lengths to check out their authenticity. Since becoming a vegetarian I no longer cook the traditional English meat dishes such as roast beef for Sunday lunch, shepherd's pie, or toad-in-the-hole, although I have sometimes made the latter with vegetarian sausages. While Rozin (1996) suggests that some vegetarians can be clearly classified as falling into one of two categories in terms of their motivation to adopt their position on food (moral-ecological vs. health), I see it more as a dimension than a dichotomy and would place myself mid-way, a little closer to the 'health' pole.

At home we have never achieved the ideal of commensality. My daughter eats healthily but she is very finicky and would not touch with the proverbial barge pole most of the dishes I prepare for myself. My partner and I tend to cook separately. In part, this is related to the fact that she eats fish and poultry whereas I do not. We take it in turns to cook for our daughter. On weekdays, we frequently eat at different times, depending on what we are doing. My daughter and my partner often eat their food while doing other things (e.g. watching films or TV, doing crosswords, reading, or listening to music). I often eat in the kitchen, rather than in the dining room, and listen to the radio. Sad but true.

I do like to cook for friends. We do not entertain very often but when we do I usually do the bulk of the cooking and try to make something special. In the house where we previously lived, the dining table was in the kitchen and I very much enjoyed that situation. In our current house, the kitchen is too small and so we eat in our dining room. In the old house because our friends were embedded in the general buzz and chaos that goes on with the preparation of any meal, the social event felt very informal. The geography of our current house seems to push the occasion in the direction of a formal dinner party. In Goffman's (1959) dramaturgical terms, the kitchen in our present house has become a separate back-stage area whereas, previously, there was no distinction between the consumption and production performance areas. Although I prefer the informal arrangement, it is not something that bothers me greatly. Having provided a thumbnail sketch of the development of my interests in food and cooking, I now turn to my background in psychology.

My Academic Background

Although I am a psychologist, I have not always been interested in the psychology of food. For many years I taught social psychology to university undergraduates and my previous book dealt with the psychology of action. I became interested in the psychology of food by a roundabout route. I was involved in the supervision of some research relating to attitude theory within social psychology and part of this was concerned with people's attitudes to healthy eating. I then began to read texts and academic papers on the topic of food, in general, beyond the narrow focus of attitudes. It was at this point that I began to find some difficulty in relating my interest in food and domestic cooking at home to the psychology of food that I was reading about in the academic texts. If anything, I was better able to relate my everyday experience in this domain to the *sociological* texts on food. I then began to think of this as something of a conundrum and that is what led me to write this book.

One of the reasons for the mismatch between my experience of mundane reality and its representation in the world of the psychological texts may be related to the fact that most of the texts appear to endorse the mainstream stance that psychology is, and ought to be, a positivist experimental science. This stance tends to be put forward most strongly by physiological psychologists. For example, Rowland *et al.* (1996) indicate their position in the following introductory statement:

> The philosophy of determinism states that a full knowledge of the content and structure of the brain will completely account for behavior. In the following, we implicitly assume this position with regard to eating behavior. (p. 173)

Interestingly, they later acknowledge difficulties in providing a physiological explanation of anorexia nervosa and bulimia nervosa partly because 'they involve complex sociocultural factors that evidently transcend the repertoire of rodents' (p.195). I think that this is where the approach of the scientific mainstream runs into difficulties. As long as the positivists stick to the explanation of behaviour and movement, determinism will do well. The mainstream scientific approach is less successful when it moves beyond behaviour and movement to grapple with the meaning of action within sociocultural contexts.

It so happens that I am not especially committed to the scientific mainstream in psychology. If anything, my interests are closer to critical social psychology. This is a term used to cover a broad mix of theoretical and methodological perspectives held together by a common antipathy for the doctrine of the objective experiment (see Spears, 1997; Smith, J.A. *et al.*, 1995a and 1995b). In my previous book, *The Psychology of Action* (Smith, J.L., 2000), I advocate an eclectic approach and I shall stand by that in this book. However, I shall rely on the published work of others to provide information relating to the laboratory and mainstream survey studies relating to food. Since these approaches are by far the most common for this topic, I shall attempt to redress the balance where I report my own research. My work has several characteristics that enable it to be placed within the realm of critical and/or critical social psychology. For example, I am fond of the idiographic case study (see Allport, 1962), incorporating participant and non-participant observation where appropriate. I like to include autobiographical associations as I generate and reflect upon these observations, in part, to force a reflexive element into my research activity. One consequence of this is to undermine the position that my psychological research might have pretensions to scientific objectivity in the sense that this term might be used in chemistry, for example (see Condor, 1997).

Smith, J.A. *et al.* (1995a) comment that the idiographic domain 'has been grossly neglected in mainstream psychology' (p. 59). There are thus few examples to hand which could act as a guide for such research. The influence of positivist psychology can often be seen to creep into qualitative approaches, even where these are supposedly closer to the hermeneutical endeavour. This is especially likely to happen if the researcher collects too much data: the temptation will be to use nomothetic techniques in order to cope with the volume. An obvious example would be the use of content analytic strategies involving counting as a way to simplify and summarise interview data, thus drawing the study away from the discursive approach. I feel deeply nervous about the use of computer text coding packages, in this regard, although they may have some application in grounded theory (see Charmaz, 1995).

Smith, J.A. *et al.* (1995c) warn that the case study should not be assessed by criteria formulated for experimental methodology. A large *n* and lots of data, by and large, is good for statistical analysis and makes people feel more confident when it comes to claims relating to universal statements and causal laws. This is a mistake for idiographic work: I hereby resolve not to collect too much data.

It is my impression that the bulk of the findings reported in the published literature on the psychology of food tend towards the nomothetic. I shall therefore seek to redress this balance with my own case study material later in the book, despite the fact that this strategy may not be welcomed by those wholly committed to the nomothetic way. Smith, J.A. *et al.* (1995c) provide encouragement in this regard:

> More pragmatically we would argue that, given the neglect of the idiographic level of inquiry and the consequent paucity of our knowledge about individual psychological functioning, there is some urgency in the need for projects which take as their task the detailed description of individual human beings. (p. 63)

Because there are so few idiographic studies available, it means that I shall have to develop my approach as I go: this is at the same time exciting and daunting for me.

JOHN L. SMITH

Acknowledgements

At home, Deborah and Natasha have been very supportive and I would like to thank them for that. At the publishers, Frances Arnold has been her helpful self, dispensing information and encouragement in equal measure.

Several people have helped me by providing suggestions for reading, lending me books and papers, talking to me, and so forth: Robert Pullen, Jacqui Rodgers, Adrian Smith (physiology and biochemistry of hunger, taste, smell and digestion); Maura Banim, Alison Guy, Sue Thornham (eating disorders, feminist theory, women's magazines); Barbara Dobson, Elizabeth Dowler, Sally Corbett (nutrition and poverty); Heather Neil, Joan Aarvold, Tony Machin (breastfeeding); Mary Dalgleish (infant spoon feeding skills); Mark Conner, Paul Sparks (social psychology of food); Kenneth Boyd (ethics of animal experimentation); Hugh Brayne, Graeme Broadbent (legal cases); Alan Hedge, Diane Westwood (kitchen ergonomics); Eliane Meyer (French translation). Even though I have not used everything, thanks anyway.

I am grateful to several of the above who read individual chapters in draft form for me and provided helpful comments and corrections: my nephew Adrian; my partner Deborah; my friends Maura and Alison.

I am also grateful to Sally Bannard of the Harrow Learning Resources Centre, University of Westminster, for giving me access to the 1954 French edition of *Elle* magazine.

In October 2000, I went to a performance of *Bella: The Story of Mrs Beeton* at the London Film and Food Fiesta in Notting Hill. This play was written and performed by Alison Neil. I subsequently wrote to her for some information and I would like to thank her for recommending further sources. While on this topic, I would also like to thank Valerie Mars (a social historian of foodways in the nineteenth and twentieth centuries in Britain) who provided me with several references relating to Mrs Beeton.

Sally Wiggins very kindly sent me the full text of a journal article (Wiggins *et al.* 2001) which, at the time I was writing my manuscript, was still 'in press' with the *Journal of Health Psychology*.

I would like to thank Dorling Kindersley and Anne Willan for permission to use her recipes for *chocolate chestnut pavé* and *Chantilly cream* which I have reproduced in Appendix 3. These are taken from her book *Anne Willan's Reader's Digest Complete Guide to Cookery* (1989).

I would like to thank Penguin Books, David Higham Associates, and Jane Grigson for permission to use her recipe for *potage au potiron* which I have reproduced in Appendix 1. This is taken from Jane Grigson's *Vegetable Book* (1979).

The recipes for *gorgonzola cheese and apple strudel with spiced pickled pears* from *Delia Smith's Winter Collection* (1995) by Delia Smith, reprinted in Appendix 2, are reproduced with the permission of BBC Worldwide Limited. Copyright © Delia Smith 1995.

JOHN L. SMITH

1

Introduction

Without food there is no life: the baby dies, the teenager becomes emaciated, famine decimates the whole population. Too much food can also be a problem: the risk of coronary heart disease, obesity, and bulimia nervosa. When approaching the topic of food, there are many things to take into account apart from the plentifulness of its supply. The huge changes in the production and consumption of food, started in the twentieth century, look set to continue in the twenty-first. The geneticists are modifying their crops; the engineers are developing ever more sophisticated machines with which to harvest them. Retailers in the Western world continue to market their produce in sheds that challenge the size, if not the majesty, of our medieval cathedrals. In terms of storage, the freezer, the can and the vacuum pack push the limits beyond the dreams of our grandparents. Global infrastructures erode the significance of season, while competition from the supermarkets threatens to destroy the traditional ways of country life. In the UK, modern industrialised farming techniques bring with them controversy, as one crisis follows another: BSE, the foot-and-mouth epidemic.

Although religion, custom and taste, solely or in combination, may dictate what is edible, how it should be prepared and how it should be eaten, the days when class or nationality provide a reliable guide to individual attitudes to food may be over as fragmentation into niche markets gains momentum. This process is not hindered by the proliferation of style gurus, media chefs and food writers.

There is no simple answer as to where and how psychology should make its contribution to an understanding of food; it is such a complex and rapidly changing topic. The problem is not made easier by the fact that psychology can in no sense be regarded as a straightforward academic discipline, as I intimated in my preface. At the millennium, psychology brings with it the twentieth-century inheritance of a disciplined, scientific approach in its mainstream, coupled with a range of flexible perspectives and looser research strategies emanating from its critical wings. In a nutshell, mainstream psychology tends to ground its explanations in the biological sciences while critical psychology has a

1

stronger allegiance to the social sciences, cultural studies and linguistic philosophy. I shall draw on both mainstream and critical approaches in this book.

Before I get down to business, I should perhaps mention that I have not singled out mainstream social psychological approaches to food (see Axelson and Brinberg, 1989) for special treatment. I have elsewhere discussed the post-positivist critique of experimental social psychology (see J.L. Smith, 2000) and, more specifically, offered an alternative interpretation (see J.L. Smith, 1999) of the influential theory of planned behaviour (see Ajzen, 1991). I do not wish to revisit these matters in the narrower context of food research, since I have nothing further to add. Conventional social psychological investigations will be dealt with alongside other mainstream studies.

I present this first chapter as something of an appetiser, prior to tackling theoretical approaches in Part One. I have chosen a rather mixed bag of topics, starting with babies, moving swiftly through child-hood, and on into adult tastes and attitudes towards food. Food can be such a joy but there are unpleasant aspects to be dealt with: I consider academic work relating to famine and poverty towards the end of this chapter; eating disorders I discuss in Chapter 4. Placing the work on famine and poverty in this chapter is, to some extent, an arbitrary decision but I feel that by dealing with it early in the book, it will serve as a reminder that much of what I talk about subsequently has to be seen in the context of the relatively affluent Western industrialised nations. I conclude the chapter with a plan of the book.

Babies and Mother's Milk

Eibl-Eibesfeldt (1970) singles out the infant's rhythmic searching movements for the nipple, where the head turns to the left or right, as one of the earliest of the fixed action patterns that can be observed in humans. After a few days this reflex changes to an oriented search for the breast. At this stage the infant turns towards whatever stimulus object touches its mouth:

> Initially the lips close firmly around the nipple area (areola papillaris) and suction is produced by a partial vacuum in the mouth cavity (pump sucking); later the tongue alone does the work involved in sucking by pressing the nipple against the roof of the mouth. During this lick sucking the corners of the mouth remain open. (p. 400)

Booth (1994) points out that this reflex sometimes consists of rapid bursts of sucks. He suggests that these tend to be non-nutritive (as would be the case where the baby is sucking on a pacifier or dummy). In normal feeding the sucking is more protracted. One way or another, the aim is to get the liquid down into the baby's stomach where it can be digested. The rate of ingestion may slow down if the milk in the stomach brings on drowsiness. Booth (1994) comments that drowsiness may occur where there is insufficient interaction between mother and baby. The remedy would seem to be more smiling, cooing and touching. Beeton (1861/1982) had some advice for middle-class nineteenth-century mothers in England (in her preface, she acknowledges help from an experienced surgeon on medical matters):

> The mother, while suckling, as a general rule, should avoid all sedentary occupations, take regular exercise, keep her mind as lively and pleasingly occupied as possible, especially by music and singing. Her diet should be light and nutritious ... Tapioca, or ground-rice pudding, made with several eggs, may be taken freely; but all slops and thin potations, such as that delusion called chicken-broth, should be avoided, as yielding a very small amount of nutriment, and a large proportion of flatulence. (p. 1034, #2473)

Her somewhat severe injunction against wind was counterbalanced by an extremely liberal attitude towards the partaking of alcoholic beverages. She felt that malt liquor would help to keep mind and body up to the required standard and recommended porter in cases where the supply of milk needed a boost. Mennella and Beauchamp (1996) describe studies they carried out where nursing women drank a small dose of alcohol in orange juice or drank some beer. They found that, contrary to folklore, the breast-fed infants consumed less milk after their mothers had drunk the small dose of alcohol.

Beeton (1861/1982) also offered a scientific explanation as to what happened to the mother's milk once it was in baby's tummy. She starts with the assumption that the process of making cheese will be familiar to most people, which, of course, it is not nowadays:

> The internal membrane, or the lining coat of a calf's stomach, having been removed from the organ, is hung up, like a bladder, to dry; when required, a piece is cut off, put in a jug, a little warm water poured upon it, and after a few hours is fit for use; the liquid so made being called *rennet*. A little of this rennet, poured into a basin of warm milk, at once coagulates the greater part, and separates

from it a quantity of thin liquor, called *whey*. This is precisely the action that takes place in the infant's stomach after every supply from the breast. (Beeton, 1861/1982, p. 1029, #2457)

That Beeton was moving along the right lines, here, is apparent from Fox and Cameron's (1961) *A Chemical Approach to Food and Nutrition*. They attribute the coagulation or clotting of milk in the stomach to the action of the enzyme rennin which brings about the conversion of caseinogen, one of the principal proteins in milk, to its coagulated form called casein which in turn reacts with calcium salts to become calcium caseinate, the tough clot (see also MAFF's, 1985, *Manual of Nutrition*, p. 36).

Beeton's (1861/1982) advice to mothers about drinking malt liquor and porter has a quaint ring to it now. The concerns of the present era tend to focus on the possibility that the mother might, through her milk, pass to baby noxious substances as a result of drug taking or smoking, for example. Eastwood (1997) reports that the breast milk of mothers who smoke cigarettes contains ten times the amount of cotinine, a stable metabolite of nicotine, when compared with non-smoking controls. On an even more serious note, further worries relate to the transmission of the HIV virus. Palmer (1993), while reporting studies which place the proportion of babies developing HIV infection from HIV-positive mothers at about 30 per cent, urges caution over interpreting such results: HIV-positive mothers tend to be discouraged from breastfeeding and therefore the sample size is often small and the results are difficult to interpret. Sachs *et al.* (2000), in an electronic letter to the *British Medical Journal*, raise more complex criticisms of controlled studies. They argue that, notwithstanding the risk of HIV transmission, it may be difficult to provide safe breast milk substitutes to children from underprivileged populations where water may not be clean and contaminated fluids may damage gastrointestinal mucosa, thus increasing the likelihood of disruption of immune barriers. In such situations, exclusive breastfeeding may still be the safest way to nourish the infant. Eastwood (1997) argues that in the Third World the benefits of breastfeeding exceed the potential risk of HIV transmission.

Setting aside the risks relating to the transmission of HIV, I turn now to the effect that the adequacy of the mother's diet may have on her milk production. Rasmussen (1992) in a discussion of the influence of maternal nutrition on lactation reports two studies involving undernourished mothers who were given a food supplement to their diet while breastfeeding. In one study (Burma) the mothers in the experimental group were given a curry of animal protein cooked in oil, delivered to their homes twice daily. In the other study (Guatemala), the mothers were given cookies. It was found infant milk intake improved in both studies, as a result of the supplement to normal diet. This suggests that an increase in the quantity of nutrition delivered to baby may be obtained from relatively simple environmental interventions (curry or cookies) without recourse to artificial formula feeds.

Palmer (1993) advances a wide range of powerful arguments in support of the view that babies should, ideally, be breast-fed. She feels that artificial feeding is especially dangerous in the poorer countries of the world. Palmer also discusses the fact that breastfeeding may cause the father to feel excluded. She sees this as a poor argument for switching to bottle-feeding. If fathers are going to be involved in bottle-feeding, she feels that they should also do all the other things that go to make up childcare. The general thrust of her argument, supported by an apt cartoon drawing against men, is that male bottle-feeders are doing it in order to satisfy their own emotional needs. I can't speak for all men, but I will say something about my own experience as a father. Of course, it must be borne in mind that I speak as a university-educated man living with my partner in a relatively wealthy industrialised Western country. Apart from having middle-class jobs, we are a small family. Still, I shall set these reservations aside and proceed nonetheless.

My daughter was bottle-fed when she and her mother came home after spending about a week in hospital since the birth. My partner had taken some maternity leave from work but I continued to go to work as normal. We had no extended family living nearby. Because my partner was going to be at home with our baby all day, we agreed that it would make sense if I did the night feeds, so that her sleep would be less disturbed. This I did for a relatively short period; our daughter quickly began to sleep through the night without waking up. As we got into the swing of parenthood, we agreed that I would participate fully in all aspects of childcare and so I did my fair share of nappy changing, bathing, burping, feeding, playing, dressing, and putting to bed. My partner returned to work after about four months.

I do not think Palmer's (1993) accusation that fathers become involved in bottle-feeding for their own emotional satisfaction applied to me. I realise that anyone of a psychoanalytic persuasion would be justified in attributing my denial to my own unconscious defence mechanisms. Notwithstanding this, I shall put forward my reasons. Firstly, there is an aspect of bottle-feeding which reminds me strongly of school chemistry classes (the measuring of quantities, the warming of liquids, the testing for temperature, the washing of bottles, the sterilisation of teats, and so on). This tends to place an extremely practical frame around the feeding episode and guards against an overly sentimental interpretation of the event. Secondly, I do not think it is helpful to classify bottle-feeding as a uniformly homogenous event in terms of emotional experience. My memory of bottle-feeding is that these occasions were like most other family interactions: there were the good, the bad and the indifferent. I think that how things turned out on any specific feed was largely down to how tired or fractious we both were at the time. Obviously, I would agree that bottle-feeding a baby is more pleasant than changing a nappy but I do not think that I would single out bottle-feeding as the supreme experience of parenthood. For example, I very much liked walking round the house with my baby daughter cradled in the crook of my arm; humming jolly tunes in the misguided belief that this might cause her to nod off to sleep. I also liked walking out with her in the pram. Palmer's (1993) view of the situation doesn't square with my experience.

Once weaned, the infant begins to eat solid foods and the study of appetite and nutrition has to take note of the difference between eating and drinking, hunger and thirst. However, Booth (1994) suggests that the distinction between hunger and thirst may not be clear-cut for the infant in the first few months of life and there may be little ability to discriminate milk from water. Interestingly, this is something that puzzled McDougall (1933) well into adulthood:

> Frequently I am at a loss to know whether I am hungry or thirsty; and I can then decide the question only by taking a drink of water. If this allays my craving, my appetite was thirst; if not, it is hunger. (p. 146)

He concludes that the one appetite requires both food and drink for its satisfaction. This is similar to Logue's (1991, p. 43) position. She argues that while eating helps to satisfy thirst, the satisfaction may also work in the other direction, with drinking taking the edge off hunger. Logue notes that the approach taken in the investigation of hunger is similar to that deployed in research into thirst (see Chapter 3 for a fuller discussion of hunger research). I now turn to consider the role that food plays in childhood socialisation.

Children and Food

Lyman (1989) reminds us that eating in childhood is not always a bowl of cherries:

We are told to eat nicely and not make a mess; or to eat so we will grow big and strong; or not to eat foods that will rot our teeth or make us obese. If we won't eat the cold mashed squash set before us, it is implied that we must somehow bear the guilt for the starving millions of the world. When parents pretend the food is really delicious, they begin to establish the child's realization that they are not always truthful. (p. 4)

I was once taken to tea with a distant aunt who tricked me into eating apricots (which were one of my least favourite fruits) by telling me that they were peaches. She seemed to gain some satisfaction when she revealed to me at the end of the meal that I had, in fact, eaten apricots and not peaches; I never trusted her again. Fortunately, I didn't have to cope with nonsense of that kind in my own home.

The concern for table manners is by no means a modern phenomenon. For example, some of the prohibitions and exhortations listed in a book of rules for children's behaviour, first published in 1701, are as follows:

Rule 1. Come not to the Table unwash'd or not comb'd.
Rule 2. Sit not down till thou art bidden by thy Parents or Superiors.
Rule 6. Find not fault with any thing that is given thee.
Rule 9. Speak not at the Table; if thy Superiors be discoursing, meddle not with the matter.
(Whalley, 1701/1983, pp. 31–2)

Visser (1991) provides an extensive discussion of the historical development of table manners. In terms of current practice, Grieshaber (1997) conducted an observational study of four Australian families and part of her work was explicitly concerned with the documentation of rules regarding table manners. She based her analysis on video records of the families in their houses, especially at mealtimes, and supplemented this with interview data. She coupled the methodological technique of analysing transcribed discourse with a Foucauldian theoretical perspective. An important part of her study was concerned with making explicit the ways in which the children's positioning within the practices of food preparation depended entirely upon their gender, but I shall not dwell upon that side of her work here. With regard to table manners, she lists a set of rules for each of the four families studied. In Table 1.1, I provide a comparison of some of the 1701 English rules with equivalents drawn from the 1997 Australian

Table 1.1 Table manners: comparison between 1701 English etiquette and 1997 Australian families

1701 etiquette book (from Whalley, 1701/1983)		1997 Australian families (from Grieshaber, 1997)	
Rule no.	*Rule*	*Family*	*Equivalent rule*
21	Lean not thy Elbow on the Table, or on the back of thy chair.	The Andersons	Elbows off the table.
22	Stuff not thy mouth so as to fill thy Cheeks; be content with smaller mouthfulls.	The Haineses	Not too much food in the mouth at one time.
37	Put not a bit into thy mouth, till the former be swallowed.	"	
24	Sup not Broth at the table, but eat it with a Spoon.	The Gordons	No drinking from the cereal bowl.
10	If thou want any thing from the Servants, call to them softly.	The Haineses	Speak nicely at the table.
26	Throw not any thing under the Table.	The Sullivans	Scraps to be put in the proper place.
34	Foul not the Table-Cloth.	The Gordons	Make as little mess as possible.
36	Drink not, nor speak with any thing in thy mouth.	The Gordons	Speak with an empty mouth.

research. I was surprised to find so many points in common, despite the cultural and historical distance between the sources. Of course, the 1701 English rules were not, as far as I am aware, based upon observational data in the formal sense that the Australian rules were. If the occasional reference to servants is anything to go by, the 1701 etiquette book was aimed at the upper classes. Grieshaber (1997) does not describe the families in her study in class terms but she does comment on their financial situation, living accommodation, and lifestyle. Two families (the Andersons and the Sullivans) were well off, while the other two (the Gordons and the Haineses) appeared to live more frugally. Some of the differences, not included in Table 1.1, referred to saying 'grace' in 1701 and not eating snacks between meals in 1997. In general, the 1701 etiquette book seemed to demand higher standards of deference and respect for elders from the children than did the 1997 rules for the Australian sample, although the Sullivans' rules (including a reference to smacking for transgressions during the meal) sounded a bit brutal to me.

Lupton (1996) discusses the part that food may play in the socialisation of the child. Where discipline is administered with a light touch, this may amount to little more than exerting some control over what the child eats and teaching polite mealtime behaviour and table manners. In Victorian England this may sometimes have been taken to extremes and used as a means to break the child's will. Mars (1993) comments that in the eighteenth century there was an emphasis on 'natural' foods for children (cultural interference through fancy cooking was seen as corrupting nature). On the basis of her analysis of child-care manuals, she argues that this attitude changed markedly during the Victorian era:

> As the nineteenth century progressed, this view shifted with nature increasingly seen as subject to man's control and subjugation. Children's food similarly became the vehicle in its turn for their control and subjugation. (p. 152)

The survival of the Victorian legacy could have unfortunate consequences. Birch and Fisher (1996) advise against coercing or forcing children to eat disliked foods since associative learning is likely to take place between the negative social context in which the coercion occurs and the targeted food and this will have the inverse effect on the child's taste preference to the one intended by the authoritarian adult. While the principles of associative learning provided Birch and Fisher (1996) with their argument as to why coercive tactics might backfire, social learning theory appears to have inspired Lowe *et al.* (1998) with ideas for a more positive approach to intervention.

Lowe *et al.* (1998) carried out an extremely creative study in which they encouraged children to eat foods (fruits, vegetables and pulses) which they had hitherto reliably refused at home. They made videos of older children, the 'Food Dudes' enthusiastically eating one of the specifically named target foods. The children on the video 'exhorted the viewer to do likewise in order to help the Dudes in their struggle against the evil Junk Food Junta' (p. 65). In general, this intervention proved to be effective in encouraging the children taking part in this home-based study to eat the targeted foods, compared to baseline consumption rates, but it was important that the children were rewarded for their behaviour, too. The effect remained when examined after two- and six-month follow-up periods, and the combination of peer group video-modelling with reward was far superior to either modelling or reward on its own. Lowe *et al.* (1998) found little generalisation effects when the vegetables or fruits were named specifically in the modelling (e.g. 'eat broccoli' or 'eat guava'). However, when they carried out another study in which general food categories were used in the modelling (e.g. 'eat all vegetables'), there was a better generalisation response. I move on now, from children, to consider preferences for foods and dishes in a more general fashion.

Attitudinal and Cognitive Basis in Choice of Dish and/or Menu

Lyman (1989) reports the findings from two surveys on liked and disliked foods. Both of these date back to the 1970s and must be regarded as culture specific to the United States. One (Meiselman and Waterman, 1978) surveyed US Armed Forces personnel; the other (Einstein and Hornstein, 1970) was based on samples of college and university students. The information so gleaned is not of great interest from a psychological standpoint, although it may have given caterers something to think about. For example, in the meat category, the Armed Forces personnel preferred roast beef to pickled pigs' feet and liked meatloaf more than pork chop suey. In the vegetable category, canned peas were seen as more preferable than Brussels sprouts (although I can't imagine why). The students had a negative view of Brussels sprouts and cauliflower, too; things like ice cream and beef-steak (although not necessarily on the same plate) were amongst their best-liked items. Lyman (1989) also reports on Moncrief's (1966) study of preferences for 132 natural and artificial odorants. Strawberries did well, coming second in the rank order, as did garden mint (21st). Onion and chives were less impressive, appearing in the middle of the ranks (52nd and 54th, respectively), but still a long way ahead of herring oil (121st).

The conventional concept of attitude and its measurement in relation to food research has recently been challenged by Wiggins *et al.* (2001) who argue that when people express a view as to the value of food in naturally occurring situations, such as mealtime conversations, it is likely that they will become engaged in a continuous process of negotiation and evaluation. They bring to bear a discourse analytic perspective to food preference and thus approach the topic from a post-positivist standpoint, emphasising the fact that food evaluations are often constructed in social interaction and should not, therefore, be seen as individual attitudes.

An interesting but non-discursive approach to qualitative data in food research is provided by Bredahl (1999) who used a laddering technique to elicit means–end chains from interviewees (from Denmark, Germany, UK and Italy) concerning their views on genetically modified products (yoghurt and beer). Although these products were described realistically, they were in fact only the imaginative creations of the investigators. Once salient attributes had been obtained, trained interviewers asked a series of 'why is that important to you?' type questions in order to reach the level of abstract values (e.g. happiness and inner harmony; responsibility for nature) at the end of the reasoning chain. This is what is meant by the laddering technique and it reminds me of Harré and Secord's (1972) procedure for obtaining second order accounts from first order explanations. Laddering is also one of the techniques used in personal construct theory (see Bannister and Fransella, 1971, p. 73). Bredahl (1999) goes on to code all the individually mentioned concepts into broader categories and then to provide hierarchical value maps. These are a form of graphic representation used to summarise data across a group of respondents and Bredahl was able to produce maps for each country, for each product. Although the respondents were aware of the benefits that had been added to the genetically modified yoghurt and beer, they regarded the hypothetical products as unwholesome and unnatural. I see this technique as lying somewhere between the mainstream and post-positivist research paradigms. Because of its reliance on coding and the fact that it does resort to a degree of quantification, it is perhaps located closer to the mainstream. The reason for my ambivalence is that the focus on constructs in the laddering technique and the subsequent production of hierarchical value maps has something in common with Q-sort methodology. Stainton Rogers *et al.* (1995, see pp. 248–53) defend Q as a bona fide method for social constructionist research and hence accept it into the post-positivist fold, despite its quantitative psychometric trappings. Following this short methodological discussion, I now return to a conventional experimental study, this time concerned with food preference as a function of mood state.

Lyman (1989) investigated food preferences and the emotions by asking students to imagine themselves experiencing a particular emotion (there were 22 in all) and then to indicate what foods they would like to eat or drink while in that state. When I examined his results, I found some evidence that common-sense expectations were confirmed. At the risk of being highly selective, I will provide illustrative examples of his findings in only two categories of foods: soup and dessert. I shall further narrow my treatment of his results by examining the percentage of respondents opting for food in each of these categories within just two of his emotion categories: happiness and loneliness. Fewer people opted for soup when happy (1 per cent) than when lonely (8 per cent). This pattern was reversed for dessert where 15 per cent chose it in the 'happy' condition compared with only 8 per cent in the 'lonely' condition (see Lyman, 1982). At a stretch of the imagination, it is possible to imagine that soup might be a comforting food to have when one is feeling lonely. Desserts, on the other hand, are perhaps more strongly associated with happy times and celebrations such as childhood birthday teas. Steptoe *et al.* (1998) studied volunteers working in a department store in order to investigate the relationship between stress at work and diet. They found that 'people ate more during periods of high work stress, and the food they ate was especially rich in fat and sugar' (p. 37). Putting this finding together with Lyman's (1982), it would appear that desserts may be multi-functional, given that they typically have a high fat and sugar content: they are the food of choice both when people are happy and when stressed.

Turning now to the process of food choice in the family, Stratton and Bromley (1999) conducted a qualitative survey involving interviews with some 80 British families. Their data yielded over 7000 coded belief statements, about personal experiences of food choice, from 149 family members. These data came from a total of 52 hours of interview tapes. It occurs to me that it would take a single researcher a full working week to hear all the tapes, assuming that he or she spends 8 hours per day listening non-stop. In order to cope with such a huge quantity of data, Stratton and Bromley (1999) used the Leeds Attributional Coding System which, as the name suggests, provided them with a standardised method for coding and classifying attributional statements identified in their data set.

Stratton and Bromley (1999) analyse the way food choices and decisions are viewed from the family perspective. They found that the mother plays a central role, not just in terms of determining her own preferences but also with regard to those of the rest of the family. They also found that the parents, as opposed to the children, take on the role of providers of food. It has to be said that these findings are not particularly surprising. More interestingly, Stratton and Bromley found that neither television advertising nor nutritional values for food appeared to have strong influence on food choices. This is good news for those who fear advertisers may be having a detrimental effect on family diet but it is disappointing for those involved in promoting healthy eating through public awareness campaigns. In general, the key issue with regard to the choice of a particular food tended to be whether or not the family would accept and eat it, as opposed to any considerations relating to nutrition or health.

The importance of the familiar has been demonstrated experimentally by Stallberg-White and Pliner (1999). They base their experiment on Rozin's (1983) idea that each culturally distinctive cuisine has its own set of flavour principles. Indian food is thus characterised by the use of spices such as cumin, coriander, chilli, turmeric, and so forth, while Italian food is more closely identified through the use of a combination of tomato, garlic, and olive oil. Stallberg-White and Pliner found that when novel foods were presented in combination with a *familiar* flavour principle sauce, participants were more willing to taste them than when they were presented without the familiar sauce (the presence or absence of the sauce for familiar foods had no effect on willingness). Returning to the work of Wiggins *et al.* (2001), for a moment, I feel that there is considerable scope for extending studies such as Stallberg-White and Pliner's (1999) into naturalistic settings where individuals negotiate whether to try or refuse novel foods at the family dinner table; such negotiations would then, once recorded and transcribed, provide data for a discursive analysis.

Attitude surveys on food preferences, for obvious reasons, tend to be carried out in societies where individuals have some degree of choice regarding what to eat. In general, it is assumed that they have access to an adequate basic diet. While this assumption may hold for most, if not all, people in the Western industrialised nations, this is frequently not the case in Third World countries.

Famine

The treatment of famine has mainly fallen to the sociologists (e.g. Mennell *et al.*, 1992) or to economists such as Sen (1981). Mennell *et al.* (1992) see a close relationship between three polarities: shortage and plenty, fasting and feasting, poverty and wealth. Famine or food shortages tend to be on such a scale as to affect whole social groups, classes or nation states. It therefore follows that psychology, which operates primarily at the level of the individual or small group, is likely to have less to contribute to problems in this area. This seems to be borne out by the lack of coverage for the topic in a number of recent texts. There are only three passing references to famine listed in the index of Booth (1994) and although Logue (1991) cross-references from famine to food-deprivation, there is no sustained treatment of the topic. Similarly there is no reference to famine in Lyman (1989) and the topic does not feature in Axelson and Brinberg (1989), although the latter do devote a chapter to a consideration of sociodemographic determinants of food-related behaviour. There is nothing mysterious about this state of affairs: there would appear to be a dearth of psychological research directly relating to famine. Rather than ignoring the topic, I have decided to offer a speculative discussion of ways in which existing psychological theory or research, whether in mainstream or critical paradigms, might be brought to bear on the issue. I fully admit that such links are tenuous and that the contribution of psychology, when compared to economics or sociology, is likely to remain slight. Nevertheless, I shall proceed.

Mennell *et al.* (1992) suggest that much empirical work in the sociology of food has been motivated by the desire to investigate poverty and to expose inequities in the distribution of nutrition, particularly in the industrialised societies. More recently such concern has encompassed poverty on the global level and, in this connection, they point to the work of Sen (1981) who has argued that people starve because they lack the entitlement to food rather than because there is not enough food per head of population. Lack of employment and hence the absence of a wage, lack of access to social security, or lack of ownership are factors which may be examined in the attempt to recast the phenomena of famine within the framework of human rights. Although Sen brings a cool economic analysis to bear on the problem, he also draws attention to the harsh realities of famine in an extremely moving fashion:

> The persistence of widespread hunger is one of the most appalling features of the modern world. The fact that so many people continue to die each year from famines, and that many millions more go on perishing from persistent deprivation on a regular basis, is a calamity to which the world has, somewhat incredibly, got coolly accustomed. It does not seem to engender the kind of shock and disquiet that might be reasonable to expect given the enormity of the tragedy. Indeed, the subject often generates either cynicism ('not a lot can be done about it'), or complacent irresponsibility ('don't blame me – it is not a problem for which I am answerable').
> (Drèze and Sen, 1989, p. 276)

Drèze and Sen's claim that people have become accustomed to the occurrence of famine suggests that a process of desensitisation has perhaps taken place. There may therefore be some potential in exploring the extent to which research carried out into desensitisation and media violence (e.g. Thomas *et al.*, 1977) has application to this phenomenon.

There may be some scope for generating research from both the mainstream and the discursive paradigms in relation to Drèze and Sen's view that cynicism and complacent irresponsibility may be common responses to news of famine. From the mainstream, Rotter's (1966) *locus of control* concept would appear to be germane, since only those with internal control in that situation will feel they can 'do anything about it'. With regard to complacent irresponsibility, both attribution theory (see Kelley, 1967), within mainstream social psychology, or accounting methodology (see Antaki, 1988), from the discursive stables, might be brought to bear on the issue. Accounting methodology could be used to explore the nature of excuses and justifications for inaction and denial of responsibility, while attribution theory could be used to investigate the way individuals attributed the cause of the famine internally to its victims. Another area of research, related to this, is concerned with the *belief in a just world* (see Lerner, 1980). Drèze and Sen (1989) say that

> The distinction between the problem of chronic hunger (involving sustained nutritional deprivation on a persistent basis) and that of famine (involving acute starvation and a sharp increase of mortality) is particularly important. (p. 7)

One prediction might be that those individuals with a high belief in a just world might be happy to help in times of famine, providing it is construed as a natural disaster (the disaster providing an obvious external cause for the plight of the victims). However, such individuals may not be prepared to help in situations of chronic hunger, since they may be at a loss to readily identify any specific factor in the situation that would invite the external attribution. Led to an internal attribution of chronic hunger, even if this is only by default, their belief in a just world will invite them to see the victims' plight as deserved (perhaps even mysteriously brought upon themselves).

Drèze and Sen (1989) place great importance on the unfettered expression of public concern and the demand for action. In their view, a free and critical press combined with a multi-party political system that provides an effective opposition to the government of the day, is one of the best safeguards against the occurrence of famine. There may therefore be some potential in exploring the way the mediated rhetoric of famine is processed by those who possess a high belief in a just world, as compared with those low in such a belief. I have deliberately entwined discursive, attitudinal and information-processing language games in making this suggestion since I feel that an eclectic approach to the research question might be interesting (I discuss eclecticism at some length in my previous book: J.L. Smith, 2000).

Drèze and Sen (1989) point out that although there will be conflict in famine situations over who is or is not entitled to the available food, there may be some degree of co-operation between the opposing factions. They coin the term *co-operative conflict* to describe the situation where the parties are each fighting against one another for a bigger *share* of the cake (conflict) while, at the same time, working together against the outside world (co-operation) in order to maximise the total size of the cake. Drèze and Sen (1989) give the example of workers and capitalists at loggerheads over the issue of share dividends and wage levels: if production is disrupted by their conflict, they will lose out to other competitors within the industry.

In mainstream social psychology, there may be some common themes with these ideas and Sherif's (1966) work on intergroup conflict and co-operation. One might think that the prospect of famine above all else (save impending invasion from hostile aliens) would count as a superordinate goal for the society under threat. Sherif was at pains to show how intergroup hostility and negative stereotypes might be exacerbated through win–lose competition over scarce resources. Sherif's work suggests the way in which a depressing downward spiral might be generated in a famine situation. Where the *haves* are in conflict with the *have-nots*, negative stereotypes and intergroup hostility might be expected to increase, thus making it less and less likely that the society, as a whole, will shift into the co-operative mode in struggling to achieve its superordinate goal (i.e. the avoidance of famine). It is here that psychological considerations become less than tangential. Drèze and Sen (1989) suggest that a vociferous and dramatic protest by the *have-nots* is extremely beneficial in providing an early warning for the possibility of famine (and obviously that is less likely to happen in highly repressive societies). In terms of Sherif's ideas, I see that as forcing a reconstruction of the situation onto the *haves* which, in turn, may lead them to embrace the superordinate goal of preserving their society. If the *haves* do not respond to pressure from the ground, they run the risk of a breakdown of their own society (their workforce may be decimated by the famine; anarchy or some other arrangement incompatible with the status quo may ensue). Another possibility is that the *haves* do hear the warning but, through their own incompetence or ineffectiveness, bodge the job of doing anything about it.

Drèze and Sen (1989) seem to think that it is better to leave the shifting and distribution of the food from one geographical region or social group to the other to the existing private commercial sector than to risk governmental inefficiency. If the government gets warning of the famine early enough, huge public works schemes involving cash for labour may be quickly put in place to ensure that the money gets through to those who need it. The demand of the labour force will then draw the supply of food to where it is required. Drèze and Sen (1989) point to India, since independence in 1947, as providing an excellent example of this approach to the avoidance of famine. Although these broader considerations lie primarily in the domains of economics, politics and, possibly, human geography, I have indicated that there is nevertheless scope for psychology to make an albeit limited research contribution to this topic.

Poverty and Malnutrition

Poverty and malnutrition are not the same as famine. However, when, as is often the case, the industrialised nations are set to one side in any discussion of Third World famine, it would be wrong to think that the provision of food was uniformly bountiful to all citizens residing within those nations. Dirks (1980) suggests that Britain, France and the German states were suffering famine in one region or another approximately every couple of years up until the latter half of the nineteenth century (i.e. around the time Mrs Beeton was advising the nursing mothers to eat up their rice pudding – see above). It is difficult to comment on the precise extent to which poverty is a now prevalent problem. Dowler and Dobson (1997) report the proportion of the populations in the UK and Europe living below 50 per cent of average national income in each country (their figures are for 1988): Greece, Italy, Portugal and Spain had high levels (17–32 per cent) whereas the UK, France and Ireland were about average at 15 per cent. I find it difficult to picture what these abstract figures mean. Dowler and Dobson (1997) give an absolute comparison of expenditure for average UK households in the top and the bottom income quintiles. The richest households spent £21.50 per week on alcohol and £73.63 per week on food; the poorest households spent £2.91 on alcohol and £21.07 on food (Dowler and Dobson, 1997, p. 54). It is interesting to note that the richest households spent as much per week on booze as did the poorest on food. Much of the research on poverty and nutrition is based on families (whether single-parent or not) whose situation enables them to be construed as households.

The relation between nutrition and poverty is complex. Dowler and Dobson (1997) point out that setting the criteria or cut-off point for inclusion in 'poverty' poses governments with a difficult problem. Given pressure to reduce public spending, the aim will be to set the threshold at the minimum level for subsistence. Because food is one of the most basic requirements for subsistence, it is tempting to look for an operational definition of poverty that is partly based upon energy intake requirements and nutrient levels. Dowler and Dobson (1997) explain how, although not an ideal approach, reference intakes based upon group average figures can serve as the basis for devising minimum food baskets. These can then be costed in terms of average prices in the sorts of shops that will exist in the neighbourhoods where those in poverty will buy their food (and these are unlikely to be the out-of-town superstores). The cost of the minimum food basket then has to be related to household income since this is likely to be the figure that will form the basis of a decision as to whether the family qualifies for social assistance or income support. Dowler and Dobson (1997), working from UK Department of Health reports, demonstrate just how difficult it is to disentangle the links between income and nutrient outcomes. Although guidance may be produced from nutritionists on how to optimise the diet on a frugal budget and a rational approach to shopping may suggest ways to cut costs, it will be almost impossible for households in poverty to act in accordance with such optimal strategies.

Dobson (1997), moving away from formal definitions and formulae for poverty and nutrient intake, describes what it is like for families struggling to subsist at or close to the minimum level. I shall not attempt to report all aspects of her work; a few points will suffice to bring home how difficult this situation is. Economies in food purchase are likely to be found in competitive prices offered by bulk buying at large supermarkets. Such a strategy will be frustrated for several reasons. It is unlikely that a poor household will have access to transport to get to out-of-town supermarkets. Even if transport could be found, the purchase of a large quantity of food in a single trip to a supermarket would result in a further set of problems. An abundance of attractive items of food lying in the fridge or kitchen cupboard may prove too tempting for hungry members of the household. It will only take a few of these items to be eaten spontaneously ahead of the planned meal schedule and all the savings from bulk purchase will be wiped out.

Some items purchased by poor families may appear as luxuries when judged by the criteria of their contribution to the minimal nutrition level. Dobson (1997) argues strongly that it is necessary to take into account the social and psychological context within which poverty is being lived out. Speaking of those participating in a UK series of case studies, she says:

All the families bought snacks such as biscuits, chocolate and crisps, items that could be seen as extravagances. However, the families all had very good reasons for these purchases. Their experience had taught them that if their children went to school without similar food and snacks as their peers they were teased and risked being ostracised. The experience of poverty can isolate and stigmatise families. These families were aware of this and wanted to protect their children. (p. 42)

It can also be difficult to introduce innovation into the family diet through the use of novel yet nutritious items or ingredients. Nutritionists may speak highly of lentils but if a family has never eaten them, and if lentils do not feature as part of the 'normal' diet within the local culture, then there is the risk of both social ostracism and food wastage if family members reject the new food as unpalatable (see Dobson, 1997, for a fuller discussion of these points). Incidentally, Dowler (1997) insists 'there is no evidence that poorer people are less well informed or worse at budgeting than the general population' (p. 89).

As with famine, so also with poverty; it is sometimes difficult to see how psychology might play a role or where it might make a useful contribution. Dowler and Dobson (1997) make the point that to set food consumption at the minimum level for survival might not be sufficient to enable a normal social, economic, and physiological life to be lived. This reminds me of Maslow's (1968) theory of personality. The goal to which human beings may aspire is that of self-actualisation where the individual's full potential may be realised. However, self-actualisation requires freedom for the development of an individual's talents and capacities and for this to be possible other needs lower in the hierarchy and closer to the fundamental bodily needs have to be satisfied. Beneath the apex of Maslow's hierarchy lies the need for respect, esteem, approval, dignity and self-respect; beneath this level lies the need for friendship, affection and love that may be provided through a sense of belonging to family or community, for example. Then comes the need for protection, safety and security. At the bottom of the hierarchy lie the basic bodily needs, including the need for food (see Maslow, 1968, pp. 199–200). If the basic needs are frustrated, this view suggests that there is not a lot of point in talking about the higher needs: it is mainly in relation to the higher needs that the relevance of psychology becomes apparent. The various definitions of poverty that have been advanced recently may be seen to relate to different levels of Maslow's hierarchy. Dobson (1997) provides the following definitions:

> *Absolute* poverty is the term used for those living below a minimum standard and is defined in terms of subsistence items and conditions. These measures are used to define a level of income necessary to meet basic biological needs and are essentially for survival ... *Relative* poverty is defined in relation to a generally accepted standard of living in a specific society at a specific point in time, and it goes beyond basic biological needs. According to this definition poverty is not simply a lack of money but it is also about exclusion from the customs of society. (pp.33–4)

The definition of absolute poverty seems to be concerned with satisfying the needs at the most basic level of Maslow's hierarchy, while the definition of relative poverty requires some satisfaction beyond that (although not far beyond, it has to be admitted). Maslow's humanistic psychology was developed many years ago and was influenced, to some extent, by the existential philosophy of Sartre. The importance of the bodily and mental health of individuals and the acknowledged potential of the environmental and social context for facilitating or frustrating the attainment of these goals is something that currently concerns critical and community psychologists.

Prilleltensky and Nelson (1997) argue that community psychology has placed too much emphasis on the values of health, caring and compassion, self-determination and participation, for example, and has allowed the value of social justice to be pushed too far into the background. They draw on the work of Rawls (1972) in relation to social justice, and consider communitarianism (Etzioni, 1993) as providing some encouraging ideas on how to move forward in the future. They see mainstream psychology as working with a person-centred orientation, as opposed to community psychology which, as the name implies, involves collaboration with groups in the neighbourhood, and in organisations. They feel that giving the concept of social justice a more prominent place in their work will shift their objectives from amelioration to transformation. They acknowledge that this will not be easy:

> Our historical analysis suggests that most of our work as community psychologists tries to ameliorate living conditions within the

existing distribution of wealth and resources. Herein lies the main barrier for the fulfilment of our mission For as long as we try to address only the consequences of an uneven allocation of resources, without looking at the problem's root cause, we confront only the surface of the issues. (Prilleltensky and Nelson, 1997, p. 170)

The fact that the richest families in the UK can spend as much on booze per week as the poorest spend on food (see my discussion of Dowler and Dobson, 1997, above) indicates that the situation is beyond amelioration and that is why I think that the position of critical psychologists, such as Prilleltensky and Nelson (1997), is relevant to the psychology of food in this context. Most of the research I have discussed relating to poverty and nutrition is concerned with households, even though they may be located in difficult conditions. Beneath this poorest stratum of society, there lie the homeless, migrants, refugees and asylum seekers. Coufopoulos and Stitt (1997) confirm that their sample of homeless respondents had lower energy, protein, calcium, iron, vitamin C and fibre intakes than average. They also had higher total fat, saturated fat and sodium intakes than average. If these groups of people slip through the net of sociological research based upon households, they also would appear to be relatively invisible in psychological research. I turn now, in the final section of this chapter, to provide some indication of what is to follow in the remainder of the book.

Plan of the Book

I have grouped three chapters into Part One on the grounds that they are mainly theoretical in nature. Three more chapters, containing research reports, comprise Part Two.

In Chapter 2, I consider a wide range of non-biological perspectives on food. It is not uncommon, when reading mainstream texts on food, to find that the material is indistinguishable from that which one might encounter in biology, physiology or neuroscience. I have already intimated that I wish to counteract an over-dependence on the mainstream with a coverage of psychological approaches closer to the social sciences. I therefore make no apology for covering material largely drawn from sociology and social anthropology, as well as psychoanalysis.

I delay presenting the scientific background to hunger, taste and digestion until Chapter 3. I have to cover some disturbing experiments as I move through this material and I take pains not to endorse the use of animals in this research. I then move on to comment, more cheerfully, on how useful a knowledge of kitchen chemistry can be to the cook. Had I left things as they stood, at this point, this chapter would have provided a straightforward sketch of the scientific underpinning of matters in the kitchen, the mouth, the nose and the gut. The temptation to muddy the waters was too great and I was unable to resist inserting a phenomenological case study at this point.

In Chapter 4, I consider three theoretical discourses relating to eating disorders, with the emphasis on anorexia nervosa. Some of the physiological material already introduced in Chapter 3 provides a good introduction to the biomedical discourse. I revisit the psychoanalytic discourse, this time in a contemporary feminist-Lacanian guise. I also examine the cybernetic discourse of control, based upon cognitive behavioural theory. I hasten to add that I am not a clinician and this is not an area where I have been involved with research. I therefore rely on my source material for all information relating to this topic.

In Part Two, I present research reports which I have carried out primarily from an idiographic stance. I devote the whole of Chapter 5 to a case study of a dinner party I gave for two of my research students and their partners. I am mainly concerned to analyse the dinner party as an exercise in skilful planned action and I pay very little attention to the dynamics of the interaction around the table. In developing my analysis I adopt a cybernetic approach where possible, drawing upon the techniques of hierarchical task and critical path analysis (there is thus some similarity with the cybernetic discourse of control previously introduced in Chapter 4 in relation to eating disorders). My approach to the dinner party draws more on these aspects of industrial psychology than it does on social psychology (mainstream or otherwise).

I move from eating in to eating out, in Chapter 6. I introduce case studies based upon field notes I collected while eating out at five varied locations. These were all idiographic records of meals that I would have eaten even if I had not been carrying out the research. Like the dinner party reported in Chapter 5, the episodes occurred naturally in the flow of my everyday life. On more than one occasion I found that my research interfered with the enjoyment of my meal and this was sometimes annoying. In Chapter 7, however, I present an analysis of food discourse. This analysis was done on purpose as a research exercise and I construe it as far from quotidian in this regard.

In Chapter 7, I examine food discourse as it appears in two categories: articles in women's magazines and cookbooks. Following my discussion of anorexia, in Chapter 4, it is hard not to be drawn into an analysis of the images of women presented in these magazines. Because the preponderance of the ectomorphic waif as photogenic model is so obviously there for all to see, I do not feel that there is any need for me to labour the point. I therefore resist the temptation to be distracted by such an analysis, save the most cursory and superficial comments, since it would take me away from the primary topic of food.

I start the concluding chapter with a discussion of multidisciplinarity within the domain of food research. I then review the way I have woven together various discourses, drawn from a range of paradigms and disciplines, in the production of this text. I go on to develop a hermeneutic framework within which this and other texts on food psychology may be placed. I finish by offering some speculative comments on the future for psychological research into food and food-related issues.

Part One

Focus on Theory

2

Non-Biological Perspectives

In the preface, I mentioned that my alignment was closer to critical social psychology than to the experimental mainstream. This being the case, my preference is to look to the social sciences, as opposed to the biological sciences, to provide a framework within which to ground the psychology of food. It is for this reason that I decided to deal with the social scientific material ahead of the biological which I explore in the next chapter; I did not want it to appear as though I endorsed the biological perspective as taking pride of place in the pecking order, as it were. However, I hasten to add that it should not be assumed that I agree with everything produced by the social scientists, be they anthropologists, structuralists, semiologists or sociologists.

I shall deal with what I take to be some of the most relevant socio-logical approaches to contemporary food consumption towards the end of the chapter, and, because Bourdieu's work is especially relevant in this regard, I single him out for separate treatment. Before I do this there are several other approaches I wish to cover. One of the founda-tions of discursive psychology is semiology and so I feel that a consid-eration of some of Barthes's writing on food is not out of place at this early stage. Although I think of Barthes primarily as a semiologist, he has roots in structuralism, and I shall cover the latter in relation to Lévi-Strauss's work on food (the culinary triangle). I have to admit that I find Lévi-Strauss's ideas somewhat fanciful: as an antidote I explore the more down-to-earth work of the social anthropologist, Douglas (she also operates within the structuralist tradition). Whereas Lévi-Strauss strains for the structure of the cosmos, Douglas contents her-self with the structure of *meat-and-two-veg*. Social anthropologists are not always concerned with deep structure and some are content to document the social function of food-related activities. For example, Mennell *et al.* (1992) discuss the case of a woman preparing porridge (taken from Richards's, 1939, study of South African tribes). They suggest that the function of this culinary activity goes beyond the preparation of a meal to the expression of her sentiments towards her male relatives. Other writers, especially those of a psychoanalytic persuasion, have concentrated not so much on the social function of eating as on the sexual function. Their approach is to speculate on how our early experiences of eating, shot through with intense sexual feelings, may affect our subsequent behaviour as adults. I fail to see how I can avoid saying something about Freud and so I will dive straight in and get it over with.

Psychoanalytic Theory and the Good Breast (Freud and Klein)

For Freud, the early experience of the child or baby is extremely important for their psychological development. He makes the reasonable assumption that with most children their first experiences of ingesting food will be at their mother's breast. He is quick to emphasise the pleasurable nature of this experience:

> When children fall asleep after being sated at the breast, they show an expression of blissful satisfaction which will be repeated later in life after the experience of a sexual orgasm. (Freud, 1963/1973, p. 355)

I often wonder how he knew that. Hmm ...

> Sucking at the mother's breast is the starting-point of the whole of sexual life, the unmatched prototype of every later sexual satisfaction, to which fantasy often enough recurs in times of need. This sucking involves making the mother's breast the first object of the sexual instinct. I can give you no idea of the important bearing of this first object upon the choice of every later object, of the profound effects it has in its transformations and substitutions in even the remotest regions of our sexual life. (Freud, 1963/1973, p. 356)

This is an argument that has not been lost on 'Page 3' editors of the British tabloid press. It has been taken up less enthusiastically by mainstream psychologists. However, the idea has been developed in an interesting fashion by Klein (1981) who introduces the concept of the good (and the bad) breast.

Klein (1981) starts from Freud's pleasure–pain principle which captures the fact that the tiny child is only concerned with immediate gratification or the lack of it:

> Thus, the breast of the mother which gives gratification or denies it becomes, in the mind of the child, imbued with the characteristics of good and evil. Now, what one might call the 'good' breasts become

the prototype of what is felt throughout life to be good and benefi-
cent, while the 'bad' breasts stand for everything evil and perse-
cuting. (Klein, 1981, p. 291)

Given that she is working from within the psychoanalytic framework,
she is able to draw upon all the usual defence mechanisms to supplement and develop her ideas around the good/bad breast. So, for
example, she argues that the child *projects* his or her own active hatred
towards the bad breast onto the breast itself. At the same time, the
child also *introjects* everything he or she perceives in the outside world:

> To begin with, the breast of the mother is the object of his constant
> desire, and therefore this is the first thing to be introjected. In phan-
> tasy the child sucks the breast into himself, chews it up and swallows
> it; thus he feels that he has actually got it there, that he possesses the
> mother's breast within himself, in both its good and in its bad
> aspects. (Klein, 1981, p. 291)

These cannibalistic tendencies lie at the heart of oral sadism. Other
things become tied more obliquely to food as this sadism develops on a
wider front:

> The child expects to find within the mother (a) the father's penis,
> (b) excrement, and (c) children, and these things it equates with
> edible substances ... Thus the child's sadistic attacks have for their
> object both father and mother, who are in phantasy bitten, torn, cut
> or stamped to bits. The attacks give rise to anxiety lest the subject
> should be punished by the united parents, and this anxiety also
> becomes internalized in consequence of the oral-sadistic introjection
> of the objects and is thus already directed towards the early super-
> ego. (Klein, 1981, p. 219)

The child's arsenal then becomes supplemented with items associated
with urethral and anal sadism:

> In phantasy the excreta are transformed into dangerous weapons:
> wetting is regarded as cutting, stabbing, burning, drowning, while
> the faecal mass is equated with weapons and missiles. At a later
> stage of the phase which I have described, these violent modes of
> attack give place to hidden assaults by the most refined methods
> which sadism can devise, and the excreta are equated with poison-
> ous substances. (Klein, 1981, pp. 219–20)

I have included reasonably extensive quotations from Klein, since I thought that readers might think that I was making it up if I merely reported the gist. It is difficult to know how to handle this material. In order to deal with it seriously, one is likely to be sucked into the psychoanalytic language game and that may well be too high a price to pay for mainstream psychologists. One possibility is to stay firmly within the bounds of common sense and to reject the whole thing as a 'load of old tosh'. The psychoanalyst would be likely to construe this as a convenient way of preventing potentially disturbing material of a personal nature seeping into one's consciousness; the outright rejection would thus be accounted for in terms of defence mechanisms. This is a very common situation with regard to any challenge to psychoanalytic theory: heads Freud wins, tails you lose.

Mainstream psychologists are likely to demand testable hypotheses that can be checked through empirical methods. The problem is that it is difficult to see how the canons of science can be applied to psychoanalytic material. Freud acknowledges that analysis uses knowledge of infantile experiences to get at the client's symptoms. At first blush, it may seem that the reports offered by clients of their early experiences might be subjected to something approaching the rigour of scientific checking. Freud blocks this avenue:

> Well, the surprise lies in the fact that these scenes from infancy are not always true. Indeed, they are not true in the majority of cases, and in a few of them they are the direct opposite of the historical truth. (Freud, 1963/1973, p. 414)

Freud is not worried by the fact that his clients' reports may not always square up with reality. For him the important thing is what the reports, *qua* phantasies, may reveal about the clients:

> The phantasies possess *psychical* as contrasted with *material* reality, and we gradually learn to understand that *in the world of the neuroses it is psychical reality which is the decisive kind.* (Freud, 1963/1973, p. 415; emphasis in the original)

This sounds deceptively close to the contemporary debate about realism and relativism which abounds in critical social psychology (I discuss this in greater detail in my previous book: J.L. Smith, 2000). However, I think that a distinction can be made, since the contemporary debate is centred on an argument about objective reality and whether it is ever possible to check statements made in language against it. The situation with Freud is more similar to that of Lewin. Freud seems to acknowledge an objective or material reality and contrasts this with phantasy. Lewin, too, contrasts the reality of his two-dimensional representations of the life space with degrees of irreality which shade off into the imaginary (see Lewin, 1936/1966).

Rycroft (1970) argues that Freud was not so much engaged in the scientific procedure of elucidating causes but was concerned more with questions of understanding and semantics (he makes the point that Freud entitled his famous work on dreams *The Interpretation of Dreams*, and not The *Cause* of Dreams):

> If psychoanalysis is recognized as a semantic theory not a causal one, its theory can start where its practice does – in the consulting room, where a patient who is suffering from something in himself which he does not understand confronts an analyst with the way in which repudiated wishes, thoughts, feelings and memories can translate themselves into symptoms, gestures and dreams, and who knows, as it were, the grammar and syntax of such translations and is therefore in a position to interpret them back again into the communal language of consciousness. (Rycroft, 1970, p. 330)

Another, less individualistic approach to deep semantics is provided by the structuralists, and I turn now to consider Lévi-Strauss.

Structuralism and the Culinary Triangle (Lévi-Strauss)

Lévi-Strauss, the French anthropologist, is perhaps the best known of the structuralists. He examines surface phenomena from a wide range of cultures in order to articulate the deep underlying structures that are responsible for the patterns at the surface. According to Beardsworth and Keil (1997):

> These patterns are the deep structures, structures which represent the unvarying foundations of the enormous diversity of surface cultural forms which we can observe. There is assumed to be an affinity between the deep structures of the human mind and the deep structures of human society. (pp. 60–1)

In this regard, there may be some similarities with Carl Jung who looked for deep patterns in relation to dreams and myths across cultures and postulated the collective unconscious.

RAW
roasted

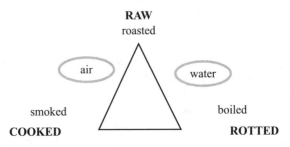

smoked
COOKED

boiled
ROTTED

Figure 2.1 The culinary triangle
Source: Adapted from Lévi-Strauss (1966).

Lévi-Strauss's major conceptual contribution to the social anthropology of food was the culinary triangle (see Figure 2.1). In this scheme, food is regarded as *cooked, raw* or *rotten*. Raw food becomes cooked by cultural transformation; both raw and cooked food may become rotten by natural transformation. Lévi-Strauss (1966) acknowledges that there may be variation between cultures in terms of what specific foods fall into these categories. He illustrates the point with respect to the term 'rotten':

> And we know from some incidents that followed the Allied landings in 1944 that American soldiers conceived the category of the rotted in more extended fashion than we, since the odor given off by Norman cheese dairies seemed to them the smell of corpses, and occasionally prompted them to destroy the dairies. (p. 587)

Lévi-Strauss (1966) regards two modes of cooking as discernible in most societies: roasting and boiling. Roasting, he deems to be close to nature since the food is directly exposed to the fire. However, boiling is seen as being different on the grounds that both the receptacle and the use of water involve some degree of cultural mediation. Within the culinary triangle, he places the roasted in the vicinity of the raw, while the boiled is positioned nearer to the rotted. Smoking, he acknowledges, is a technique that has something in common with roasting: both expose the food directly to fire. He argues that the principal distinction between the two methods is that the layer of air that separates food from fire is smaller for roasting than it is for smoking. Of course, smoking requires some form of culturally produced apparatus and thus has something in common with boiling. However, the product (e.g. smoked meat or fish) is more durable than most other cooked foods and in this regard may be regarded as a form of cultural acquisition. Lévi-Strauss takes the method of smoking used by American Indians as his primary illustration for his argument. He notes that the wooden frame they use to position the meat above the fire is about five feet high. This frame is then destroyed immediately after use. He contrasts this procedure with the way pots and pans are carefully cared for. He summarises the main aspects of his scheme as follows:

> The smoked and the boiled are opposed as to the nature of the intermediate element between fire and food, which is either air or water. The smoked and the roasted are opposed by the smaller or larger place given to the element air, the roasted and the boiled by the presence or absence of water. The boundary between nature and culture, which one can imagine as parallel to either the axis of air or the axis of water, puts the roasted and the smoked on the side of nature, the boiled on the side of culture as to means; or, as to results, the smoked on the side of culture, the roasted and the boiled on the side of nature. (Lévi-Strauss, 1966, p. 594)

He then deals with a number of other cooking techniques, of a less basic nature. Grilling, because the distance between fire and meat is less than for roasting, will be placed closest to the raw apex, with roasting lying between grilling and smoking. Steaming, because the water is at a distance from the food, is located halfway between the boiled and the smoked. In order to cope with frying, he has to introduce a third axis for oil (the other two being for air and water). He thus replaces the recipe triangle with a tetrahedron. It may be easiest to picture fried at the top of this triangular pyramid (and at the three corners of the base there still remains the roasted, the smoked, and the boiled). In the middle of the edge joining smoked and fried, he places roasted-in-the-oven (with fat). Midway on the edge between fried and boiled he locates braising (in a base of water and fat).

I'm not sure how Lévi-Strauss would deal with some of the techniques derived from modern technology. Freezing, because it prolongs storage, could be regarded as similar to smoking in some ways, although because it arrests the slide into the rotten by inhibiting the chemical processes based on water, it could also be regarded as similar to drying. Although the freezer is a cultural artefact, people did use ice, especially in winter, prior to the invention of the technology. The microwave oven would appear to be without natural precedent and microwaving is mediated culturally. Given that the radio waves operate mainly by heating water molecules in (and around) the food and that they then heat the other food fibres, the technique appears closest to boiling or steaming. I shall make no further attempt to discuss the science of food storage or cooking techniques at this point since Lévi-Strauss's (1966) work is more likely to lead the reader towards the mystical aspects of cooking than to the scientific, as can be seen from the following remark on boiling:

> Because boiling takes place without loss of substance, and within a complete enclosure, it is eminently apt to symbolize cosmic totality. (p. 591)

Food Codes and the Grammar of Eating (Douglas)

Another social anthropologist operating within the structuralist tradition, but perhaps in a more down-to-earth fashion than Lévi-Strauss, is Douglas. She treats food as a code conveying information about social events and social relations:

> The message is about different degrees of hierarchy, inclusion and exclusion, boundaries and transactions across the boundaries. Like sex, the taking of food has a social component, as well as a bio-logical one. Food categories therefore encode social events. To say this is to echo Roland Barthes on the sartorial encoding of social events. (Douglas, 1975, p. 249)

I shall come to Barthes later in the chapter. Douglas (1975) uses Halli-day's (1961) linguistic ideas on food to get her started. This is based upon a hierarchically organised framework of categories going from the daily menu, to the meal, the course, the helping and, at the bottom, the mouthful. The mouthful is analogous to the morpheme in linguistics. Douglas extends Halliday's work to provide the equivalent of a grammar of eating by looking not only for the underlying structure of English family meals (admittedly based on her own middle-class life in London) but also for echoes of that structure in related social activities. Owing to limitations of space, I can do no more than provide an extremely brief indication as to how she does this.

I will start by saying something about the structure. Elements of the primary structure *Daily Menu* comprise *early*, *main*, *light*, *snack*. An exponent of the element *early* would be breakfast. Within the unit *Meal*, there exists the class *Dinner*. This has a primary structure of *first*, *second*, *main*, *sweet*, and *savoury*. An exponent of the *savoury* element would be cheese. Permissible ordering rules in terms of the sequence of elements are also set out. Thus *Main, Sweet, Savoury* is an acceptable structure. The full scheme is quite lengthy, as Douglas (1975) comments:

> This advances considerably the analysis of our family eating patterns. First, it shows how long and tedious the exhaustive analysis would be, even to read. (p. 253)

Douglas's (1975) quest for structure is aroused when her family rejects the suggestion that soup followed by pudding might count as a meal. I construe this informal piece of research as a spot of Garfinkelling by thought experiment (see Garfinkel, 1967). She articulates the structure as follows:

> Now I know the formula. A proper meal is A (when A is the stressed main course) plus $2B$ (when B is the unstressed course). Both A and B contain each the same structure, in small, $a + 2b$, when a is the stressed item and b is the unstressed item in a course. A weekday lunch is A; a Sunday lunch is $2A$; Christmas, Easter, and birthdays are $A + 2B$. Drinks by contrast are unstructured. (Douglas, 1975, p. 259)

This is rather strange since, by her own definition, she appears not to count the weekday or Sunday lunches as proper meals. An alternative strategy would be to acknowledge them as proper meals and admit that the formula $A + 2B$ wasn't up to much. Clearly it is possible to think of examples which will match this formula, especially at the level of the individual course. Thus meat a and two veg $2b$ would do nicely providing you don't count the gravy as a third b. Fish a & Chips b poses a dreadful problem, since it is short of a second b. If you add in the vinegar as a second b, then you would also have to add in the salt and that would take it to $3b$.

Douglas argues that $A + 2B$ is not peculiar to her family but is one that was current in her social environment at the time:

> It [the formula] governs even the structure of the cocktail canapé. The latter with its cereal base, its meat or cheese middle section, its sauce or pickle topping, and its mixture of colors, suggests a mock meal, a minute metonym of English middle-class meals in general. (pp. 259–60)

When I checked out this formula for canapés with a couple of recipe books drawn roughly from a period in the 1970s, to be equivalent to

Douglas's time of analysis, I found a reasonable degree of agreement for *base + topping + garnish*. Patten (1972) gives a recipe for *cheese whirls*: pipe the cheese topping onto the biscuit, bread or pastry base, and sprinkle with paprika. Thus the sprinkling of paprika secures the second *b*. Her recipe for *caviar canapés* involves covering the base with rings of hard-boiled eggs onto which the caviar is placed. The second *b* in this case is thus the caviar. I am unhappy about giving a sprinkling of paprika the same weight or formulaic status as a topping of caviar. Turning to a City and Guilds of London chef's compendium of recipes from around that time (Fuller and Renold, 1972) I was forced to the conclusion that allowing the canapé only 2 *b*'s might be erring on the cautious side. For example, *Canapé des gourmets* (No. 1176) has ham with mustard butter, cream and paprika *a* heaped onto the base b_1 and garnished with a sprig of parsley b_2. However, it seems a little arbitrary to swallow the paprika into the main *a* component. If the paprika were to be construed as a secondary garnish, then the recipe would shift into the $a + 3b$ category. Fuller and Renold's (1972) *Canapé écossais* (No. 1178) provides a better example of the formula being breached. A scrambled egg mixture *a* is heaped onto toast b_1 and is then garnished with a criss-cross of anchovy b_2. Next, a caper is placed in each section (counting the four capers as one unit gives b_3). Finally, a garnish of parsley b_4 is added.

Douglas (1975) deals with the sweet course, one of Halliday's (1961) categories, in the context of Sunday lunch (Halliday gives exponents of the sweet course as fruit, pudding or ice cream and lists steamed pudding as a sub-class of the sweet course):

> But Sunday lunch has two main courses, each of which is patterned like the weekday lunch – say, first course, fish or meat (stressed) and two vegetables (unstressed), second course, pudding (stressed), cream and biscuits (unstressed). (Douglas, p. 257)

Of course there is no arguing with what Douglas ate in her house in the 1970s. However, it really does seem to be pushing things too far to insist that the sweet course conform to the $a + 2b$ formula. In my opinion, one of the major contenders for the title of the quintessential post-war English middle-class pudding has to be Spotted Dick. Stewart (1972/80) in *The Times Cookery Book* provides a recipe for this dish (the requirement for two hours' steaming pegs its date prior to the era of the microwave oven). Her instructions are to serve the pudding hot with a custard sauce (b_1). This produces the formula $a + b$ and not $a + 2b$. I think there may well be countless other examples to weaken confidence in the formula. Bread-and-butter pudding (e.g. Turner *et al.*, 1997) may be eaten on its own or, if absolutely necessary, served with a drop of custard (I think custard spoils that particular pudding). This would put bread-and-butter pudding as an *a* or, at most, an *a + b*. Again, I would find it very odd to eat an apple pie with anything more than custard *or* cream (another *a + b*). In sum, I feel that Douglas's (1975) *A + 2B* formula is surrounded by too many contradictions and borderline cases to be taken too seriously. I now leave geometric (Lévi-Strauss) and algebraic (Douglas) models and move on to the heartland of French semiotics.

The Semiology of Food and Cooking (Barthes)

Mennell *et al.* (1992) point out that Barthes sought a grammatical code for people's food preferences and approached this goal from a semiotic analysis of food advertising and cookery writing. Barthes's analyses are not solely concerned with images and meanings, since he packs a good political punch from time to time. For example, in his essay on wine, Barthes (1973) points out that whereas people in countries other than France may drink to get drunk, drunkenness for the French is merely a side effect. Drinking wine is a decorative gesture that helps the drinker achieve a range of other mythical goals. For the intellectuals, wine will bring them nearer to the proletarian way of life and will help them to escape from the curse of romanticism (whatever that may be). It is near to the end of his essay that he adopts an overtly political stance:

> The mythology of wine can in fact help us to understand the usual ambiguity of our daily life. For it is true that wine is a good and fine substance, but it is no less true that its production is deeply involved in French capitalism, whether it is that of the private distillers or that of the big settlers in Algeria who impose on the Muslims, on the very land of which they have been dispossessed, a crop of which they have no need, while they lack even bread. (Barthes, 1973, p. 61)

In another essay, on ornamental cookery, he takes the French magazine *Elle* to task for peddling a dream-like and over-elaborate form of cookery to its working-class readership. He makes the point that whilst the working-class reader of *Elle* is expected to cook fancy partridges which they can ill afford, the middle-class readers of *L'Express* are given recipes for salad niçoise which they will almost certainly be able to afford and prepare. He attacks *Elle* for presenting

to its working-class readers the dream of smartness, since they will
not be able to afford it in practice. He hates the smooth coating of
food: glazes, creams, icing and jellies. He also dislikes the ornamenta-
tion which is then placed upon the smooth-coated surfaces of the food
(chiselled mushrooms, cherries, carved lemon, silver pastilles, glacé
fruit). While this removes the dish from the natural state, there is also
a tendency to imitate nature as happens with the Yule log. Barthes
(1973) thinks that these contrary tendencies are understandable:

> This is because here, as in all petit-bourgeois art, the irrepressible
> tendency towards extreme realism is countered – or balanced – by
> one of the eternal imperatives of journalism for women's magazines:
> what is pompously called, at *L'Express*, *having ideas*. Cookery in *Elle*
> is, in the same way, an 'idea'-cookery. But here the inventiveness,
> confined to a fairy-land reality, must be applied only to *garnishings*,
> for the genteel tendency of the magazine precludes it from touching
> on the real problems concerning food (the real problem is not to have
> the idea of sticking cherries into a partridge, it is to have the part-
> ridge, that is to say, to pay for it). (p. 79)

Barthes (1973) states in the preface to his book that he wrote the
essays at the rate of about one per month for about two years from
1954 to 1956. I became curious as to how bad the cookery articles in
Elle magazine really were and so I traced some bound copies of
the Paris edition for 1954 to one of the academic libraries in the UK
(I figured that this would have been around the time he was writing the
essay on Ornamental Cookery). Indeed, I found the article on partridges (*Elle*, 1954, 461, p. 52). There were three recipes given and only
one involved cherries (*perdreaux aux cerises*); the other two (*perdreaux
Normande aux pommes-fruits* and *perdrix au chou*) would appear to
involve apples and cabbage, respectively. The general tenor of the
articles on cookery in *Elle* at that time was not especially grand, as far
as I could see. For example, there was a feature on quick meals for
young couples ('Service rapide jeunes ménage'), most of which were
estimated to take between 15 and 30 minutes to prepare (*Elle*, 1954,
463, pp. 58–9). One of these, *Les croque-monsieur*, involved 2 slices of
ham, some butter, bread and gruyère cheese: scarcely the epitome of
bourgeois fare. Elsewhere I found a recipe for roast pork and Bussels
sprouts (*Elle*, 1954, 466, pp. 48–9: *Cotes de porc – choux de Bruxelles*).
I even found a 10-minute recipe for Welsh Rabbit (*Elle*, 1954, 464,
pp. 59), although I have to say that my Mum never put in a spoonful
of kirsch or a dash of Cayenne pepper when she made this for me

when I was a kid; I like the sound of the French version.[1] Another article extolled the nutritional value of mushrooms (*Elle*, 1954, 462, pp. 64–5) while elsewhere there was a comprehensive article on good soups (*Elle*, 1954, 467, pp. 46–7). The recipe for *pot-au-feu* did not strike me as extravagant: apart from beef this included carrots, leeks, onion, a stick of celery and, it almost goes without saying, several cloves of garlic.

Barthes (1973) also accuses *Elle* of using food photographs of a mythical nature:

> This is an openly dream-like cookery, as proved in fact by the photographs in Elle, which never show the dishes except from a high angle, as objects at once near and inaccessible, whose consumption can perfectly well be accomplished simply by looking. (p. 79)

This is complete nonsense. There are sometimes explicit instructional photographs arranged 'cartoon frame' style with clear explanatory captions beneath each frame indicating which aspect of the cooking process is being illustrated. One example occurred for two savoury dishes (see *Elle*, 1954, 454, pp. 50–1: *Petits soufflés individuels* and *Artichauts-surpise*) with another relating to the icing of chocolate cake (*Elle*, 1954, 456, p. 55). In the latter example, the chocolate icing is shown being dolloped on with a long spatula and the finished product appears neither fussy nor fancy (at an estimated preparation time of 11 minutes, I can't see how it could be).

My difficulty with Barthes is that he seems to have such a hatred of petit-bourgeois tastes. I guess partridges were expensive in France in the 1950s but making a chocolate cake, a stew, or a roast would not be beyond the reach of many working-class families, surely. When my daughter was little I used to make a Christmas cake each year. I enjoyed creating the smooth coating from the white icing, although I found it quite difficult to get a flat, even surface. We then had great fun adorning the cake with what Barthes would, no doubt, describe as petit-bourgeois trinkets. I can't see what the problem is; it sounds like a case of intellectual snobbery to me. I had always thought of Barthes as one of the leading semiologists of his time and it came as something of a disappointment to find that he approached his textual data in what appeared to me to be such a cavalier and careless fashion. While some

---

[1] David (1986, p. 161) provides a recipe for French Welsh rabbit which, although differing in several respects from the one in *Elle*, also includes kirsch and Cayenne pepper. David's recipe is attributed to the Comtesse Mapie de Toulouse-Lautrec.

difficulties may be due to translation problems, I remain convinced that he wrote more out of his own preconceived ideas than from a close analysis of the culinary articles published in *Elle* magazine.

The Sociology of Contemporary Food Consumption (Warde)

Warde (1997) provides an excellent distillation of four theoretical approaches to food consumption. I shall cover his account of the first three approaches in this section but the fourth (Bourdieu) I treat separately in the following section.

The first thesis he calls *towards arbitrary diversity* and he bases this primarily on the work of Fischler (e.g. 1980). It is assumed that there has been widespread disintegration of the traditional rules and norms governing social life in many societies. This anomic state of affairs leads people to behave unpredictably and idiosyncratically. Food habits seem to have followed this general trend. With the collapse of norma-tive regulation, people have started to snack and 'graze' in individual ways. Fewer families are enjoying the social episode characterised by the family meal that Douglas (1975) wrote about (see above). Apart from this, there has been a huge increase, for the more affluent sectors of the industrialised world, in the choice and availability of foods. The constraints of the seasons are overcome by flying food in from other parts of the world or by storage based on freezing techniques.[2] Items that were once exotic are now to be found on a regular basis on the shelves of the local supermarket. The individual is left alone to make decisions about what to eat and how to cook it. Frequently there will be conflicting advice on what to do. The desire to eat lots of nice things is set against the desire to have a lean body. Warde (1997) sums up this thesis as follows:

> As a consequence of individualization and deregulation, people are deprived of confidence in foodstuffs, in expert advice and in their own abilities to select what to eat. In this view the current period is not one of flourishing styles, plural market niches, or the aestheti-cization of everyday life, but a mire of personal uncertainty and discomfort. (p. 32)

Warde's (1997) second thesis is concerned with *post-Fordist* food. With Fordist (as opposed to post-Fordist) mass consumption what

---

[2] An interesting account of this process in the UK food retail and distribution industry is provided by Wrigley (1998).

folk consume is mainly determined by considerations of production. Taking cars as an example, most people who can afford a car will have the same sort (perhaps a Ford) and, within a given price range, there will be little difference between the alternative brands available. In post-Fordist consumption, the consumers have more to spend and a wider range of goods is produced. Production becomes much more consumer-driven as individuals develop distinctive lifestyles and open up the possibilities of niche consumption and neo-tribalism. Warde (1997), speaking of the situation in the UK, points to fashions which come into being for various foreign cuisines and restaurants or distinctive diets (sometimes supported by brand labels). He also suggests that the rise of vegetarianism provides an example of a social movement that is related to a range of other social, political and ethical attitudes. However, this thesis suggests that people become connoisseurs and make complex purchasing decisions in accordance with their chosen lifestyle script. Although it could be argued that supermarkets are doing their best to provide the consumer with information that will render him or her equal to the task, Warde (1997) remains sceptical:

> British supermarkets provide free recipe cards for unfamiliar meals and leaflets on what to do with a mango or a guava. There are, obviously, many people so involved, journalists and marketeers, as well as nutritionists and political campaigners. The extent to which they deliver information that will encourage or allow people to construct a coherent food style is, however, debatable. (p. 36)

Warde (1997) thus pulls away from the view that neo-tribalism and niche consumption offer the best ways of explaining contemporary food consumption.

The third thesis Warde (1997) discusses is that of *mass consumption in a mass society*. The idea behind this is that as class cultures have collapsed, the population has moved into an increasingly larger 'middle-class' society. Providing that groups such as the very rich, the very poor, and some of the ethnic minorities are set aside, the remaining mass of the middle consensus has become basically homogeneous. This thesis is very much in accord with the ideas set out in Ritzer's (1996) *The McDonaldization of Society*. Globalisation is resulting in some brands and items being sold in exactly the same format around the world (McDonalds, Coca-Cola, and so forth). However, Warde (1997) also points to some degree of uniformity within nations. Sometimes this will be reinforced in order to promote heritage trade and tourism (Warde gives the example of the 'A Taste of Scotland' campaign, run in 1992). On a different note, governments may also play a role in promoting campaigns for healthy eating and so forth which will, if followed, result in some degree of homogeneity within the nation's diet. Warde (1997) thus acknowledges a number of ways in which the drift towards stylisation or individualisation may be overpowered.

Warde's (1997) fourth thesis is the persistence of social differentiation. In this approach, the importance of social class in determining tastes in food is asserted. The accounts based upon neo-tribalism and niche markets are thus dismissed. One of the major proponents of this view is Bourdieu and I go on to describe his work in the following section.

Food Consumption, Class, and Cultural Capital (Bourdieu)

Warde (1997) points out that class was once regarded as the major determinant of consumption and, until comparatively recently, that extended to the consumption of food. This is a position which finds less support among sociologists than it used to, with many arguing that there has been a demise of class cultures. Warde (1997) singles out Bourdieu (1984) as being the most sophisticated exponent of the view that consumption behaviour is best accounted for by class position:

> Taste knowledge and the desire for particular commodities are necessary elements in the process of class formation and class reproduction. Classes can be identified by their consumption patterns; and consumer behaviour can be explained in terms of the role of display and social judgement in the formation of class identities. (Warde, 1997, p. 9)

I see Bourdieu as a cross between Marx and Goffman. Marx lends weight to the importance of class and material production; Goffman takes care of the self-presentational aspects of class identities.

Bourdieu (1984) suggests that two forms of capital contribute to the competition between classes: economic and cultural. This opens up the possibility of distinctive factions within the dominant class and also within the middle class who may be richer in the one form than the other:

> The fact that in the realm of food the main opposition broadly corresponds to differences in income has masked the secondary

opposition which exists, both within the middle classes and within the dominant class, between the factions richer in cultural capital and less rich in economic capital and those whose assets are structured in the opposite way. (p. 177)

Bourdieu (1984) illustrates this by indicating that the diet of foremen in factories remains closer to popular taste than does the diet of clerks, even though the foremen earn more than the clerks and thus occupy a relatively dominant position in terms of economic capital. The clerks, on the other hand, are richer in cultural capital and incline to the leaner, lighter diets of the middle class. Bourdieu sees the taste of the working class as one of necessity; culture develops in middle- and upper-class taste as a result of freedom and luxury. The power of the dominant classes can be deployed in a number of ways in order to ensure that the working class is kept at a distance:

Thus, within the dominant class, one can, for the sake of simplicity, distinguish three structures of the consumption distributed under three items: food, culture and presentation (clothing, beauty care, toiletries, domestic servants). (p. 184)

Bourdieu (1984) argues that the class characteristics of the family into which a child is born largely shape the child's tastes. For example, a child born into a family of teachers is likely to develop cultural capital in line with his or her parents' dominant position in that regard. Mennell *et al.* (1992) comment on how this preoccupation with the reproduction of culture means that Bourdieu's theory appears rather static. I feel that this is a little unfair, since Bourdieu (1984) certainly spends some time discussing the possibility of class mobility and I shall now go on to explore this aspect of his work.

There are two ways whereby someone attempting class mobility might run into difficulties. Firstly, it is extremely difficult to learn how to behave convincingly and genuinely as a member of a class that is different from the class of one's birth, so to speak. This is where Goffman's (e.g. 1959) work is of relevance. In the presentation of the 'upclassed' persona, there will be many opportunities to make gaffes and to lose face. A very similar point is made by Garfinkel (1967) when discussing the case of one of his trans-sexual patients, Agnes, who needed to learn to pass as a woman (having been born male). The consequences of failure for someone 'passing' as a member of another economic or cultural class group may not be as severe as for someone undergoing gender realignment but they may nevertheless be real enough.

The second problem is that the members of the dominant class will probably have changed the rules by the time the 'upshifters' have equipped themselves with what they took to be the appropriate economic or cultural qualifications:

> What makes the petit-bourgeois relation to culture and its capacity to make 'middle-brow' whatever it touches ... is not its 'nature' but the very position of the petit-bourgeois in social space, the social nature of the petit-bourgeois, which is constantly impressed on the petit-bourgeois himself, determining his relation to legitimate culture and his avid but anxious, naïve but serious way of clutching at it. It is, quite simply, the fact that legitimate culture is not made for him (and is often made against him), so that he is not made for it; and that it ceases to be what it is as soon as he appropriates it – as would happen tomorrow to the melodies of Fauré or Duparc if the development of suburban and provincial Conservatoires caused them to be sung, well or badly, in petit-bourgeois living rooms. (Bourdieu, 1984, pp. 327–8)

I find Bourdieu's analysis extremely depressing, partly because I also find it persuasive. I shall conclude with a brief summary of Bourdieu's (1984) findings and views on what typifies the food tastes of the various class factions that he studied in France in the 1960s based upon a survey by questionnaire, carried out on a sample of some 1200 people.

Bourdieu (1984) claims that the working classes have a familiar conviviality which is expressed through an indulgent attitude to eating and drinking. This flies in the face of the more sober and restrained diets of the middle class, which are consonant with positive attitudes to healthy bodies and slim physiques (I return to discuss the issue of class and body image in Chapter 4, in relation to eating disorders). When clerical workers are compared with skilled manual workers, they spend more on health and beauty care; this highlights the possibility of differences surfacing within the same socio-economic strata. In line with this, the clerks spend less on pork and charcuterie but more on fish and fresh fruit than do the manual workers.

Bourdieu comments that the modest diet of the 'upshifters' is based upon delayed gratification, underpinned by a Benthamite calculation of the benefits and costs (of e.g. health and beauty). It occurs to me that this can be related in a direct fashion to the psychological expectancy-value theories of reasoned action such as Ajzen's (1991) theory of planned behaviour. Bourdieu's assessment seems to be that the working class will grasp the opportunity for a good blowout or a booze-up should the opportunity arise:

> The hedonism which seizes day by day the rare satisfactions ('good times') of the immediate present is the only philosophy conceivable to those who 'have no future' and, in any case, little to expect from the future. (1984, pp.180–3)

Bourdieu argues that the positive attitude to sobriety embraced by the petit bourgeois underpins a desire for social isolation from working class, and thus constitutes an important break with collective solidarity:

> The café is not a place a man goes to for a drink but a place he goes to in order to drink in company, where he can establish relationships of familiarity based on the suspension of the censorships, conventions and proprieties that prevail among strangers. In contrast to the bourgeois or petit bourgeois café or restaurant, where each table is a separate, appropriated territory (one asks permission to borrow a chair or the salt), the working-class café is a site for companionship (each new arrival gives a collective greeting, 'Salut la compagnie!' etc.). Its focus is the counter, to be leaned on after shaking hands with the landlord – who is thus defined as the host (he often leads the conversation) – and sometimes shaking hands with the whole company; the tables, if there are any, are left to 'strangers', or women who have come in to get a drink for their child or make a phone call. (1984, p. 183)

Bourdieu (1984) does articulate one path upwards through the class structure which involves no qualitative change in diet or taste, merely the opportunity to buy increasingly heavy and rich food. This chain starts with manual workers, and then moves through foremen and craftsmen to industrial and commercial employers. The higher the status, the more likely that game and foie gras will be encountered. Bourdieu (1984) singles out teachers, by way of contrast, to these other groups:

> Finally, the teachers, richer in cultural capital than in economic capital, and therefore inclined to ascetic consumption in all areas, pursue originality at the lowest economic cost and go in for exoticism (Italian, Chinese cooking, etc.) and culinary populism (peasant

dishes). They are thus almost consciously opposed to the (new) rich
with their rich food, the buyers and sellers of *grosse bouffe,* the 'fat
cats'. (p. 185)

Bourdieu (1984) also comments on the sexual division of labour.
Women of the dominant class tend to avoid labour-intensive dishes,
such as pot-au-feu (made by stewing cheap meat for a long time), and
opt for quicker dishes involving grilled meats or fish. In this way they
free up more time to be devoted to childcare and the transmission of
cultural capital. In sum, Bourdieu (1984) suggests that class provides a
useful basis for articulating and distinguishing between the food habits
of groups separated within society on the basis of their acquisition and
entitlements to economic and cultural capital.

Conclusion

I started the chapter by declaring my allegiance to critical social
psychology and explained that that was the reason why I had chosen to
give precedence in my order of treatment to the non-biological perspectives on food. I engaged in many sorties and excursions across
disciplinary boundaries in the course of this chapter but I regret that I
return at the end without very much to show for it: I cannot take
seriously Klein's (1981) ideas about good and bad breasts; Lévi-
Strauss's (1966) journey into the cosmos via the culinary triangle sounds
fanciful; Douglas's (1975) formula for meat-and-two-veg doesn't work;
and Barthes's (1973) analysis didn't square with the data. I did find
Warde's summary of the various sociological approaches to food consumption to be particularly interesting, and Bourdieu's ideas appear
directly relevant to social psychology insofar as he stresses the importance of the *self-presentational* aspects of class identities.

It is possible that some of these earlier approaches will resurface
in the future as critical or post-positivist social psychological research
is deployed in contemporary studies into food-related topics. For
example, semiotics is one of the foundations of discursive psychology.
While the work of Wiggins *et al.* (2001) is founded on discourse analysis, semiotics does not feature in their work since they are mainly
concerned with the analysis of mealtime conversations. However, if
the discursive approach were to focus upon food imagery, as opposed
to food talk, then its semiotic roots may well be brought to the fore.
Similarly, although I do not see a contemporary application of Freud's
work to the psychology of food (setting aside psychoanalytic and

Lacanian approaches to eating disorders), it is possible that Billig's (1999) discursive reformulation of repression and the unconscious may open the way for a resurgence of interest in this approach, possibly in relation to food choices and preferences.

I shall leave the sociological perspectives on the back burner for the time being and move on in the next chapter to consider the physiological research.

3

Hunger, Flavour, Digestion and Kitchen Chemistry

I shall start the chapter with a brief review of research relating to hunger and its role in the regulation of food intake. This work has largely been carried out by physiological psychologists and most of it involves experimentation with animals. Skating over this unseemly material as quickly as possible, I shall move on to present the conventional scientific account of flavour and digestion. A biochemical perspective is brought to bear on both these topics, although with regard to the former some of the work on taste and smell is carried out using the experimental approach typically found in psychophysical research in general. Having discussed flavour and digestion, I shall then consider the way in which food preparation and cooking may be regarded as applied organic chemistry in the kitchen. Owing to limitations of space my treatment of some of these topics will be highly selective. For example, when I talk about digestion I shall focus solely on carbohydrates, mentioning fats, proteins and other nutrients only in passing, if at all. As for kitchen chemistry, I shall deal only with egg cookery. I conclude the chapter with a short case study: my experience of cooking and eating a simple lunch at home.

In approaching the topics of this chapter I am conscious of the fact that I shall be pulled towards the outlying boundaries of the discipline of psychology, in the direction of the biological sciences. Some drift into the language games of biochemistry, physiology and organic chemistry will be inevitable. Rather than provide a comprehensive review, I shall draw upon a relatively small number of sources relating to hunger, taste, smell, nutrition and kitchen chemistry. As far as texts on food are concerned, I shall use Lyman (1989), Logue (1991), and McGee (1984). With regard to taste and smell, slightly more specialised coverage is provided by Bear *et al.* (1996) and Bartoshuk and Beauchamp (1994). For an earlier treatment of these topics, I particularly like Woodworth and Schlosberg (1954).

Hunger

Research into hunger seeks to uncover the mechanisms by which food intake is regulated: what causes an animal to start eating, to continue eating and, finally, to stop eating. Most people can recognise the pangs of hunger associated with contractions in the stomach on those occasions when they have gone without food for a long time. At other times, people may feel 'stuffed' or 'bloated'; they may even admit that they 'pigged out'. Feelings of hunger and satiety indicate that food intake is regulated with some degree of success in everyday life. I start by considering some of the research that examines the physiological mechanisms underpinning this regulation.

Stomach distension

In reviewing studies on hunger, Logue (1991) starts with Cannon and Washburn's (1912) experiments on hunger pangs. In order to detect contractions in his own stomach, Washburn swallowed a tube with a partially inflated balloon. Cannon and Washburn describe the method as follows:

> Almost every day for several weeks W. [Washburn] introduced as far as the stomach a small tube, to the lower end of which was attached a soft-rubber balloon about 8 cm. in diameter. The tube was thus carried about each time for two or three hours. After this preliminary experience the introduction of the tube, and its presence in the gullet and stomach, were not at all disturbing. (Cannon and Washburn, 1912, p. 449)

This allowed them to measure any stomach contractions in Washburn's body, using the balloon that lay in the stomach to record changes in pressure. The timing of the subjective reports, when compared to that of the contractions, confirmed the hypothesis that the feeling of hunger was caused by the contraction of the stomach (and not the other way round). More recent research suggests that neither stomach contractions nor a stomach is absolutely vital for the experience of hunger and therefore casts doubt on the strength of this relationship (see Logue, 1991, p. 19). Setting aside the scientific merit of this work, I feel that Washburn is to be applauded for subjecting himself to his own experimental procedures.

I regret to report that much of the work in this area has been carried out using some appalling methodological techniques on animals. For example, esophagostomy was performed on dogs in order to provide a way to separate out the chewing and the swallowing of food (as one factor) from the distension caused by the food filling the stomach (as a second factor). In this procedure the esophagus is brought out through the dog's neck and a hole is made so that food eaten will pass out of the hole instead of continuing to the stomach (see Logue, 1991, p. 20). This procedure is known as sham-feeding and goes back to Janowitz and Grossman (1949) who worked from a method recommended by Dragstedt and Mullenix (1931) who, in turn, claimed to have improved Pavlov's (1910) procedure. On reading about this at textbook level, I assumed that the procedure was straightforward. Scrutiny of the primary sources revealed that it takes about 10 days to prepare the animal properly and that (at least at the time the pioneering research was carried out) a mortality rate of 50 per cent obtained. This provides an example of the way the scientific story is sometimes expurgated of its more unpleasant details as one moves from primary source to textbook summary.

Another variation on this experimental theme is to use a gastric fistula. This is a hole in the stomach through which food, inert gunge, or inflatable balloons can be inserted. Janowitz and Grossman (1949) demonstrated that sham-feeding dogs would eventually result in the cessation of eating and this provided support for the fact that oral factors are implicated to some extent. Large intragastric feedings decreased sham feeding, although the inflation of a balloon in the stomach had no effect. This suggests that it is the absorption of nutrients from food in the stomach that may be crucial and not stomach distension *per se*. Summarising these and other experiments conducted with rats, Logue (1991) states:

> There is no single, perfect mechanism; a regulatory system malfunctions more readily if it has only one way of collecting and using information. Instead, the body uses several ways of determining how much has been eaten and how much should be eaten. All of this information, including oral factors and stomach distention, plays a part in initiating and terminating eating. (p. 23)

Homeostatic mechanism in the blood

One hypothesis relating to control of food intake is that animals are provided with a homeostatic mechanism which adjusts the eating of food (in terms of quantity or nutrients) and modifies storage of energy (through body fat) as a function of the body's energy needs. Research on parabiotic rats indicates that the appropriate signalling function of such a mechanism must be carried in the blood. Logue (1991) describes parabiotic rats as:

> pairs of rats that have been surgically joined side to side so that blood circulates between the two animals where the incision heals together. Their appearance is simply that of two normal rats, joined together at the side. (Logue, 1991, p. 25)

This sounds deceptively harmless but even the most cursory reading of the primary source literature was enough to disabuse me of that conclusion (see Fleming, 1969; Bunster and Meyer, 1933). Logue (1991) reports that Fleming (1969) was able to demonstrate the involvement of the blood in this information transfer:

> When one member of a pair was fed for 3 hours, beginning 2 hours before the start of the other member's 3-hour-long feeding, over a period of weeks the second rat came to eat significantly less than the first. (Logue, 1991, p. 25)

The glucostatic theory of hunger postulates blood sugar level as one of the mechanisms crucial to the successful operation of the homeo-static process. While this may account for short-term variation, the longer-term involvement and adjustment of body fat stores requires a complementary system. This has been postulated as the lipostatic theory of long-term regulation. The story does not end here. Glycogen has been put forward as a more reliable indicator than blood glucose level. The situation appears to unravel into great depths of complexity and Logue (1991) concludes that:

> A theory involving a single, simple mechanism is inadequate to describe the roles of blood sugar and body fat in the consumption of food. (p. 28)

Perhaps not surprisingly, the research shifted the locus of the investigation to the central nervous system.

Hypothalamus as centre for control

Logue (1991) reports that, for various reasons, the hypothalamus was suspected as being one of the control centres for hunger. One procedure used in this area of research is to lesion the appropriate part of

a rat's brain using electrodes to burn out the desired area. Hetherington and Ranson (1940) found that rats subjected to lesions of the
ventromedial hypothalamus (VMH) ate excessively and became obese.
Taking into account some further studies, which amplified the original
findings and also tied glucose in to the VMH, Logue (1991) suggests
that the results imply a central integrating mechanism (p. 31). Momentum to the idea that there might be hunger and satiety centres in the
brain was gained when it was found that lesions to the lateral hypothalamus (LH) resulted in rats that would never eat again (see Anand
and Brobeck, 1951):

> Death by starvation is not a necessary consequence of an LH lesion,
> however. LH-lesioned rats at first refuse to eat any food or drink
> any water (aphagia and adipsia). But if the rats are carefully
> handled, after several weeks they will eat wet palatable foods, then
> dry foods, and finally drink water. Apparently the tissue surround-
> ing the lesion aids in this recovery. If recovered LH-lesioned rats are
> lesioned again in the areas surrounding the original LH lesion, the
> aphagia and adipsia return. (Logue, 1991, p.31)

This seems to be a particularly nasty line of research since, having
taken the rats to the brink of death, they are nursed back to health
only to be lesioned once again. There have been a number of scientific
difficulties with the hunger and satiety centres hypothesis. Logue
(1991) comments that VMH-lesioned rats do not always put on or lose
weight as the theory says they should. She concludes her discussion of
this issue as follows:

> Finally, various sorts of peripheral manipulations (for example,
> manipulations involving stomach distention or injections of nutri-
> ents) affect hunger in VMH-lesioned rats just as they do in non-
> lesioned rats. These and other results are difficult to reconcile with
> the hypothesis that destruction of the VMH is simply the destruction
> of a satiety center. (p. 33)

It is possible that the heyday is long gone for techniques such as the
gastric fistula, the esophagostomy, or the VMH lesion and that death
by starvation is no longer entertained as a humane dependent variable
measure. But as we move into the age where neuroscientific research
increasingly draws upon techniques involving biosynthesised gene
products, the sacrifice of animal life may fall ever further into the taken-
for-granted background. Against such stunning scientific advances, it
seems churlish to make a fuss over a few mice.

Neuropeptide Y and obese gene product

Kalat (1998), in his text *Biological Psychology*, reports the discovery of the *obese* gene in mice and how this led to finding a previously unknown protein, leptin. Leptin circulates in the blood and, when its levels are low, it seems to be involved in signalling the need for food. Kalat (1998) goes on to tie this in to recent work relating to *Neuropeptide Y* (NPY):

> Leptin activates receptors in the brain, especially the hypothalamus, to inhibit the release of Neuropeptide Y (NPY) (Stephens *et al.*, 1995), a neurotransmitter that (among other effects) powerfully inhibits the paraventricular nucleus (PVN) of the hypothalamus. Inhibition of the PVN, like damage, increases feeding, and prolonged inhibition can produce extreme overeating. (p. 291)

Stephens *et al.* (1995) showed that obese rats when injected daily with biosynthetic mature human and mouse obese gene product reduced their food consumption and their body weight fell to near normal, compared with control rats injected with saline solution. Just to recap: more leptin means less NPY; less NPY means a lack of inhibition for the PVN; only the inhibited PVN is associated with increased feeding, therefore food intake trims back to normal.

Satiety signals

Woods *et al.* (2000) suggest that tremendous advances are being made in this area, although these are occurring in the disciplines of biochemistry and molecular biology, rather than in psychology or physiology (as is evident from the discussion of leptin and NPY, above). The earlier glucostatic and lipostatic mechanisms for governing the ingestion process now seem to be wanting:

> A key point is that under usual circumstances, the supply of energy in the blood does not decrease to anywhere near the threshold necessary to trigger eating. Rather, animals initiate meals even though ample energy is readily available. Eating is in fact a relatively inefficient way to get calories into the blood rapidly. (Woods *et al.*, 2000, p. 258)

There are now thought to be many correlates of meal onset, including blood glucose, temperature and metabolic rate, all of which show some changes just before the ingestion of a meal. Environmental triggers may thus stimulate the synthesis and secretion of hormones and neurotransmitters (such as insulin and NPY) which, in turn, help to control intake.

Satiety for individual meals is thought to be signalled by the secretion of the peptides in the gut, including cholecystokinin (CCK). The satiety peptides may combine with other factors, such as gastric distension, in order to signal termination of the meal. This mechanism does not appear to control long-term weight:

> Although satiety peptides can alter the size of individual meals, their repeated administration does not alter body weight. For example, when CCK-8 is automatically administered to rats at the start of each spontaneous meal, the size of each meal is reduced, but the animals compensate by initiating more meals and thereby maintain body weight. (Woods *et al.*, 1998, p. 1379)

In sum, the physiological psychology of hunger and the homeostatic mechanisms controlling both ingestion at individual meals, and body weight in the longer term, appear to be more complex than was at first anticipated. Gastric distension is not ruled out as irrelevant but is seen as one factor among many in signalling meal termination. Attention has moved from glucostatic and lipostatic mechanisms in homeostatic regulation to the secretion of hormones and neurotransmitters, such as NPY. I shall return to the regulation of body weight (as opposed to ingestion at a single meal) in Chapter 4, where I discuss eating disorders. For the moment, I move on to the flavour of food, as opposed to its ingestion.

The Biochemistry of Flavour

Flavour is a complex perception stemming from sensations deriving from taste (tongue), smell (nose) and what might be loosely described as mouthfeel (including texture). Duffy and Bartoshuk (1996) comment on the fact that there is no verb in the English language to express the perception of flavour, resulting from the integration of oral sensations, and they use the term 'mouthsense'. It is convenient to parcel out the components of mouthsense when reporting the research and I shall follow this procedure, starting with taste.

Taste

Several writers in the past have provided sensation maps of the tongue, focusing on the four tastes of sweet, bitter, salty and sour. Although

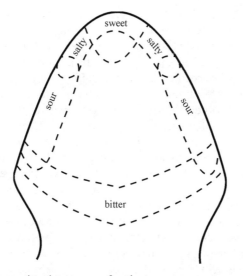

Figure 3.1 Conventional taste map for the tongue

this view no longer seems to be in vogue within the academic community, I shall briefly describe it since it appears to have drifted into culinary culture. Woodworth and Schlosberg (1954, p. 300) provide a negative map which highlights the areas *not* receptive to each of the four tastes. I prefer McGee's (1984) positive map and I have based my own on his (see Figure 3.1). The rule of thumb for the tongue, if that doesn't sound too silly, is that sweet is tasted on the tip, salty up at the front edge, sour along the middle edges, with bitter across the back as you move towards the throat. The bit in the middle of the tongue, away from the edges, is not very responsive to taste. Contemporary writers point out that the conventional taste map conveys a false impression, since most sites are now thought to be sensitive to all of the basic tastes. Bartoshuk and Beauchamp (1994, p. 438) claim that the origins of the taste map myth can be traced back to a mistranslation of a German article by Boring in the 1940s. Bear *et al.* (1996, p. 191) are not quite so dismissive and would appear to go along with the idea that there is a tendency for greater responsiveness to specific tastes at particular sites, as set out in the conventional tongue taste map, even though all tastes can be detected at all sites. One further update in terms of the contemporary picture is that a fifth basic taste quality is sometimes included: *umami*, meaning 'delicious' in Japanese. The most common source of umami in culinary form is monosodium glutamate.

The tastes coming from the tongue remain independent and do not, like colours, combine when mixed in combination to form new categories. Whilst blue and yellow paint may be mixed to form green, the sweet and sour ingredients in a Chinese dish, for example, will remain sweet and sour. According to McGee (1984), sourness tends to be caused by acids. Saltiness is not only brought about by sodium chloride but by other chlorides, too. He suggests that bitterness is largely the result of alkaloids, with quinine and caffeine being two common examples. Sweetness is produced by a variety of products apart from the various sugars, including synthetic substances such as saccharin. Lyman (1989), reflecting on this, makes the interesting point that people who munch with their front teeth may have a different taste experience from people who chew with their molars, even when eating identical food. I assume that this would be caused by the food being in primary contact with different areas of the tongue for the front vs. molar chewers and that this would have an effect on the overall taste profile delivered by the specialised receptors on the tongue. Although this idea appears to be based upon the false assumption of the conventional tongue taste map, there could, in any case, be a difference resulting from 'mouthfeel'.

Apparently, we are much more sensitive to bitter substances than to natural sugars. Woodworth and Schlosberg (1954) say that a per cent concentration of 0.7 is needed before sugar can normally be detected; for quinine the concentration is much lower at 0.00003 per cent concentration. Most writers seem to feel that our heightened sensitivity to bitterness may have served us well in evolutionary terms since this taste may provide warning of poisonous substances to be avoided. Woodworth and Schlosberg (1954) also suggest that adaptation to taste is fairly rapid, with salt needing only about 30 seconds.

There has been some controversy more recently concerning the fact that taste adaptation may not happen to the same extent in everyday life as it does within the laboratory setting. Theunissen and Kroeze (1996) found that mouth movements diminished taste adaptation to sucrose solutions in the laboratory. The experimental introduction and (strict) control of mouth movements was an attempt to simulate the real world experience of chewing when eating. Further investigation (Theunissen *et al.*, 2000) revealed that mode of presentation of the stimulus taste could have an effect on adaptation. When the taste medium remained in constant position on the tongue (for example, a filter paper soaked with a sucrose solution), greater adaptation occurred compared with other presentation conditions:

Among the three presentational methods, a sucrose-soaked filter paper on the tongue produced more adaptation than either sipping the solution or flowing it over the tongue. This suggests that even mouth movements far more subtle than those still present in the no-movement condition of a sip-and-spit experiment can disrupt the adaptation process. (Theunissen *et al.*, 2000, p. 607)

In everyday life it is unlikely that the static mouth situation used for filter paper adaptation studies will be an appropriate model for the majority of eating episodes (I reflect on this later in the chapter when I present my case study). The experimental findings may therefore give an exaggerated impression of the rapidity of adaptation.

To get some idea of the scale involved in detecting taste, only about 1 per cent of the surface of the tongue contains taste cells. These are arranged in groups of about 50–150 into taste buds which, in turn, are grouped together in units of between one to several hundred buds to form the papillae or 'bumps' that can be inspected by sticking out one's tongue in front of a mirror (see Bear *et al.*, 1996, p. 191). Information detected in the taste cells is carried away for further processing via the gustatory axons. It would be elegant if different kinds of receptor were used to detect a particular taste and that information was then trans-mitted by separate sets of axons to neurons in the brain. This arrange-ment is sometimes referred to as the labelled line theory but it seems that taste is unlikely to work on this principle. Individual taste cells tend to be broadly tuned to stimuli and not narrowly responsive to par-ticular taste substances. Bear *et al.* (1996) say that this broad response pattern exists also at the level of the primary taste axons, right up to the central taste neurons leading to the cortex.

Smell

The general consensus seems to be that establishing odour primaries is proving to be a difficult, if not impossible task (when compared to the establishment of the four taste primaries). Although there has not turned out to be too much support for it, Henning's odour prism, described in Woodworth and Schlosberg (1954, p. 306) caught my eye (see Figure 3.2). The base of the prism is fairly unremarkable, with the four corners labelled as fragrant, ethereal, resinous, and spicy. What excited me were the two peaks at each end of the roof, as it were: putrid and burned. These bear a close resemblance to aspects of Lévi-Strauss's culinary triangle (see Chapter 2). Putrid equates with rotten and burned with cooked. The similarity with the treatment of oil is less

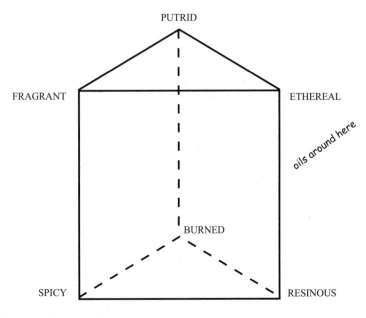

Figure 3.2 Odour prism
Source: Adapted from Woodworth and Schlosberg (1954).

direct. Lévi-Strauss found it necessary to convert his triangle to a tetrahedron in order to accommodate oil as a third axis to air and water. Henning places oils along one of the sides of his odour square at the base of his smell prism, lodging them between resinous and ethereal (I have indicated the approximate position in Figure 3.2). I can only speculate that, in this scheme of things, rancid chip fat would be elevated to the putrid end of the prism away from the position occupied by fresh oils on the resinous–ethereal axis.

Smell receptors are located at the extreme top of the nasal passage at the olfactory epithelium. The receptors (arranged as two small patches about 2–4 cm^2 in size) are tucked out of the way of the main breathing pathway. Because of this we need to take a sharp sniff in order to pull molecules emanating from an odorous substance over the receptors when we want to check out its smell. Molecules are also born upwards from the mouth into the nose, and that is very important with regard to food (see Woodworth and Schlosberg, 1954; McGee, 1984). The reason why foods appear to lose their flavour when we have a head cold is because the air pathways in the nose get bunged up and a layer of mucus gunge lies over the sensitive patches on the epithelium, rendering them ineffective.

I have already intimated that the classification of odours is a much more difficult problem than the classification of tastes. Lyman (1989) favours a rating system developed by Harper *et al.* (1968). The food sample is rated on a six-point scale for each of 44 qualities. Although this sounds a simple approach, I have found it takes a little too long if one is actually eating the food. It is not possible to hold a bite of food in the mouth for very long without registering subjective changes in the experience. For example, the action of the saliva may turn the food mushy, or the fact that chewing has stopped may restrict the circulation of air around the mouth and upwards to the receptors in the nose, thus reducing olfactory cues.

Some of these practical problems may be avoided if the food is merely sniffed. The problem with sniffing is that if a second sniff is required, a certain amount of adaptation may have taken place. I have already referred to the fact that the process of adaptation in taste is very rapid, even if some laboratory techniques may exaggerate the effect (see above). If anything, adaptation in smell seems even speedier. Lyman (1989) suggests that a decline in sensation may occur at the rate of 2.5 per cent per second until the odour has only 30 per cent of its original intensity. The adaptation effect has been acknowledged for some time. Woodworth and Schlosberg (1954) report that Zwaardemaker in 1895 found that

> Exposure to a rubber odor of moderate strength doubled the stimulus threshold for this odor in 15 seconds and quadrupled it in 45 seconds; but exposure to a stronger rubber odor raised the threshold still faster. (Woodworth and Schlosberg, 1954, p. 316)

The fact that we can adapt quickly to odours has the benefit that by the time we have moved on to dessert we are probably no longer registering the odours of the main course we have just eaten. However, speedy adaptation poses problems for research. A second bite of the cherry will not produce the identical sensation to the first (insofar as the flavour is affected by smell), unless a sufficient break is allowed for all adaptation effects to dissipate and for the sense of smell to regain its full edge. But the moment we start to introduce timings between bites, we move even further from the naturalistic setting in which food is eaten. When a bite is defined as a 'research' bite, the context is changed and ecological validity is challenged. I shall return to a discussion of this issue when I present my case study, later in the chapter. For now, I move on to consider what happens to the food, once bitten, as it journeys through the body.

Digestion

Fox and Cameron (1961) describe the body, metaphorically, as a slow combustion stove, with carbohydrate as the fuel:

> The digestive system is essentially a long tube open at both ends: food enters at the mouth, passes down the gullet into the stomach, the small intestine, the large intestine, being digested and absorbed in the process. Any that remains is excreted through the anus. (pp. 26–7)

The UK Ministry of Agriculture, Fisheries and Food (MAFF) has provided a manual of nutrition that has been updated through many editions since 1945. They make the point that food cannot be regarded as having entered the body until it has been digested and absorbed. By this they mean that the food substance first has to be broken down into its simple chemical constituents in order to pass through the walls of the digestive tract into the blood or lymph. I shall presently dip my toe into the science of this, but before I do, it is worth bearing in mind that ingestion, a necessary prelude to digestion, takes place in a social and psychological context:

> Appetite is a sensation which relates to the smell and taste of particular foods and their ingredients, and is influenced by the surroundings, habits and emotional state of the individual, all of which can also increase or decrease the flow of saliva and other digestive juices. Thus, where there is freedom of choice, more attractive foods are likely to be eaten in preference to others, and it can be seen that good cooking and pleasant surroundings are important in nutrition. (MAFF, 1985, p. 33)

As mentioned at the start of the chapter, I shall deal only with one category of food in depth and I have chosen carbohydrates as my primary example. A good food to bear in mind might be bread, which contains about 46 per cent starch, according to MAFF (1985).

A classification of carbohydrates based upon their chemical complexity and molecular size yields three categories: monosaccharides, disaccharides and polysaccharides. Examples of monosaccharides are glucose and fructose both of which may be found to occur naturally in some fruits (fructose is also present in honey). Disaccharides are formed from linking two monosaccharides together. Sucrose, present in common sugar, is a chemical combination of glucose and fructose, for example. Moving on to greater complexity, some of the starches are best thought of as polysaccharides made up from a combination of many units of glucose. Not all starches are digestible in the raw state. Flour needs cooking with the addition of water in order to render it more easily digestible (see MAFF, 1985, p. 7). Eastwood (1997) points out that finely milled flour is more easily digestible than the coarser product. Toasting bread also helps the digestion, apparently.

The process of digestion begins the moment the food enters the mouth. The general thrust of the biochemical activity is to have the carbohydrates broken down into their component monosaccharides by the time the food arrives at the large intestine. By far the majority of the absorption in the gut will have occurred before the enteric (i.e. gut) contents enter the right colon. The first step in this process is for saliva to be mixed into the food as it is chewed in the mouth. Conventional wisdom suggests that this enables the enzyme ptyalin (alpha amylase) to hydrolyse the starch to maltose and other disaccharides. However, given the short time food stays in the mouth (perhaps about 2 minutes), there may be insufficient time for the starch to be broken down since this process is thought to take about 20 minutes. The function of the saliva may thus be primarily one of lubrication. On reaching the stomach the masticated food is acidified as it is mixed with the gastric juices. This denatures a large proportion of the amylase and effectively slows carbohydrate digestion until a second burst of amylase, from the exocrine pancreas, enters in the second part of the duodenum. Once through the stomach and into the small intestine, pancreatic amylase continues the conversion of the starch to maltose and other disaccharides. This is real progress, since maltose is a disaccharide with two connected glucose units. Intestinal juices, rich in maltase, then hydrolyse the maltose (and other disaccharides) into its constituent parts. The hydrolysis of maltose to glucose may be represented as follows:

$$C_{12}H_{22}O_{11} \text{ (maltose)} + H_2O \rightarrow 2C_6H_{12}O_6 \text{ (glucose)}$$

One reason why it is necessary for the starch compounds to be broken down into their constituent components is because the molecules are too big to be absorbed through the gut wall. Once the food has been reduced to glucose it can be passed into the blood stream and carried away to the liver or to the muscles. At this point it may be useful to reflect on how the glucose provides the body with energy for immediate use or storage.

With plants, carbohydrates are built up by photosynthesis from carbon dioxide and water. The process may be symbolised, using the conventional chemical formula, as follows:

$$6CO_2 + 12H_2O \rightarrow C_6H_{12}O_6 \text{ (glucose)} + 6O_2 + 6H_2O$$

The energy from sunlight that is required to synthesise glucose may be retrieved at a later stage through the reverse process of oxidation. While it is true that animals are unable to synthesise carbohydrates, it is possible for them to utilise the energy stored within them. Energy may be obtained by the oxidation of glucose to lactic acid and then on to carbon dioxide and water by a complicated series of reactions. However, glucose, as a source of energy for humans, is wanting in two aspects: firstly, it is not an ideal storage medium; secondly, it is not capable of providing the speedy delivery demanded by a muscle with a job of work to do. With regard to the storage problem, the liver converts some glucose to glycogen and some to adipose tissue for use at a later date. Because the oxidation of glucose takes too long to be utilised in muscular contraction, the energy it releases is used to build (and rebuild) the compound adenosine triphosphate (ATP). This compound contains three phosphate groups and it is when these are split off that large amounts of energy are liberated. When the ATP has been relieved of its energy, more glucose can be used to replenish and restore the compound to its former state. Stored glycogen is broken down in order to furnish the glucose necessary for this process.

I have provided this sketch of how carbohydrates are used by the body as an illustration of the digestive process. A similarly complex story could be told about the digestion of fats, proteins, and other substances. Eastwood (1997, p. 362) states that there are six main phases in the digestion and absorption of proteins, moving from whole protein absorption through to their breakdown into amino acids and peptides and the eventual transfer of end products into the bloodstream. It is not necessary for me to elaborate on each of these six phases since it would take me too far into the language games of biochemistry for my present purposes. In any case, I have scant qualification to make that journey. On similar grounds, I shall forgo the temptation to describe the process of fat digestion whereby lipids are degraded into forms capable of being absorbed by the gastrointestinal tract. If the digestion of food involves chemical activity within the body, food preparation frequently requires chemical changes effected in the kitchen and it is to this topic that I now turn.

Kitchen Chemistry

Skill in the kitchen is helped not only by the development of culinary techniques requiring practice and manual dexterity, such as filleting fish or icing cakes, but also by the acquisition of a sufficiently broad knowledge base in the form of recipes. An additional advantage to the cook is provided by the possession of an understanding of the scientific principles that account for what happens to food when it is cooked. Just as I limited my treatment of digestion to the single topic of carbohydrates, I shall deal only with one topic in depth in relation to kitchen chemistry: egg cookery. I shall draw mainly from McGee (1984) in my exposition.

There are many ways in which eggs play a part in cooking. The two obvious components of an egg are the yolk and the white (albumen). One of the most interesting aspects of eggs from the point of view of their chemistry is the way they coagulate. The egg contains proteins in the form of amino acids and these come in the form of long chains, folded into themselves. When they are heated some of the chains unfold but, being in close proximity of other unfolded chains, they then start to become enmeshed with one another. In this process, fresh bonds are formed between the stranded chains, and the new mesh of molecules will, providing the process is not taken too far, contain pockets of water within its boundaries. The clustering together of these solid molecules can be seen as the albumen changes its appearance from a colourless liquid to an opaque white solid (the change depending to some extent on how long the cooking has gone on for). If coagulation is taken to extremes, the mesh becomes so tight that the water contained within its pockets is squeezed out and the result may be observed in several manifestations, such as a rubbery egg or curdling.

The temperature at which the egg white begins to coagulate is about 63°C and the white as a whole will be properly cooked at about 71°C. It should be born in mind, however, that eggs are often mixed with other ingredients, when they are not being eaten as a dish in their own right. Custard, for example, requires the additional ingredients of milk and sugar. McGee (1984) suggests that the addition of the extra liquid raises the temperature at which coagulation begins and that this is because the protein molecules are effectively diluted in a larger solution. The upshot of this is that it is more difficult for them to bind on one another.

According to McGee (1984), salt and acid have the reverse effect of milk or sugar, thus speeding up the process of coagulation:

Acid – cream of tartar, lemon juice, or the juice of any fruit or vegetable – lowers the pH of the egg, and thereby lowers the mutually
repelling negative charges on individual protein molecules. The lower
this charge, the smaller the repulsion, and the less force required
to overcome it; the protein molecules can then bond together more
easily. Salt, by dissociating into positive sodium and negative chloride ions, disturbs the electrical environment in its own way, again
encouraging coagulation. So, diluting or sweetening eggs delays
coagulation; salting or acidifying them accelerates it. (McGee, 1984,
p. 68)

Applying this idea to the skill of cooking egg custards, it can be seen
that the addition of milk and sugar will raise the point at which
coagulation starts. The use of a water bath limits the temperature of
the pan containing the custard to 100°C and this is important since it
provides protection from the ambient temperature of the oven which
might otherwise take it beyond that level. There is very little margin
for error in custard-making and the speed with which the custard
mixture is heated can have an effect on this. McGee (1984) reports that
custards cooked by placing the mixture into a pan of already boiling
water might start to thicken at 88°C and curdle at 91°C (a latitude
of 3°C). When the custard is cooked more gently, by slowly bringing
the custard up to temperature at the same time as heating the water
in the bain marie, thickening happens at 82°C and curdling at 88°C
(doubling the range to 6°C). With the slower approach to cooking the
custard, McGee (1984) argues that the cook has a better chance to get
the pan out of the heat and cooled in a bowl of cold water to arrest
cooking before curdling occurs.

Another important use for eggs, especially the separated whites, is as
a foam in the making of soufflés (sweet or savoury), meringues, or
sponge cakes. When egg whites are whipped, air is incorporated into
the mixture to form a relatively stable mass of bubbles. McGee (1984)
regards egg whites as stabilising the foam 'by introducing a kind of
reinforcement into the bubble walls, a culinary equivalent of quick-
setting cement' (p. 73). There are various proteins in eggs. Ovalbumin
plays no role in the creation of the egg foam at room temperature but
when the foam is cooked in the oven, it is ovalbumin that fixes the
liquid foam into the solid texture that resists collapse once the dish is
out of the oven. If the whites are beaten for too long (beyond the stiff
peaks stage) the bonding of one protein molecule to another becomes
excessive and the water-holding capacity of the mixture will decline to
the extent that water will be leaked from the foam. If even a drop of fat

is present in the bowl when whites are being beaten, this can reduce the volume of the foam considerably. The reason for this is that fat, including fatty molecules from the egg yolk, interferes with the way the protein–protein bonds of the albumen form the coagulated lattice.

Even when the cook has succeeded in creating the perfectly beaten foam, a soufflé can still collapse as it is removed from the oven. When the steam and air begin to cool, this can be enough to bring down the precarious foam created by the web of proteins and starch. Although sponge cakes are also made with whipped egg whites, the addition of flour into the mixture provides both strength and stability for the end product, when compared with soufflés.

All processes in kitchen cookery may be considered from the standpoint of organic chemistry. McGee (1984) covers many interesting aspects of preparation and storage. For example, he is concerned with the chemical changes in making ice cream and bread. He provides two accounts of the processes involved in sauce-making, depending on whether the sauces are starch-thickened (e.g. béchamel) or emulsified (e.g. hollandaise). Beyond this he covers cheese, batters, cakes, meat and fish cookery.

My aim, in this section, has been to illustrate the advantages of bringing to bear a perspective based upon organic chemistry to mundane problems that the cook may experience in the kitchen. I chose to use egg cookery as a way to illustrate this largely on the grounds that I found it to be interesting. Both carbohydrate (discussed in relation to the section on digestion, earlier in this chapter) and egg (the focus of this section) will feature in the case study which I report below, although this was entirely fortuitous.

The act of eating sits between food preparation and food digestion. From animal and vegetable sources the chemical compounds are transformed and absorbed into human bodies where they provide energy, some of which may be stored for future use. Residues not taken up by the body are then eliminated as waste matter. Given that eating is the point at which this chemical process touches consciousness, one could argue that psychology might best be construed as occupying a conceptual space somewhere between agribusiness and the sewage industry.

In one sense, psychophysical studies of taste and smell do deal with conscious experience. However, the assessment of taste on a rating scale in the laboratory is an activity that is far removed from the experience of flavour in mundane reality. In order to provide a counterpoint to the laboratory and survey studies, I conclude this chapter with a case study of my experience of lunch at home. In reporting this quotidian kitchen event, I shall allow myself the indulgence of drifting away from the objective style of reporting, from time to time, and shall try to remain phenomenologically true to the ebb, flow and contents of my stream of consciousness.

Case Study: A Simple Lunch at Home

I report this case study on the basis of notes that I made while preparing and eating a simple lunch (extracts appear as boxed text).

> I intend to boil an egg and have that on one slice of toast, with a glass of still spring water. I shall not put any butter or margarine on the toast, since I am trying to keep to a low-fat diet.

This marks the start of the episode. Had I not designated this lunch as a research event, I doubt whether I would have articulated this intention in such an explicit fashion.

> I've just boiled the kettle. Kettles make an interesting noise when boiling. Now I can hear the gas on the stove, the egg water bubbling in the pan, and the wind howling down the extractor vent through an old disused chimney outlet in the kitchen.

I must resist the temptation to bracket off these noises as irrelevant. Although I am going to focus upon taste and smell (both topics which I dealt with from the scientific standpoint earlier in the chapter), I want them to feature merely as part of the gestalt of the lunch episode.

> I've put the bread in the toaster. I'm just getting into this episode when my neighbour switched on his garden vacuum machine to pick up the autumn leaves. It's making a nasty noise and has completely shattered the tranquillity of this Sunday morning.

I have to say that this was an unusual occurrence; it didn't last long but unhappily it coincided with my lunch. I note that a distraction of this nature would be unlikely to occur at an experimental tasting session.

> I get a slight sniff of burning plastic, probably the handle of the egg saucepan.

This is the first reference to olfaction in my notes. This smell (which was unpleasant) was generated by mistake and was not directly related to the food. Again, I am sure it would not be present in a controlled tasting environment. The smell is difficult to position with regard to the odour prism (see Figure 3.2). I do not think that the use of the word 'burning' in my description 'burning plastic' is equivalent to what is meant by burned (at the apex of the odour prism). I think of burnt toast or bonfires in that context.

> My 5-minute timer has gone off, so I'm peeling the egg and I've propped up the slab of toast to let the moisture out (just as Delia Smith advised on her TV show).

My timer is a small electronic gadget that sticks to the fridge with a magnet; it displays a countdown of the time set on a small screen and beeps shrilly when it's done. As I sit writing this chapter, I remember that we had a sand-filled egg-timer at home when I was a child. This thought did not occur to me at the time when I was writing up my notes and now I am not sure whether I should legitimately include it here. I can't see why not and so I have not deleted this paragraph from my manuscript. It provides a simple example of the way in which my lunch episode is embedded in a broader cultural and technological epoch. My memories put down a marker as to progress made in readily available timing devices for use in kitchens over the course of the past 50 years or so.

Propping the toast up is an example of the way in which an expansion of my knowledge base through exposure to a recent TV cookery programme altered my behaviour. The rationale for this strategy is grounded in kitchen physics, if not chemistry. In the book accompanying her series, Delia Smith (1998) advises:

When the toast is done, remove it immediately to a toast rack. Why a toast rack? Because they are a brilliant invention. Freshly made toast contains steam, and if you place it in a vertical position, in which the air is allowed to circulate, the steam escapes and the toast becomes crisp and crunchy. Putting it straight on to a plate means that the steam is trapped underneath making it damp and soggy. If you don't possess a toast rack you really ought to invest in a modest one. Failing that, stand your slices of toast up against a jar or something similar for about 1 minute before serving. (p. 83)

I don't have a toast rack, so I stood the toast against the metal toaster.

> Next, I deliberately break the egg on the toast and spread the yolk. On goes the seasoning and I'm preparing to take my first mouthful. The sound of toast being cut on plate is quite distinctive and fairly noisy.

I am surprised by how important audition was in this lunch episode. I feel that this is something that would be lost in a laboratory setting.

> I've definitely got the tastes of salt and burnt toast, up at the front of my mouth. Another bite. I notice that the egg dries out my mouth, somewhat. This may be because I have put no margarine on the toast. I have some water. This racket from my neighbour's garden is getting on my nerves.

Duffy and Bartoshuk (1996) emphasise how the liking or disliking of odour combinations for particular dishes is subject to the processes of positive and negative conditioning. Looking back with hindsight, I am pleased to report that the pairing of the garden vacuum noise and the eating of egg on toast did not result in a single trial learning experience. Apparently, single trial learned food aversions are not uncommon in humans, although surveys indicate that these are often where a gastrointestinal upset follows the ingestion of the food (see Schafe and Bernstein, 1996, for a discussion of taste aversion learning).

In reporting the fact that my mouth had dried out, I am assuming a shared linguistic knowledge and a common cultural experience. You perhaps know what a dried out mouth feels like, maybe one dried out while eating egg. I assume that you can imagine that drinking water will alleviate this. In a sense, I am banking on the fact that you will be able to carry out a replication of my experience based on your memories, perhaps using a little imagination too. Brentano (1874/1995) feels that this is one area where psychology may have the advantage over the physical sciences:

We really can focus our attention on a past mental phenomenon just as we can upon a present physical phenomenon, and in this way we can, so to speak, observe it. Furthermore, we could say that it is even possible to undertake experimentation on our own mental phenomena in this manner. For we can, by various means, arouse certain mental phenomena in ourselves intentionally, in order to find out whether this or that other phenomenon occurs as a result. We can then contemplate the result of our experiment calmly and attentively in our memory. (p. 35)

Brentano acknowledges that this procedure will not be fully equivalent to the observation of currently occurring events and, in particular, that distortions may be introduced through memory.

> Now I've taken a bit of egg on its own, without toast. I let my tongue roll over the smooth surface of the white. It's really very sensuous and it seems a shame to bite into it. I take another forkful.

I can't remember getting sensuous pleasure from rolling my tongue over cooked egg white before. I don't think that I would have stumbled across this experience, had I not designated this lunch as a research episode. It wasn't anticipated and it's difficult to know what construction I should place upon it now.

> The crunching up of the crusty toast is very loud in my jaw and nearly drowns out the sound of the garden vacuum.

Internal noise, conducted through the jaw, is a very interesting aspect of the eating experience. Here I have competition between the internal and external sources. In passing, I think that this could be approached using the laboratory methods of psychophysics, even if establishing just noticeable differences (see Woodworth and Schlosberg, 1954, p. 193) between crunching toast and garden machinery does seem a trifle eccentric.

> Writing up my paper-and-pencil notes is making my food get cold.

This is something that I have noticed, since doing research for this book. It is a classic case of the Heisenberg principle in physics, applied to psychology: the act of observation affects that which is observed.

> Now I've taken a bit of egg with lots of pepper showing on it. It does feel a bit hot. The peppery taste seems to be up at the front of my mouth.

McGee (1984) suggests that one of the reasons that we enjoy hot foods is that they may trigger the production of endorphins (an opiate substance) in the brain. I think McGee was mainly talking about chilli peppers and not necessarily the ground black pepper that I put on my lunch. Setting that aside, tasting pepper on egg creates competing flavours. The pepper fights the smoothness and the blandness of the egg and, in so doing, challenges the sense of reassurance that I sometimes get by association when I eat eggs. To speak of a taste being reassuring is to go way beyond the boundaries of laboratory descriptors for taste and smell. The term is loaded with autobiographical associations for me, possibly relating to those occasions when I was ill and had lost appetite when a child: a boiled egg and 'soldiers' of bread and butter would often do the trick. Perhaps it is to rid myself of such associations that I use the pepper as an adult.

> To some extent all the various tastes have been masked or overshadowed by the taste of egg yolk which I find very dominant.

I found it extremely difficult to think of my experience of eating the egg in terms of the basic tastes of bitter, sour, salty and sweet. It is the case that I tasted salt, but then I seasoned the food before I ate it.

> I am only about halfway through my lunch and I've suddenly noticed that time is slipping by. I shall have to curtail this research episode. The reason for this is that I have to wake up the girls (my daughter's friend's mother is coming to collect her daughter from a sleep-over in 20 minutes). I clearly failed to allow enough time. I think it took far longer than I expected to make my notes.

This was, perhaps, an example of bad research organisation. However, it also illustrates how intrusive the research process can be on the event under consideration.

Concluding Discussion

By way of conclusion, I shall attempt to relate what happened in the case study I have just described to the findings reported earlier in the chapter. The experimental investigation of the effects of stomach distension indicates that it is the absorption of nutrients in the food that may be crucial in terminating a bout of eating. In the case of my lunch, I stopped eating partly because I had eaten everything that was on my plate and partly because I had something else to do. Neither of these reasons is directly related to stomach distension or the absorption of nutrients. An explanation of why I stopped eating in my luncheon episode would also appear to be otiose, if couched in terms of blood glucose levels.

The attempt to explain eating behaviour, in animals, in terms of cortical activity in the ventromedial or lateral hypothalamic regions appears not to have been wholly successful. I shall therefore set that material aside and move on to speculate as to whether a psychological (as opposed to a physiological) explanation of my lunchtime behaviour could be fashioned from knowledge relating to leptin levels and neuropeptide Y.

Given that my body weight was high-ish at the time of the case study, let us assume that my leptin–NPY control system was set in such a way that I was secreting too much leptin. This would inhibit the release of NPY that in turn would inhibit my PVN (paraventricular nucleus) in the hypothalamus, thus generating an appetite for larger meals. But this physiological explanation could not account for the fact that I deliberately chose not to put butter on my toast and cooked only one egg, instead of two (which I could have eaten with ease and relish). To find a psychological explanation for my lunch it is necessary to leave physiology to one side and to construe what I did as intentional action. At one sweep, the explanation leaps across a paradigm barrier (I discuss the distinction between action and behaviour in my previous book, *The Psychology of Action*). I refrained from putting butter on the toast because I wanted to lose weight and I thought a low-fat diet would be a good way to do it. My knowledge of physiology influenced the tactic I chose to follow in the pursuit of my goal. I chose this course of action, despite what may or may not have been going on in my cortex in terms of leptin secretions. I claim that what I did was under my conscious control and was not necessarily determined by physiological events in the hypothalamus.

Had I been suffering from a head cold when I ate my lunch I would not have been able to taste the egg and toast as well as I did. In that case, the physiology of taste and smell could have been brought in to furnish an explanation. As it was, I was in good health and so my smell receptors were in as good a working order as ever. This made it hard for me to separate out impressions of taste from those of smell. Having said that, I did smell the burning plastic and the burnt toast independently of tasting them (of course, I did also taste the toast). My choice of food handicapped me in terms of exploring the taste of sweetness. Although I noticed the taste of salt, it was the peppery taste that came through more strongly. I thought that I got this on my tongue, up the front somewhere. It is impossible to account for this in terms of the physiological literature, which allows only sweet, sour, bitter and salty as tastes for the tongue. As I write this discussion, this matter of the pepper is really annoying me. I've just gone down to the kitchen and ground some black pepper onto a small plate. I took a drink of water to cleanse my mouth, dabbed my finger in the pepper and put some on my tongue while holding my nose with my other hand. I definitely felt a hot burning sensation on my tongue. When I released my nose and started breathing again I did get a better sense of a 'peppery' taste but the hotness was definitely up the front of the tongue. I can't understand why 'peppery' has not been included in the taste maps of olden days.

One of the main findings to come from the notes on my lunch was how important audition seemed to be for the episode as a whole. My guess is that this was because I was on my own. Admittedly, in my episode it was the unpleasant noise of garden machinery that was the main competitor with the intra-cranial crunch. In retrospect, it is surprising that I did not switch on the kitchen radio during lunch, since I often listen to news magazines on BBC's Radio 4 or music on one of the other channels, be it classical, jazz, or popular. Talk or music would have competed for my attention in terms of both eating and preparing the food. This is something that will have to await further investigation but my recollection of similar kitchen and food episodes is that such distractions sometimes result in my preparing and eating the meal on automatic pilot, rather like driving to work and not being able to recall the details of the journey.

With regard to kitchen chemistry, I think the situation is rather like statistics on the undergraduate curriculum in psychology. It is possible to cook by following recipe books, without a deep knowledge of the principles of organic chemistry, in the same way that an adequate statistical analysis may be achieved by executing the correct commands in a computer statistical package, without knowing anything about the underlying formulae or why they are as they are. Indeed, this style of statistical analysis is known as 'cook book stats'. Problems arise for the statistically naive psychologist when something goes wrong or when there is a pile of data but no clue as to how to go about the analysis. Similarly, in the kitchen, the chemically naive cook may be slow to associate the rubbery egg with time or temperature of cooking, or the reluctantly whisked egg whites with traces of grease in the bowl. Such a cook may also run into difficulties where a meal has to be made from the ingredients at hand, in a fashion not dissimilar to the TV show *Ready, Steady, Cook* (popular in the UK). The point that I wish to make in this regard is that kitchen chemistry may provide the cook with an important knowledge base. Obviously, kitchen chemistry is not psychology. Organic chemistry becomes integrated into the psychology of food only when it is blended with cognitive psychology. An examination of the utilisation of the chemical knowledge base in kitchen problem-solving and in the generation of intentions to cook specific dishes (influencing the choice of ingredients and the mode of cooking, for example) is a topic for future research. Weaknesses in the knowledge base (relating to organic kitchen chemistry) may be examined for the part they play in frustrating the enabling conditions that need to obtain in the execution of kitchen plans of action (see Abelson, 1975, for a discussion of enabling conditions).

In discussing the scientific research into food psychology in the context of my case study, I have been drawn to the view that in some cases the scientific research lies beyond the boundaries of the discipline of psychology. The case study was an example of the idiographic method, with leanings towards the phenomenological approach, and should not be seen as running in direct competition with experimental laboratory studies. What seemed to be gained from the idiographic stance was a different perspective on what might be interesting to explore in further psychological studies. In this regard the case study might best be regarded as heuristic. Some of the scientific work concerning hunger provides a foundation for the biomedical discourse on eating disorders and this I explore more fully in the next chapter.

4

Eating Disorders: The Feminist, Control and Biomedical Discourses

As a teenager and young man I could eat as much of anything as I liked and still stay as thin as a beanpole. I never thought about my body weight because it always remained constant. In middle age, I do have to keep an eye on what I eat in order to keep my weight down to a reasonable, if not ideal, limit. However, while I regard this as a bit of a nuisance, it in no way causes me serious problems. I therefore have some difficulty in coming to grips with the major eating disorders of our times, such as anorexia or bulimia nervosa. This may be due, in part, to my gender since these disorders are predominantly experienced by women (that situation may be changing to some extent).

Although I have chosen to consider eating disorders in general, I shall focus primarily upon anorexia nervosa, since there is not sufficient space to cover all disorders in detail. Malson (1998) traces the genealogy of anorexia nervosa through to the nineteenth century, using a Foucauldian perspective, and then articulates a dozen or more different academic discourses on the topic, which she claims to be in use in the late twentieth century. She also provides a feminist, social psychological account of anorexia nervosa based on an analysis of interview data collected from women diagnosed as anorexic. She approaches her interview material from the discursive standpoint (as developed by Potter and Wetherell, 1987). I shall provide a fuller account of this work a little later in the chapter. I find the idea of breaking down the academic literature on eating disorders into cognate discourses to be an attractive one and I shall adopt it as a way of organising the material in this chapter. Rather than attempting an exhaustive coverage of all possible approaches to eating disorders, I shall focus on the following three broad conversations:

- The feminist discourse (this to include talk of a psychoanalytic and societal nature).
- The discourse of control (this to include the parlance of cognitive behaviour therapy and cybernetics).
- The biomedical discourse (this to include biochemical and genetic talk).

I shall start with a brief introduction to anorexia nervosa, before dealing with each of the above.

Anorexia Nervosa

Logue (1991) distinguishes the psychological conditions of anorexia nervosa and bulimia from the medical conditions involving extreme weight loss attributable to the effects of cancer and chemotherapy. She also sets aside cases of anorexia where the cause may lie with the side effects of drugs such as amphetamine, possibly prescribed as an antidepressant. She endorses Bruch's (1973) definition of anorexia nervosa as 'the relentless pursuit of thinness through self-starvation, even unto death' (Logue, 1991, p. 177). Vandereycken and Deth (1990, pp. 1–2) set out the following diagnostic criteria with regard to anorexia nervosa:

- An intense fear of becoming fat, even though underweight.
- Disturbance in the way in which one's body weight, size, or shape is experienced, e.g. the person claims to 'feel fat' even when emaciated.
- Refusal to maintain body weight over a normal minimum weight for age and height, e.g. weight loss leading to a body weight of 15 per cent below that expected.

Most writers seem to agree that this is something that happens predominantly to girls or women (especially in the younger age range from the teens through to the 30s) with only about 5–10 per cent of the identified cases being male. Furthermore, the incidence appears to be higher within the middle and upper classes than among the working class (see Logue, 1991; Vandereycken and Deth, 1990; Colman, 1987).

Vandereycken and Deth (1990) make the point that the behavioural characteristics associated with anorexia nervosa, such as obsession with food, eating on the sly, hoarding, constipation or amenorrhoea, are the same phenomena that arise from instances of prolonged fasting, whatever the situation, including controlled studies with volunteer fasters. Vandereycken and Deth (1990) argue that many of these characteristics were manifested by the fasting saints of medieval times and the hunger artists who performed during the nineteenth century and early twentieth century. If too much emphasis is placed upon the behavioural characteristics, the temptation may be to apply the modern diagnostic label of anorexia nervosa inappropriately where the context is quite different:

> In mediaeval hagiographies we vainly look for the relentless pursuit of thinness which is currently considered to be an essential characteristic of anorexia nervosa. There is no trace of saints 'dieting' from a fear of becoming fat. The highly valued ideals in which both saints and anorexics are completely absorbed are time-bound and widely divergent in content. Fasting saints were not obsessed by the exterior, outward appearance. By contrast they strove for an inner, spiritual fusion with Christ's sufferings. It was not a cult of slenderness but a religious-mystical cult that dominated their life. (Vandereycken and Deth, 1990, p. 221)

Feminist writers also tend to take a broad view of eating disorders, placing them within a cultural and historical context, and I move on to sample their approach, below.

The Feminist Discourse

I shall break this discourse down into three sections: the post-structuralist approach; Malson's discursive analysis of anorexic women's talk; Orbach's approach.

Post-structuralist, Lacanian discourse

Malson (1998) introduces her feminist post-structuralist perspective as follows:

> Briefly, this perspective builds upon the work of Saussure (1960) and the work of French structuralism. Rather than taking the view that language is a transparent medium through which we can view the world, I am viewing language as constructive of reality (see Potter and Wetherell, 1987). To paraphrase Foucault (1972: 49), discourses systematically constitute the objects, the individuals, the bodies, the experiences of which they speak. That is, from a post-structuralist

perspective, discourses do not simply reflect some reality existing elsewhere: they actively and systematically construct particular versions of the world, of objects, events, experiences and identities. (p. 6)

This approach leads Malson (1998) to challenge the notion that anorexia can be regarded transhistorically as an enduring medical entity (cf. the above quotation from Vandereycken and Deth). Indeed, she is critical of those who apply the contemporary psychiatric label of anorexia nervosa to medieval cases of women engaged in religious self-starvation.

Moving on from fasting as a holy expression of piety, Malson (1998) traces the way the general category of nervous disorders is formed from a convergence of talk relating to hysteria, on the one hand, and hypochondria, on the other. This took place over the course of the eighteenth and nineteenth centuries and the link to anorexia is provided through the concept of gastric disorder (a subcategory of nervous disorders, in general). The symptoms of gastric disorder include lack of appetite and this was regarded as a manifestation of nervousness. Malson, building on previous critiques which establish that these disorders are highly gendered, is able to expose the way 'femininity' featured as a causal explanation of the disorders within the nineteenth century medical discourse. She argues that anorexia nervosa, far from existing 'out there' (awaiting its scientific discovery) was a linguistic construction born of a fusion between medical and cultural discourses and, as such, has socio-historical specificity.

It seems to me that Malson achieves two things through her historical analysis. Firstly, by showing how the medical discourse evolves, she makes it difficult to accept realist accounts of a universal medical condition called anorexia nervosa and this has implications for the acceptance of the more recent scientific accounts advanced within the twentieth century. Of course, this is what one might expect from a discursive psychologist. Her second achievement is to tie anorexia to gender politics and the position of women in patriarchal society.

The perspective she adopts on gender and feminine identity is subtle and flows from a sympathetic reading of Freud's theory of sexuality where both masculinity and femininity are problematised as not being the natural consequences of genital sexual difference, even though femininity is conceptualised as a negative term. In this connection she draws upon Lacan's interpretation of Freud. While the active connotations of masculinity and the passive connotations of femininity are unconsciously acquired as a result of working through the Oedipus complex, these gender identities only become meaningful in the context of a patriarchal human society. This I can follow. However, I am one of those readers who find Lacan's writing difficult to penetrate (admittedly, I read him in English translation). There is some debate as to whether there is anything there to penetrate, anyway. Norris (1996) alerts us to the fact that the Lacanian king may, beneath the rhetoric, be devoid of clothes:

> We are therefore hopelessly mistaken if we hold psychoanalysis accountable to standards of enlightened truth-seeking thought. It is the sheer opacity of the Freudian text – its resistance to any kind of lucid expository treatment – which Lacan views as the purveyor of truth, albeit a 'truth' that can scarcely be expressed in conceptual or rational-discursive terms. This is also (though some would consider it a charitable reading) why Lacan's own texts go out of their way to create syntactic and stylistic obstacles for anyone who looks to them in hope of discovering an easy route of access to the Freudian corpus. On the contrary: such access is everywhere denied by a style that raises difficulty into a high point of principle, or which (less kindly) takes bafflement as a guard against the requirements of plain good sense. (p. 5)

Bowie (1991, p. 12) makes the point that Lacan attempted to express his theoretical ideas in a language that sounded like the unconscious; there is something satisfyingly reflexive about that goal. Bowie (1991) provides a sympathetic and enthusiastic introduction to Lacan. For the time being, I will proceed as though I am not completely baffled by this approach.

Malson starts by drawing on Lacan's rereading of Freud:

> Lacanian theory emphasises that masculinity and femininity do not arise from the real body but from the way in which male and female bodies are *signified* within a Symbolic order. (Malson, 1998, p. 16)

The *Symbolic order* is expressed in language and this provides the bridge to Saussure's (1960) work on the arbitrary nature of linguistic signs. In Lacan's theory, human identity, as the first person singular 'I', is signified through the phallus:

> The phallus defines identity, the 'I', as masculine. As that which represents the effect of the Symbolic order, it designates the masculine as the position of 'Oneness', of knowing and of being. (Malson, 1998, p. 18)

This forces the negative definition of femininity, in relation to masculinity, as 'Not-I' or 'Not-One'. Talk of the phallus flags up Lacan's creative incorporation of psychoanalytic theory into the semiological discourse.

In order to unpack the Lacanian discourse, it is necessary to think about babies and infants prior to the point at which they have acquired a human identity. Of course, when that is acquired, it will be acquired through the pre-existing linguistic signifier 'I'. Because language is a system (*langue*) which is handed down to us through our culture, human identity is therefore essentially a social identity (this is an anti-humanist position). There is no basis for distinguishing between individual and society since, through language, society inhabits each individual. This means that there can be no 'real' individual, since the human identity will be based on a misidentification: the first person indexical comes ready-made, off-the-peg from the pre-existing system of symbols in language (*langue*):

> The human animal is born into language and it is within the terms of language that the human subject is constructed. Language does not arise from within the individual, it is always out there in the world outside, lying in wait for the individual. (Mitchell, 1982, p. 5)

It seems that some degree of alienation is guaranteed by this inevitable mismatch. Apparently, the start of the rot is when the infant reaches the 'mirror stage' and identifies its fragmented body image with the integrated gestalt that appears in the mirror. This involves a distortion because the infant's fragmented experience becomes transformed into a whole gestalt:

> The mirror image is central to Lacan's account of subjectivity, because its apparent smoothness and totality is a myth. The image in which we first recognise ourselves is a *misrecognition*. (Rose, 1982, p. 30)

The mirror stage also facilitates alienation since the 'I' is an image in the mirror and is thus distanced from primary experience. Malson states that the acquisition of this 'specular I' happens prior to the moment when the subject is constituted in language.

This still doesn't account for why the phallus enters into this story and plays such a central role. I turn to a definition of the phallus from Roustang's (1990) glossary, in the hope that it might shed some light on the problem:

The term allows Lacan to link his own theory of the signifier to the Freudian theory of the libido; in it, language and sexuality are joined together. For reasons that are never made explicit, reasons dictated by the requirements of Lacanian systematization, the phallus becomes the signifier *par excellence*, and all other signifiers in the language are dependent on it. (p. 129)

I will try to explain this, as I understand it. Any human wishing to identify themselves in talk or thought will have to use the term 'I' as given to them in (the English) language. This is a special signifier because it can be thought of as lying at the heart of the symbolic order. The reason why this is so is that the infant has to start somewhere and the starting place will be the very first distinction she or he makes between 'I' and the rest of the world ('The Other'). I think this is the point at which Lacan finds it useful to hook into psychoanalytic theory. The reason for this is that Freud has already drawn attention to the importance of the mother in this process. Given that all infants start from the position of existing in a state of physiological and psychological symbiosis with the mother, a moment must come when the infant distinguishes him or her self from the mother as different or separate in some way. Because Lacan defines the signifier (the 'I') in this first moment of signification (where 'I' is distinguished from the 'Not-I') as masculine, this creates a problem for women's identity. If Lacan's assertion is allowed, then women (because they are not masculine) have to receive the identity of 'Not-I'. This puts women in the impossible situation of being defined as exclusion. Yet they are not outside the symbolic system any more than they are outside society. The twisted logic of their identity results in them being inside while at the same time having an identity that excludes them ('Not-I').

Let me just go back a couple of sentences to reconsider Lacan's insistence that the 'I' be construed as the phallus (and therefore masculine). I will present a quotation from 'The Signification of the Phallus' (Lacan, 1977) in order to throw light on this (even if I do say this with a touch of irony):

> The demand for love can only suffer from a desire whose signifier is alien to it. If the desire of the mother *is* the phallus, the child wishes to be the phallus in order to satisfy that desire. Thus the division immanent in desire is already felt to be experienced in the desire of the Other, in that it is already opposed to the fact that the subject is content to present to the Other what in reality he may *have* that corresponds to this phallus, for what he has is worth no more than

what he does not have, as far as his demand for love is concerned because that demand requires that he be the phallus. (p. 289) (emphasis in the original)

I had great difficulty in selecting any quotable paragraph from the text of this lecture. I feel that the above quotation is no more unintelligible than the bulk of Lacan's writing and it certainly provides an illustration of its opacity. Mitchell (1982) indicates that such opacity is deliberate:

> The preposterous difficulty of Lacan's style is a challenge to easy comprehension, to the popularisation and secularisation of psychoanalyis as it has occurred most notably in North America. (p. 4)

Setting aside stylistic difficulties, let us go along with the notion that the identity signified by 'I' is, indeed, masculine. I shall now proceed to explore the way in which Malson (1992) brings out the significance of this for female anorexics.

Malson's (1992) framework for anorexia assumes a subjectivity that is both gendered and socially located:

> Hence an understanding of anorexia, in which identity-disturbances and 'diffused sense of ego-boundaries' are ubiquitously acknowledged, must incorporate an examination of social prescriptions of gender, and particularly of 'femininity', in terms of the implications, social and psychological, of being positioned as 'the Other', the 'not-I' and in terms of the socio-historically specific ways in which those negative relations of 'femininity' are lived. (p. 83)

Central to her account of anorexia is the paradox of identity, which Malson (1992) clarifies, in the following passage:

> In as much as the 'I' contains identity, femininity is (impossibly) contained within an exclusion; is defined in terms of that from which it is excluded. It is not that 'the woman' is outside of the symbolic order, but that she is excluded within it: 'Her being not all in the phallic function does not mean that she is not in it at all. She is in it not not at all. She is right in it ...' (Lacan in Mitchell and Rose, 1982, p. 145) 'Femininity' stands then as an impossible contradiction, an identity as 'not-I', a subject positioned as Other. (p. 74)

I think this is as far as I can go with this discourse. Malson (1998) makes the point that Lacanian theory tends to deal with the symbolic order as given in the abstract system of language (the Saussaurian *langue*). Although this provides a framework in which gender is thought of as a construct existing in a socio-historical context, she feels that the step forward is to pay closer attention in future to the actualities of speech (the Saussurian *parole*) and it is this aspect of her work that I next consider.

Conversations with anorexic women: Malson's analysis

Malson (1998) concludes from her analysis of conversations with anorexic women that

> the many discourses that converge upon the female body and the 'anorexic' body, that interpellate these women, are discourses that are profoundly embedded in contemporary Western culture and that permeate all our lives. (p. 104)

This squares with her general theoretical stance (see above). I shall now summarise some of her findings.

Not surprisingly, fat bodies were thought to be ugly and shameful whereas a beautiful woman with a thin body might expect a perfect life and happiness. The point is made that the duty to reach the ideal of a slim body is not as pressing for men as it is for women. Malson found that thinness signified femininity characterised by meekness and delicacy. The petite woman is almost childlike; an anorexic woman with reduced breasts and hips becomes literally so. This image is reinforced and sexualised in the fashion media through the use of 'child-waifs' on the catwalk and in the magazines. Malson comments on the fact that the thinness and beauty tips given in women's magazines are presented more in terms of self-care, than as steps towards successful heterosexual liaison. She sees this as confirmation of the fact that physical appearance is an essential part of femininity. Remembering the psychoanalytic roots of feminist theory, narcissism is thus seen as the norm and reflected in the magazine images.

It is not the case that Malson's analysis generates a hermeneutically neat account of anorexia. For example, although anorexia may be regarded as an extreme and over-enthusiastic pursuit of the feminine ideal of thinness, she argues that it is also possible to construe the attainment of the anorexically thin body as boyish. In this way, self-starvation can be seen as an act of rebellion in which the cultural norms of femininity are rejected. Malson found that the 'amenorrhea-ic body' was regarded as a rejection of womanhood by some of her interviewees.

Malson also found that some participants saw dietary restraint as a testimony to virtuous self-control:

> It is within this discursive context that I would argue one might understand better the immense significance of thinness and food refusal as signifiers of self-control. For body management becomes central to the maintenance of self-integrity, and eating becomes an occasion when the body, something that is 'not me', 'takes over' and triumphs in the discursively produced conflict between mind/self and body. (p. 125)

Malson argues that body fat can be construed as morally bad and even leads to the signification of the self as being a 'bodily', as opposed to a 'spiritual' entity. Some interviewees spoke of wanting to cut off their body fat. In this way, the discourse of Cartesian dualism is combined with that of Christian asceticism in Western culture to promote the ideal of a bodiless subject. This is thinness taken to its ultimate extreme.

Malson makes the point that 'starving' is something quite different from 'dieting':

> It signifies not the pursuit of feminine beauty but the achievement of power. Whereas the fat body signifies an identity-less 'big bad blob', the subject position of 'anorexic' is articulated here in strongly positive terms as 'very powerful ... good and in control'. It is a construction which converges with readings of 'the anorexic body' as phallic symbol. (pp. 134–5)

In general, Malson's interviewees did not regard themselves as caught up in something trivial (as implied by the term 'slimmers' disease'). Sometimes anorexia may amount to a central facet of the individual's identity. This can put the person in conflict with the doctor who may wish to construe her as a patient, when the 'patient' feels more like an 'agent'. Once again, Malson is able to refer back to her post-structuralist Lacanian theoretical framework to make sense of her data:

> This metaphorical geography of identity thus becomes yet another element of a (patriarchal) discursive order which constitutes and regulates women's lives, problematizing their/our experiences of subjectivity, gender and embodiment, contributing to women's 'deep' distress and simultaneously serving to dismiss that distress as trivially superficial. (p. 150)

In the last resort, anorexia may sometimes be seen as a form of self-punishment, sharing some of the territory occupied by masochism and suicide. While extreme thinness can be interpreted as the vanishing of the body, ironically the person becomes more noticeable at the same time.

Malson acknowledges that talk of mothers did not feature in all of her interview transcripts. However, in two cases the mother of the interviewee had recently died:

> ... the discursive relationship between 'anorexic' death and the mother's death is also of wider significance because in these autobiographical accounts the trope of 'the dead mother' is associated with themes of identity, resistance and escape; themes which, as we have seen, frequently emerge in the discourses surrounding 'anorexia', gender, subjectivity and embodiment. (p. 181)

The mother features strongly in Orbach's classical feminist stance on fat. I consider this aspect of the feminist discourse, below.

Orbach on female fatness

Orbach (1988) argues that female fatness has, since the Second World War, been diagnosed by psychoanalysts in ways which suggest that the problem lies with the woman and not with the patriarchal culture in which she is embedded. Whilst acknowledging that the development of sexual identity is important for an understanding of conscious or unconscious acts that may be of relevance to food-related behaviour or body weight, she feels that a new feminist psychotherapy needs to be developed which moves beyond the conventional psychoanalytic concern with the Oedipus complex. She interprets fat as a possibly ineffectual solution to women's oppressive political situation. I have decided to deal with Orbach's work here, even though this chapter takes anorexia nervosa as its main focus. In accounting for fatness in women, Orbach (1988) develops a range of interesting arguments that link eating to cultural norms, politics, and the gendered organisation of society: as such her thesis has some bearing on eating disorders in general, and not just the situation where people are overweight.

Orbach (1988) sets out the ideological justification for differences in gender roles in order to gain some purchase on the reasons why some women might engage in compulsive eating. While she acknowledges that giving birth and breastfeeding are things that only women can do, on biological grounds, she does not think that this warrants the institutionalised division of labour whereby women are relegated to the care and socialisation of children (see my discussion of breastfeeding in Chapter 1). However, given that women are destined for this function in life, they must first get their man if they are to become wives and mothers. This leads her to place great emphasis on appearance; she comes to regard herself as a sex object. The operational definition of sexual attractiveness is provided through images in the mass media. Magazines provide plenty of advice on bridging the gap between how a woman actually looks and how, ideally, she ought to look (this is also reinforced in organs of the male-dominated fashion industry).

It might be thought that Orbach (1988) is doing no more than stressing the importance of modelling in social learning theory (e.g. Bandura *et al.*, 1961) but I do not think that this would be a fair interpretation, since she moves beyond the constraints of behaviourist theory in order to make the stronger political point:

> In this way, women are caught in an attempt to conform to a standard that is *externally* defined and constantly changing. But these models of femininity are experienced by women as unreal, frightening and unattainable. They produce a picture that is far removed from the reality of women's day-to-day lives. (p. 31)

The marketed image of women requires that they be thin. This viewpoint is still endorsed in the contemporary literature:

> Although several studies have shown that contemporary American women accept the current beauty ideal (believing that thin bodies are most attractive), it is readily evident that this is a heterosexually based definition of attractiveness ... Men, therefore could be seen as directly or indirectly implicated in this mainstream definition of female beauty. In the most obvious interpretation, heterosexual women might be striving for beauty and thinness to appear sexually attractive to men. Or at a subtler level, the behaviors of women might be influenced by a patriarchal order that controls the means of shaping popular tastes and standards. (Asher and Asher, 1999, p. 136)

Orbach's (1988) thesis is that one way for a woman to resist this social pressure is to be fat. At this point I shall briefly interrupt my summary of Orbach's position to comment on anorexia nervosa. When Orbach argues that a woman can show resistance to social pressures by becoming fat, it is important to recognise that this account has not been fashioned from within the biomedical discourse (see below). It is human agency, and not neuropeptide Y, that she invokes in her account of becoming fat. The notion that becoming fat is a conscious act of rebellion is undermined to some extent when she draws upon the psycho-analytic discourse to fill out the details of her argument. Setting that aside, if the focus is on rebellion, it could be argued that slimming to excess (or starving) ranks as an alternative strategy to becoming fat. This is so, since it also ruptures accepted norms and constitutes a challenge to patriarchal imperatives. I feel that some support for this notion is provided in the conversations with anorexic women reported by Malson (1998) (see previous section).

The second stage of Orbach's (1988) treatment of the problem assumes that the woman has been successful in becoming a wife and mother. This is when questions of the domestic division of labour come to the fore. Women, having had their babies, are then required to look after both them and their husbands. Society provides a wide range of prescriptive advice on how to go about this task, especially through the media. She services her husband so that he can go to work and she prepares her children to become the next generation of the workforce. Society demands that she does this unselfishly, expecting and getting scant reward or praise. There is little status in being a woman in a patriarchal capitalist society.

Because a mother is constantly looking after the needs of the other members of her family, she may lose sight of her own needs even to the extent of becoming confused about her own bodily needs. Orbach (1988) argues that one way the woman can gain some recompense is through food. If she is constantly giving others so much time, care, love and attention she can at least give herself something nice to eat. Orbach then connects the increase in body weight from over-eating to the political status of women in society, using a spatial metaphor:

> The resulting fat has the function of making the space for which women crave. It is an attempt to answer the question, 'If I am constantly giving myself to everyone, where do I begin and end?' We want to look and be substantial. We want to be bigger than society will let us. We want to take up as much space as the other sex. 'If I get bigger like a man then maybe I'll get taken seriously as is a man.' (p. 35)

Orbach (1988) then moves on to cover further functions of fatness. For example, women may use fat as a means to neutralise their sexual identity at work. If they are seen as sex objects this may result in their not being taken seriously by male co-workers or bosses.

One of the more subtle aspects of Orbach's (1988) thesis concerns the relationship between mothers and daughters. This is possibly the most difficult part for a middle-aged, male academic to grasp and I make no apology for being tentative in my attempt to summarise her arguments at this stage.

A mother is required to socialise her daughter into the female social role, just as her own mother did before her. An important part of this will be for the mother to ensure that her daughter does not explore to the full her desire for autonomous, self-directed, powerful and productive activity. The little girl must learn to accept her inferior status and her energies must be channelled into taking care of others. By way of contrast, little boys merely learn to accept emotional support while being placed under no obligation to offer love in return:

> To be a woman is to live with the tension of giving and not getting; and the mother and daughter involved in the process leading to this conclusion are inevitably bound up in ambivalence, difficulty and conflict. (Orbach, 1988, pp. 37–8)

Orbach suggests that the ambivalence of motherhood stems, in part, from the fact that to succeed as a mother means to prepare her daughter for marriage and motherhood. But the moment of success, for the mother, signals the end of motherhood as the daughter leaves the family to start her own. The one morsel of power available to women in society is that over which they have some control within the confines of their own family. Their success as a mother is thus a dead-end success, leading nowhere; they lose what little power they ever had. Consciousness of this state of affairs heaps on further ambivalence at what might be described as the meta-level. A mother aware of woman's poor deal in society must surely want something better for her daughter. Yet, if they discern signs for hope (be they better educational opportunities for women or equal opportunities in employment) these very grounds for optimism may lead to jealousy. From the mother's point of view, her daughter may be looking at options which the mother would have dearly loved to have had when she was young but which did not exist then; such a state of affairs may appear unfair.

Orbach (1988) then deals with the daughter's perspective. A daughter's ambivalence about leaving home is due to the fact that she both does and does not want to be like her mother. If her socialisation has been at least partly successful, she will want to be a nurturing care-taker. However, she may want to get a life for herself which goes beyond the confines of the conventional female role. The fact that she has been ill-prepared for this heaps further anxieties upon her situation. Orbach's (1988) theoretical challenge is to show how this ambivalence and anxiety translates itself into compulsive eating.

Although feeding is an important aspect in the mother–child relationship, no matter what the sex of the child, Orbach (1988) asserts that mothers hold back in giving support and sustenance to their daughters in order to teach them the self-denial they will need in their future role as women (and she supports this argument with empirical evidence relating to differential practices of breastfeeding with boys compared to girls). As a daughter grows up, compulsive eating may become a symbolic response to the physical and emotional deprivation she suffered earlier in her life. The daughter also begins to see the possibility of a life independent of her mother. The attractiveness of this option is spoiled by the guilt that flows from the knowledge that to take it would be to destroy her mother's only role.

Moving on to a scenario where the daughter has left home, she may then look for emotional support in her adult relationships but find none there, especially with regard to her husband who will not have been socialised to provide the love and support for which she craves. Once again, an opportunity is provided for her to seek compensation by turning to compulsive eating:

> For the compulsive eater, fat has much symbolic meaning which makes sense within a feminist context. Fat is a response to the many oppressive manifestations of a sexist culture. (Orbach, 1988, p. 43)

Compared with the post-structuralist, Lacanian discourse, I find Orbach's account clear and coherently argued. The problem with Orbach's thesis is that it tends to be cast in general terms and, as such, should apply to all women. However, it is not the case that women in general are happy to be fat. Some estimates suggest that approximately 80 per cent of women in countries such as the USA or UK may be dieting at any moment (Malson, 1998). This suggests that Orbach may need to extend her account to deal more directly with the question of individual differences. In other words, it is necessary to explain why some women protest by becoming fat when others manifestly do not. One problem that could occur is that some women may end up being fat when in fact they are trying to be thin. It seems to me that this would disqualify them as political protesters: rather, they should be construed as failed dieters. In the next section I consider the discourse of control in relation to ordinary dieting and then go on to explore control in relation to anorexia nervosa.

The Discourse of Control

Earlier in the chapter, I referred to Vandereycken and Deth's (1990) insistence that the broad historical picture be borne in mind when thinking about anorexia. One advantage of doing this is that it becomes clear that anorexic behaviour may be linked to goals other than thinness *per se* (such as a spiritual fusion with Christ's suffering, in the case of medieval saints). Lupton (1996) sees contemporary anorexics as being obsessed with control. Whereas hunger is regarded as a temptation to abandon control over food intake, its denial is taken as a sign of triumph for the will. The physical manifestation of this triumph is there to be witnessed as extreme thinness. This view of anorexia nervosa has much in common with the cognitive behavioural theory put forward by Fairburn *et al.* (1999).

A central feature of Fairburn *et al.*'s (1999) theory is the person's extreme need to control their eating. They focus on the process by which anorexia nervosa is maintained, rather than on how it develops. They see control over eating as a convenient and almost fortuitous way in which self-control in general may be effected. This is not to say that food consumption is an arbitrary domain in which to demonstrate self-control, since there are a number of background factors that make it an appropriate choice. Research has shown that people with anorexia nervosa tend to have low self-esteem, they tend to be perfectionists and they value asceticism. Dietary restriction sits well with asceticism and a perfectionist attitude, especially when coupled with a punitive exercise schedule. Some success may come early and may be detected visually by observable thinness, as well as by measurable weight loss. This will provide direct and immediate evidence of self-control which, it is hoped, will improve self-esteem. On the surface, this seems harmless enough. Fairburn *et al.*'s control theory provides a clue as to how things might get out of hand and lead, in some cases, to self-starvation unto death.

A novel aspect of Fairburn *et al.*'s (1999) theory is its emphasis on feedback mechanisms in the control process. Because the theory is essentially cybernetic, it lends itself to symbolic expression in the form of flow charts incorporating feedback loops, branching decision nodes and so forth. While Fairburn *et al.* (1999) provide two flow diagrams in their paper, they concentrate mainly on embedding their theory in the clinical literature and quite rightly so. However, once the theory has been placed within the cybernetic language game, as it were, there is no reason why that perspective should not be brought out to the full. For example, if broadly interpreted, Miller *et al.*'s (1960) TOTE unit (an acronym for *Test Operate Test Exit*) may be useful in highlighting particular aspects of the dietary control process, as may the process engineering and business techniques relating to task analysis (e.g. Kirwan and Ainsworth, 1992) or critical path analysis (e.g. Lockyer and Gordon, 1991). I shall draw on these broader perspectives in my discussion of Fairburn *et al.*'s (1999) cognitive behavioural theory.

Before proceeding, I should stress that I write not as a clinician. The reason why I am attracted to Fairburn *et al.*'s cybernetic model of anorexia has more to do with my broader interests in the psychology of action (the topic of my previous book, J.L. Smith, 2000). My goal in approaching Fairburn *et al.*'s model is to extend it more fully in terms of its being a model of action; I have little to say about its efficacy as a therapeutic tool.

In order to bring out the way in which the control process might become relentlessly vicious in the case of anorexia, I shall first provide a cybernetic description of ordinary dieting. To this end, let us assume that I wish to lose about 10 pounds and that I decide to restrict my food intake per day to 1800 calories in order to accomplish this. Any potential snack or meal will have to be scrutinised for its energy value in calories and a decision will then have to be made as to whether or not it can be eaten, given the target of 1800 calories per day. I provide a schematic representation for this in Figure 4.1.

In the case of eating a meal or snack, it is crucial to estimate the calorific content in order to check to see whether the 1800-calorie limit would be reached if the food were to be consumed. From a functional point of view, the calorie computation stands in for assessing thinness by looking in the mirror or checking body weight by reading the scales. While the tests of mirror and scales may be appropriate for the meta-assessment of progress over a period of a week, they are not sufficiently sensitive to be used on a meal-by-meal basis.

A test within the framework of my hypothetical diet might run along the following lines (see Figure 4.1):

- Shall I eat a plate of baked beans on toast for my evening meal?
- I figure it will come to 400 calories.
- How many calories have I eaten today? Looks like 900.
- So, $900 + 400 = 1300$ (projected cumulative total *after* eating beans).
- And $1300 < 1800$.
- Good! It passes the TEST and I can go on to OPERATE.
- I'll just put that pan of beans on the stove and whack the bread into the toaster.

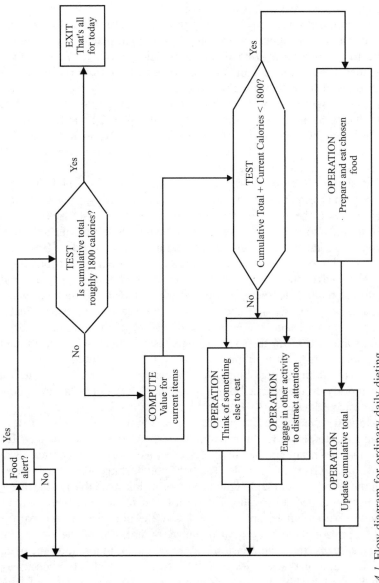

Figure 4.1 Flow diagram for ordinary daily dieting

The daily dietary restriction plan I have set out, above, is operating at the bottom level of a plans hierarchy. In ordinary dieting, when I decide to lose 10 pounds within a specific time limit (say, over the course of five weeks), it is on the basis of my general knowledge about nutrition, dieting and my own situation that I fix the target for my total daily calorie consumption. In doing this, I might take into account my starting weight (compared against population norms for people of my gender, height and age) and any experience I have from previous diets in terms of the rate of weight loss I might reasonably expect to occur. In the present example, I am to restrict my daily intake to a total of 1800 calories in order to produce a weight loss of 2 pounds per week. That gives me a time frame of 5 weeks for the execution of the diet plan as a whole. Strictly speaking, these are considerations at the meta-level regarding the execution of the plan.

A superordinate test is required to cover the point at which the daily diet plan is terminated and that can be achieved very simply with a test based upon the criterion of the target body weight (start-weight less 10 pounds, in this case). The daily diet could be left to run until that goal was attained; at which point I would exit from the diet. However, it is much more likely in practice that dieters will implement something like a weekly monitoring of progress. At such times, progress and matters relating to the execution of the diet plan, considered in the round, may be reviewed and any fine tuning to the test criteria levels can be made. I have therefore included some of these executive decisions and actions in the superordinate test in Figure 4.2, even though I acknowledge that a simpler version could be produced.

There are many possibilities for tweaking the daily calorie criterion or modifying the planned duration of the diet if things are not going quite according to plan. If the diet is repeatedly failing against the total calorie test for the day, then a meta-decision may have to be taken to raise the total calorie limit (from 1800 to 2200 calories per day, for example). This might then require a revision of the estimated time it will take to complete the diet plan (perhaps going from 5 weeks to 8 weeks, in the present example). It could be that the time available for the diet is not open-ended. For someone with a ticket to the sun, there may be only 5 weeks left before the holiday by the pool arrives and with it the opportunity for the flesh to bulge, or not, out of the swim suit. In a case like that, the decision may be taken *not* to abandon the plan. If so, additional strategies may have to be invoked. The dieter may make fresh resolve to draw more strongly upon the reserves of will-power. Alternatively, a secondary, yoked plan could be incorporated in which goals are set for jogging, gym, or other exercise. Of course,

93

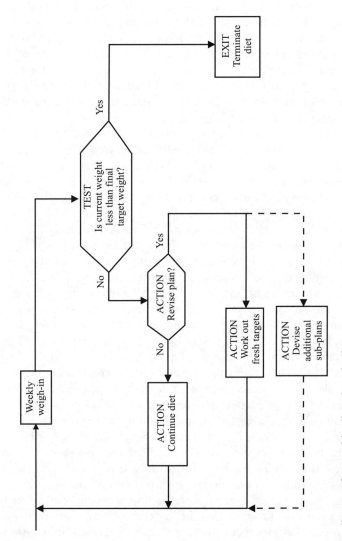

Figure 4.2 Flow diagram for weekly diet plan check

the possibility that the plan be abandoned is ever present and may become the default option where monitoring and testing in the TOTE unit ceases to occur.

Let us look on the bright side and assume that everything works out just fine; I adhere to my target of 1800 calories per day. After approximately 5 weeks of the daily execution of the plan, coupled with the weekly meta-review of progress in its execution, the plan is successfully terminated. I now want to consider what would have to be done to a nice sensible plan like this in order for it to reflect what reportedly goes on in anorexia nervosa. I shall do this by drawing on Fairburn *et al.*'s (1999) cognitive behavioural theory.

According to Fairburn *et al.*'s (1999) control theory, the anorexic's goal is first and foremost to achieve self-control. Weight loss or control over eating is used as a major index of self-control but it is of secondary importance. I provide a simplified version of what I shall call the anorexic plan in Figure 4.3. There are several aspects of this plan which give cause for concern. Firstly, there is no exit, and therefore, as written, it could run forever (or until death). Secondly, although the test criterion is explicit, the result of both success and failure is likely to amount to the same thing (i.e. more dieting). In the case of failure, increased effort may be demanded, along with additional related tactics such as engaging in an intense schedule of exercise. In the case of success, the person may not be able to escape the no-win situation, since the perception of success may be subject to a law of diminishing returns. In other words, if a weight loss of 2 pounds per week is regularly attained, this may be dismissed as being too easy to achieve from the point of view of demonstrating successful self-control. The pressure will therefore be to ratchet up the severity of the targets in the diet plan. It is possible that a particularly vicious short circuit could be introduced into this model by linking successful outcome *automatically* to the operation of increasing the demands of the diet plan. In sum, the main characteristics of the anorexic model are that there is no exit and that there is an inbuilt tendency for the targets of the diet plan to be revised upwards, but never downwards, in terms of their severity.

There are several additional factors that I wish to comment on, mainly with regard to the embedded dietary control plan. Fairburn *et al.* (1999) argue that aspects of starvation act as a further mechanism to encourage dietary restriction. In particular, they focus on several aspects of the starvation state which may assume increasing importance once the regular loss of weight is well under way. They make the point that the experience of intense hunger may be perceived as a threat to control and the heightened sense of fullness after eating may

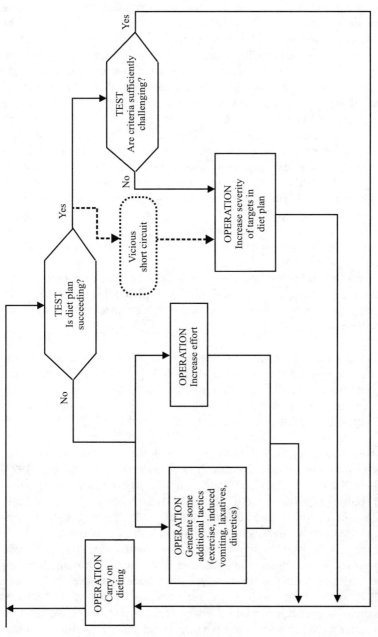

Figure 4.3 Self-control (dieting) feedback loop

be interpreted as failure. In terms of the way I have been developing my own analysis of the situation, I feel that these factors can be accommodated within the existing structures of the control model.

Fairburn *et al.* (1999) point out that anorexia brings with it, especially in Western culture, a heightened concern for shape and weight. In my description of ordinary dieting (see above) I suggested that weight on the scales was ill-suited as a criterion for monitoring meal-by-meal progress in a diet and that this is best used at the macro level of a weekly check (a similar argument might be made for taking a visual mirror check on body shape). Fairburn *et al.* (1999) argue that sufferers of anorexia monitor their weight too closely in the early stages. This is likely to lead them to increase the severity of the dietary regime unnecessarily in response to random upward fluctuations in weight which would not be noticed if checking was done at longer intervals and in a less obsessive fashion.

It is possible to construe the short-term weight fluctuations and the too frequent checking procedures as a feedback control problem. Carver and Scheier (1998) describe the way feedback systems, in general, may be sloppy or tight. I think that applying this to the frequency of weight checking suggests that the feedback control may be too tight in the case of anorexia:

> A question that's rarely raised, but has clear implications for the functioning of the system is this: How good is the comparator's ability to detect differences? There must be variability in this capability, such that sometimes a comparator can detect minor deviations but sometimes it can detect only substantial ones. (p. 15)

The problem with close self-regulation is that the dieter could alter behaviour when it is not necessary to do so. Carver and Scheier (1998) also talk about lag time and the fact that it may take some time before an output (i.e. the reduction of body weight) results from the input function (i.e. the reduced calorie intake). In dieting, a reasonably long lag time (a week might be a sensible period) should be assumed. Therefore testing at shorter intervals should be avoided, since this could lead to erroneous conclusions (e.g. the diet is not working). While focusing on feedback control, a further distinction made by Carver and Scheier (1998) is between positive and negative feedback loops. The loops depicted in the diagrams I have generated for this chapter have involved negative feedback where there is a target goal and the aim is to negate or reduce the discrepancy between the actual and the target values. Positive feedback loops involve a discrepancy amplifying system:

Discrepancy amplifying loops try to move the currently perceived value away from the reference value. They are believed to be less common in naturally occurring systems than discrepancy reducing systems, because they're unstable. That is they push away, and awayness goes on without limit. Whereas the conformity caused by a negative loop has a specific goal, the anticonformity caused by a positive loop doesn't. This creates instability, as they go on forever trying to create larger and larger deviations. (Carver and Scheier, 1998, p. 18)

It occurs to me that the situation in anorexia nervosa may, perhaps, be better captured through the notion of a positive feedback loop whereas that which obtains in ordinary dieting is best described using the concept of a negative feedback loop. The situation where ordinary dieters increase the severity of their target goals would remain within the negative feedback model, since they would still be trying to reduce the discrepancy between their actual weight and the ideal target weight.

Fairburn *et al.* (1999) also suggest that hypervigilant body checking may become aversive. This could subsequently lead to an avoidance of monitoring altogether. If sufferers then continue to feel that they are failing to control their shape and weight, they will continue to diet and yet there will be no opportunity to disconfirm their pessimistic assessment of the situation since monitoring has ceased.

In relation to the monitoring of body weight and shape targets, some research suggests that the judgements of people suffering from eating disorders are likely to be prone to distortions such as *Thought–Shape Fusion* (TSF). Shafran *et al.* (1999) state that TSF:

is said to occur when merely thinking about eating a forbidden food increases the person's estimate of their shape or weight, elicits a perception of moral wrongdoing and makes the person feel fat. (p. 167)

Shafran *et al.* (1999) developed their ideas for TSF from the notion of *Thought–Action Fusion* (TAF) which was identified in work on cognitive distortions in obsessive-compulsive disorder (see Rachman, 1993; Rachman, 1997; Shafran, 1999). If, as Fairburn *et al.* (1999) suggest, anorexics avoid objective monitoring once their condition has moved into an advanced stage, TSF will ensure false feedback whenever the sufferer thinks of forbidden food, and this may be frequently for someone experiencing extreme hunger. In this connection, Kulbartz-Klatt *et al.* (1999) have provided some evidence that body width estimations may be distorted by mood changes. Although their research was carried out in relation to bulimia, it would add another complicating factor into the situation were their research to be generalised to cover anorexia.

Fairburn *et al.* (1999) note that as people move further into a state of starvation, the rate of weight loss is likely to slow down and once this happens it will be taken as a failure to control weight reduction by the sufferer. They suggest that it is at this point that some may turn to the misuse of laxatives or diuretics, self-induced vomiting, or excessive exercising as a way of regaining a sense of self-control, and it is at this stage that I feel the link between such phenomena and the psychology of food becomes tenuous. While the discussion of anorexia nervosa is relevant to the psychology of food, since it is an *eating* disorder, there comes a point where consideration of the topic begins to shade away into matters more appropriate to general counselling or psychopathology. I shall return to this point in the discussion at the end of the chapter. The third and final discourse I shall consider is the biomedical discourse. In this I shall focus less on anorexia than on the regulation of body weight in general.

The Biomedical Discourse

The choice of 'biomedical' as a label for the scientific discourse relating to food intake and body weight is somewhat arbitrary. Woods *et al.* (2000) indicate that the major research effort in this area is moving from psychology and physiology to biochemistry and molecular biology. They also point out that a shift in policy by the Federal Drug Administration in the United States has now meant that the pharmaceutical industry is able to bring its immense research resources to bear on the quest for anti-obesity drugs. The biomedical discourse thus contains an increasing contribution from molecular biology and pharmacology, with much talk of neuropeptides and gene products running through the conversational flow.

My treatment of the biomedical discourse relating to eating disorders moves on from the section on hunger, in Chapter 3, where I briefly considered the role of blood glucose as a homeostatic signal for the regulation of food intake. It is now thought that animals typically do not wait until glucose levels in the blood decrease to such an extent to act as a metabolic trigger before starting to eat. This is not to say that glucose levels are of no relevance. Apparently, they decrease a few minutes prior to the start of a meal, only to increase again just before the animal begins to eat. The shift in glucose levels is but one signal among many that occurs prior to the onset of a meal:

All these parameters (blood glucose, temperature, metabolic rate, and no doubt others as well) begin a slow change 10–15 minutes before meals begin, and all are therefore highly correlated with meal onset. (Woods *et al.*, 2000, p. 260)

The idea is that animals anticipate the onset of a meal, possibly through habit, past learning or environmental cues, and the brain then initiates some general changes in order to get the system ready to receive the meal. So, for example, if an animal is fed regularly at a particular time of day, it will learn to produce, on cue, appropriate hormones and neurotransmitters (such as insulin or neuropeptide Y) which are important in the control of food intake. There is also some evidence that animals can learn the calorific content of foods they have eaten in the past and that this enables them to control how many calories are consumed at a given sitting.

The control of meal size is also dependent on the current body weight of the animal:

The point is that an individual who has recently eaten insufficient food to maintain its weight will be less sensitive to meal-ending signals and, given the opportunity, will consume larger meals on the average. Analogously, an individual who has enjoyed excess food and consequently gained some weight will, over time, become more sensitive to meal-terminating signals. (Woods *et al.*, 2000, p. 261)

An example of a meal-suppressing signal that is generated towards the end of eating is the secretion of the gut peptide cholecystokinin (CCK) by the intestines. If an antagonist to CCK is given to animals before they start eating, they subsequently eat more. On the other hand, if CCK (not the antagonist) is administered, the animals end up eating less. CCK is not the only signal involved in triggering the termination of a meal. It is believed that a range of gut peptides have a role to play in this, as does stomach distension (see Chapter 3).

The fact that there are mechanisms in place to control the termination of a specific meal does not help directly in explaining how body weight is held constant over long periods, given the fluctuations which can occur in daily energy expenditure through physical exercise and heat production. Food intake is adjusted in response to changes in the amount of fat stored in the body and this applies even to the situation where fat is surgically removed. Information conveying the degree of adiposity is signalled to the brain by circulating compounds, such as insulin and leptin (see Woods *et al.*, 2000, for a fuller discussion of this topic).

In Chapter 3, I outlined the role of neuropeptide Y (NPY) in the regulation of adiposity. To recapitulate: an underweight animal secretes less leptin; low leptin levels trigger the production of NPY; NPY promotes increased food intake and body weight. The process works the other way for overweight individuals. The problem with NPY is that it operates as a control mechanism in the central nervous system and therefore any therapeutic manipulation of its levels, irrespective of the technique used, has the potential for causing unknown but potentially serious side-effects by disrupting other control systems in the brain. Some researchers have focused their attention on substances directly involved in setting the metabolic rate but at peripheral locations within the organism.

Uncoupling proteins (UCPs) have been found to play a part in the generation of body heat in hibernating animals during frigid weather. It is now thought that proteins that are similar to the animal UCPs are produced in the fat and muscle tissue of humans. UCPs uncouple the synthesis of adenosine triphosphate (ATP – see Chapter 3) by abolishing the hydrogen ion gradient across the inner mitochondrial membrane, which is essential for the process to work properly. The upshot of this is a reduction in efficiency: fewer ATPs can be made from a given amount of food. As a result, metabolic rate rises and the energy leaked from this process becomes manifest as dissipated heat (so useful for hibernating animals). According to an editorial article in *Science* (Gura, 1998), researchers are now looking for drugs that could be used to achieve a slight increase in the level of uncoupling (perhaps just one or two per cent). This would be enough to boost the metabolic rate and would provide a way to reduce body weight without interfering with brain mechanisms. It would also obviate the need for incessant conscious dieting in humans.

Because much research into obesity is concerned with regulatory mechanisms (whether involving NPY or UCPs), the possibility lurks in the background that any advance in this area might be helpful not just for obesity but also for anorexia. Discovery of a mechanism to turn up metabolic rate, for instance, may well lead to another complementary technique to turn it down. Walsh and Devlin (1998) seem to think that it is possible to demonstrate that pertinent physiological disturbances do occur as anorexia progresses and, indeed, in some cases a reversal of the observed changes may be detected where the person subsequently regains the lost weight (they point to serotonin and leptin levels, by way of illustration). However, it is almost impossible to disentangle what physiological abnormalities are consequences and what are causes of the disorder.

Within the biomedical discourse, being fat is beginning to be explained in terms of a mistuning of the metabolic mechanism. For some individuals and/or groups, the mistuning is fundamental insofar as it is coded into their genes. Comuzzie and Alison (1998) report that estimates based on twin, adoption, and family studies indicate that 40–70 per cent of the variation in obesity phenotypes (such as the body mass index) is attributable to heritability. Indeed, they suggest that the case for heritability has been accepted by scientists and that the emphasis has now switched to finding out which specific genes are responsible. Given this goal, particular populations for whom gene pools may be assumed to be relatively homogeneous and for whom obesity rates are high are being studied in some depth (such populations include Pima Indians, Old Order Amish, and Mennonites). This is very much early days and so far results are tentative. An example of progress is given by Comuzzie and Alison (1998) as follows:

> Thus far, a total of nine humans have been reported to carry mutations in homologs of three rodent obesity genes, LEP (encoding leptin), LEPR (encoding the leptin receptor), and FAT (encoding carboxypeptidase E). (pp. 1375–6)

I feel that I have provided a sufficient introduction to the biomedical discourse, in the context of the present chapter. To move more deeply into the language of central control mechanisms would bring me into contact with the mysteries of proopiomelanocortin (POMC), the melanocortin (MC) receptors, and so forth (see Woods *et al.*, 2000, for a fuller treatment): this may be a step too far.

Concluding Remarks

One problem which strikes me about Malson's Lacanian position is that it does not appear to get to grips with individual differences. If society, in general, is patriarchal and if language (setting aside minor variations in terms of local dialects) is universally shared by all women, and if these factors come together in a causal cocktail to generate anorexia nervosa (although I have to admit I still can't quite see how it does that), then why is only 1 per cent of the population anorexic? Why not all women? Furthermore, I cannot see how this Lacanian–Saussurian Cocktail (LSC) can be used to account for the higher incidence of anorexia among women in the higher classes. Feminist colleagues have put it to me that the middle-class woman is more 'in it' than the working-class woman because, being middle class, she will have more invested in the status quo. I take this to mean that she has a greater stake, relatively speaking, in wealth, status and power. Being more 'in it' she will then feel the paradox of exclusion (i.e. being 'not in it') more strongly. I find it difficult to see how this could be translated into the language of the LSC. Presumably, the argument would hinge on a differential outcome of the castration complex for middle- and working-class women, since this is where the desire of the Other becomes equated with the phallus (see Lacan, 1977, p. 289). This, I find difficult to comprehend.

Turning to the biomedical discourse, the first thing to say is that this is essentially a modernist discourse and is thus likely to be dismissed by the post-modernists. Malson's (1998) argument that anorexia nervosa was constructed out of medical and cultural discourses over a particular socio-historic period is very persuasive. If anorexia and bulimia are culture-specific, then a scientific account of the phenomena is unlikely to be successful. I think that the reason for this is that in both conditions the anorexic or bulimic person is acting more as an agent than as a patient (I am using the term 'patient' in its technical philosophical sense and not in the medical sense). They are consciously causing a deviation from *ad libitum* ordinary food intake rhythms. In the case of the anorexic, willpower is used to refuse food and, possibly, to take excessive exercise. In the case of the bulimic, bingeing has to be planned and executed (as does the purging, to some extent). In other words, there is a sense in which people 'do' anorexia or bulimia nervosa. Scientific explanations work best when accounting for what *happens* to a person physically or physiologically; causal explanations fare poorly when it comes to action.

In order to force a more even-handed comparison between the feminist and biomedical discourses, I shall therefore focus on obesity (I return to anorexia later in the discussion). Orbach (1988), from the feminist discourse, provides a reasonably direct account of being fat. In a nutshell, this can be seen as a symbolic act of rebellion by women who are oppressed in a patriarchal society. Let us assume, in terms of the biomedical discourse, that genome scanning proceeds apace and the research proves to be successful. Perhaps, for a given population at least, the biomedical discourse delivers a persuasive genetic account of obesity. In this situation there would be a danger that female fatness could be incorrectly interpreted as an act of rebellion against patriarchy when, in fact, the adiposity is merely an apolitical nuisance. The possibility would also exist for a person to eat heartily for feminism, only to be thwarted by a high, genetically determined metabolic rate. I turn now to the discourse of control.

The cybernetic models I produced for this chapter are idealised descriptions of how the anorexic process might work. Flow diagrams may be regarded as the symbolic language of cybernetics. Any particular instance of the anorexic process may match the formal model only imperfectly. A Saussurian parallel might be drawn between the formality of *langue* and the fuzziness of *parole*.

Starting with ordinary dieting, failure is a very common experience. The cybernetic model I set out earlier in the chapter cannot be used to predict the success or failure of any particular dieter or diet, and cannot, as it stands, take into account the phenomenon of weight cycling where the pounds lost on any given occasion are subsequently regained with interest. For yo-yo dieters, the average body weight may increase steadily over a long period of time and it is thought that this pattern generates even more negative health problems than not dieting in the first place (see Ogden, 1992, pp. 72–3, for a discussion of this issue).

It would be wrong to assume that the path to anorexia starts with ordinary dieting for all women. One of Malson's (1998, p. 134) research participants explicitly stated that her objective was to starve, not to diet, right from the start. Malson also reports that for some of her participants, food refusal was but one technique amongst several (including, for example, excessive exercise or cutting/self-mutilating behaviour) in the wider strategy of self-punishment and self-destruction.

It is important to note that while the cybernetic model might prove to be a reasonable representation of the anorexic process, it is not designed as a model of the therapeutic process. The therapeutic process might be described in terms of effecting changes such that the cybernetic model of ordinary dieting, as opposed to the anorexic model, is the scheme that is effectively operating. The model of ordinary dieting may easily be adapted for weight gain, simply by setting higher, as opposed to lower weight and calorie intake targets. The therapeutic process would focus on sorting out inappropriate feedback short-circuits, putting in place the proper feedback loops, and ensuring that the feedback control was not too tight for the job in hand. I am not saying that this would necessarily be easy but a far harder problem may be to get the anorexic person on board for the therapeutic goal in the first place.

It seems to me unlikely that there will be a biomedical account of the cause of anorexia, in terms of the metabolic rate. If that were a problem, there would be no need for the iron self-control and no need for excessive physical exercise: the weight would fall away all by itself. If the biomedical account is rejected as a causal mechanism, then the person has to be seen as a powerful agent, generating her own anorexic behaviour (or, less frequently, his).

If, as in some cases of anorexia, the person is intent on starvation as a route to self-destruction, it seems to me that the relatively light therapeutic techniques of cognitive behaviour therapy, based upon cybernetic models, may be inadequate. This is because the cybernetic models implicitly contain an assumption of rationality, and this tends to involve lip-service to hedonism. Other things being equal, rational beings are not expected to voluntarily harm themselves. An argument might be made, therefore, that a therapeutic strategy shot through with the discourse of rationality is not ideally suited to the task of dealing with a self-destructive anorexic person. It is at this point that I can see the attraction of a therapeutic discourse that is steeped not in the language of rationality but in the language of the unconscious. And that is why I cannot bring myself to dismiss the psychoanalytic discourse out of hand.

Part Two

Post-Positivist Research Reports

5

Dinner Party
(Agentic Participant Observation
Case Study)

In order to cast light on various aspects of eating out and entertaining at home with food, Warde and Martens (2000) interviewed 33 principal food providers in 30 households in the Preston area, England, in 1994. Apart from conducting interviews, they also carried out a questionnaire survey involving approximately 1000 people drawn from London, Bristol and Preston (three cities in England). With regard to entertaining people with a meal at home, Warde and Martens (2000) state:

> Either explicitly or implicitly, most interviewees drew upon a cultural template of a dinner party against which their own social practices were described ... [The middle-class dinner party] is a highly structured event which includes an elaborate menu, a prescribed set of rituals, a particularly defined set of companions whose patterns of interaction are set out, and an injunction of exceptional care and attention on the part of the host and gratitude on the part of the guest. (p. 57)

Their interviewees suggest that the meal should have at least three courses and that these would be more special than those eaten on an everyday basis. Warde and Martens (2000) suggest that while the template for the dinner party seems to be universally held, few people follow it to the letter.

They estimated the incidence of dinner parties in their sample, on the basis of a strict definition (a meal with three or more courses, lasting two or more hours), as follows:

> Dinner parties so defined occurred on only 15 per cent of all occasions of hospitality. The proportion changes if different conditions are set, of course. Relaxing the criteria by allowing all meals with two or more courses lasting an hour or more gives a proportion of

52 per cent. Dinner parties are not the most common manner of entertaining guests. *Improvisation on the cultural template is the norm.* (emphasis added) (pp. 60–1)

Although there are many interesting questions raised in Warde and Martens's (2000) data which deserve to be followed up through further interview and survey studies, I have chosen not to go down that path here. I adopt an idiographic research stance, based upon participant observation (see Preface). While I do not seek to emphasise autobiographical experience, I shall not shun from reporting it where appropriate. Although a dinner party invites the analysis of interpersonal interaction at the dinner table, this is not where I place the emphasis in my study. Instead, I adopt a skills and planning focus for my observations on the cooking and preparation, leaving the social psychology to one side.

The episode that I chose to study was a dinner party, planned for eight persons, at my home. The guests were two of my research students, together with a new member of staff (and their partners). In the event, only my research students and partners were able to attend, thus making four guests on the night. Although this dinner party follows the standard template described by Warde and Martens (2000) reasonably closely (see above), it will be seen that serious disruptions (of an entirely agreeable nature) act to force an improvisation into the unfolding episode after the main course has been eaten. I shall say no more for the present; I now provide a brief note on the way in which I collected data for the case study.

The analysis is based upon approximately 8000 words of research notes. These notes were typed up from hand-written notes jotted down on a reporter's pad (e.g. while cooking in the kitchen). Additional material based upon memory was also added into the research record while typing up. The typing-up of notes always occurred as soon as possible after the events, usually within the same day. Limitations of space prevent me from presenting these notes in full: I shall, however, provide as many extracts from these data as possible.

A-priori Hierarchical Analysis of the Dinner Party Episode

Kirwan and Ainsworth (1992) recommend that hierarchical task analysis should not be carried out by first collecting data, since this is likely to result in a mass of unstructured information. In an idiographic study, such as this (in terms of the number of dinner party episodes,

$n = 1$), there is no sense in which data will be averaged over large numbers. It would also be silly to pretend that I did not have some idea of the general structure of the episode: advanced cooking will take place before the main dinner event; the starter will be served before the main course; and so forth. In presenting my case study, I shall therefore put forward an a-priori structure that captures the hierarchical nature of the dinner party episode. I shall provide extracts from my research notes at intervals, as this structure unfolds, to provide comment on the structure and to flag up ways in which the real event deviated from the prototypical structure.

Task and critical path analysis

In order to begin to talk about a domestic dinner as a social episode and a manifestation of skilful planned behaviour, it will be useful for me to adopt some of the descriptive conventions of task and critical path analysis. Task analysis, embodying a loosely related collection of techniques, is deployed in a wide range of domains: ergonomics, operations and process management, organisational psychology, artificial intelligence, structured computer programming, cybernetics, and time management. Perhaps the most common of these techniques is the production of a flow chart to depict the way a process unfolds through a series of stages. Where the timing of some tasks is crucial to the successful completion of others, managers sometimes use the technique of critical path analysis in order to generate optimal ways to schedule all the contributing tasks. Many projects lend themselves to hierarchical task analysis, especially where the main task may be broken down into a cascading series of subordinate goals, tasks and plans. Where such tasks are spread across the duration of the superordinate episode, partly in series and partly in parallel, time line analyses and charts may be generated to supplement the structural hierarchical task analysis.

Harré and Secord (1972) define an episode as follows:

> An episode is any sequence of happenings in which human beings engage which has some principle of unity. Episodes have a beginning and end that can usually be defined. (p. 10)

I regard the start of my dinner party as the moment of conception and the end as the point at which everything has been cleared up (the day after the meal). This provides reasonably clear temporal boundaries within which the superordinate episode may be broken down into a series of sub-episodes. In terms of a dramaturgical analysis (see

Goffman, 1959; Harré and Secord, 1972) these would approximate to the acts and scenes of a play. The a-priori episodic breakdown for the dinner party is as follows:

    A. Conception
    B. Advanced preparation
    C. Penultimate chores
    D. The home stretch
    E. Main dinner
    F. End game

In Figure 5.1, I set out a vertical timeline (improvising, somewhat, from the examples provided in Kirwan and Ainsworth, 1992, pp. 137–40) for the superordinate dinner episode. I have represented the day of the dinner party as *D-Day*, with *Episode E (Main Dinner)* taking a 3–4 hour stretch of linear time. *Episode F (End Game)* may spill over to the next day, in terms of clearing up: I have therefore marked the end of this episode as *D-Day (+1)*. The activities carried out on *D-Day*, prior to *Episode E (Main Dinner)* I have brought together within *Episode D (The Home Stretch)*. I have represented time in a quasi-logarithmic fashion falling back some 2–3 weeks from *D-Day*, since more space will be needed for all the cooking and preparations in the day immediately prior to the dinner, and progressively less the further away from the dinner one moves. In passing, it may be noted that the vertical timeline in Figure 5.1 is very similar to what is sometimes referred to as a Gantt chart in critical path analysis (see Lockyer and Gordon, 1991). I shall use the prototype, set out in Figure 5.1, to provide a structure for reporting my case study, even though events did not unfold quite as neatly as portrayed in the diagram. Before I do this, I shall first present the dramatis personae.

Dramatis Personae

I have decided to use pseudonyms to refer to the people involved in the dinner party episode. I group them into three teams: *The Home Team*, *The Guests*, and *The Visitors* (who were not formally part of the dinner party). I shall use Mr/Ms to designate gender. Apart from that, I have given everybody food-related names (thus I am called Mr Broccoli).

   The Home Team
     Mr Broccoli (myself)
     Ms Eggplant (my partner)
     Ms Pancake (my teenage daughter)

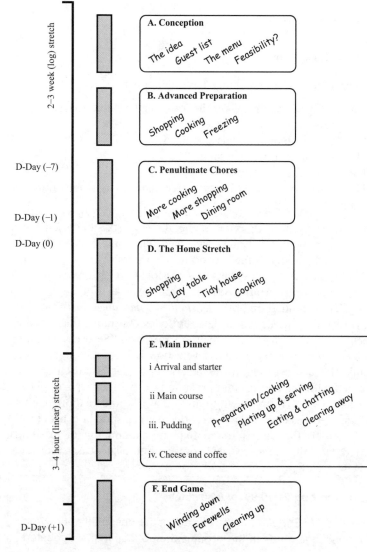

Figure 5.1 Dinner party vertical timeline chart

The Guests	The Visitors
Ms Mint and Mr Beef *	Ms Waffle (Ms Pancake's friend)
Ms Thyme* and Mr Bacon	Ms Watercress (Ms Waffle's mother)
Ms Tarragon and Mr Lime	Mr Mango (Ms Waffle's stepfather)

* My research students

Episode A: Conception

In this episode at least six things have to happen:

1. The host needs to articulate the idea for the dinner party
2. The guest list needs to be fixed
3. The date and time must also be fixed
4. The invitations must be issued
5. The menu must be defined
6. The feasibility of the dinner party plan as a whole must be examined

There is no harm in thinking of the above as six sub-episodes (see Figure 5.2), providing it is acknowledged that some of them may be closely related and that some may occur in parallel, rather than in strict temporal sequence.[1] It would also be possible to regard *fixing the date* (A^3) and *issuing the invitations* (A^4) as sub-episodes of *fixing the guest list* (A^2). The examination of the *feasibility of the dinner party plan* (A^6) assumes prior knowledge of the later episodes. Assuming that this does happen at some point in time, then, on Harré and Secord's definition (see above), it may be regarded as an episode. However, it might be best to think of it as operating at the meta-level: this is because it is more concerned with the control and execution of the dinner party plan of action as a whole. At first I had thought that it would be more likely to occur towards the end of the *Conception* (A^0) episode but this did not turn out to be the case: I found that an examination of feasibility occurred within the first recorded conversation of my case study:

Research Log 21.10.99 @ 8.30 a.m.

Spoke to *Ms Eggplant* in the car about the possibility of having a dinner as a study in the organisation of cooking. Suggested

---

[1] I shall adopt the convention of using numerical superscripts to indicate sub-episodes of the alphabetically labelled main episodes (A–F) using zero to designate the main episode as a whole. Thus *issuing invitations* (A^4) is a sub-episode of *Conception* (A^0).

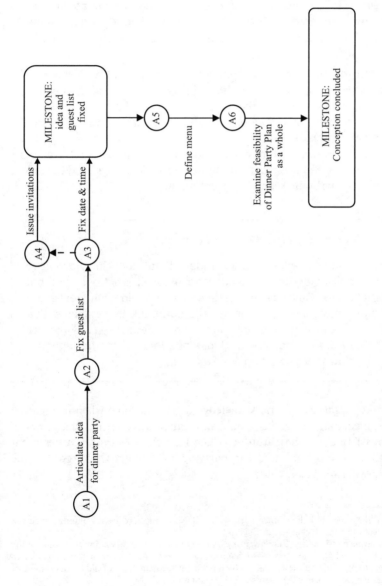

Figure 5.2 Network diagram for dinner party sub-episode A (Conception)

> *Mr Beef*, *Ms Tarragon* and *Ms Thyme* as possible guests. Acknowledged that there would be no guests from her side. She said OK but that she might go off and get on with her stuff after the meal. We noted that we'd have to explain to *Ms Pancake* that she wouldn't be able to watch cable that night. Proposed taping and a full evening on the internet as alternatives. I suggested it would be a Saturday in a few weeks' time.

Already, at this early stage, potential dramaturgical problems for the dinner party are emerging. Cable TV playing in the dining room might disrupt the ambience of the meal (Episode E). I therefore build in a sub-plan giving *Ms Pancake* an attractive alternative (time on the internet,[2] instead).

Once the guest list has been agreed (A^2), the guests have to be invited (A^4). If one or more guests cannot make a suggested date (A^3), there may be some scope for negotiation.

> **Research Log 21.10.99 @ 9.00 a.m.**
>
> ... I then checked the calendar. Saturday 13th November seems about right. I could have made it 6th November but that's the 'Guy Fawkes' weekend and I might as well avoid that. I have therefore resolved to email the three guests. I've also made a mental note that I shall need to assemble the table from the garage for this, since there could be eight sitting down, not counting *Ms Pancake*.

I draw upon my general knowledge to avoid a time when it might be assumed that the guests would have alternative social engagements. Thus I rule out the Saturday which falls close to Guy Fawkes night (5th November: a time for partying in England) and go for the following weekend.[3]

---

[2] At the time that the dinner party took place, connection to the internet incurred metered telephone charges, in England.

[3] In terms of Ajzen's (1991) *theory of planned behaviour*, I am assuming that some of my guests would have low *perceived behavioural control* with regard to their *intention* to come to my dinner if they already have a prior engagement. This would be an example of negative gating, using Abelson's (1973) terminology.

My invitation plan begins to interface with events in mundane reality, as the resolve to email becomes manifest as an item in a *to-do* list. I am already problem-solving in terms of setting the stage for the main dinner (Episode E): my regular table is too small to seat eight guests so I must assemble a larger temporary table which I keep dismantled in the garage. This can be regarded as another manifestation of feasibility checking (A^6).

Research Log 21.10.99 @ 1.36 p.m.

Phoned *Ms Tarragon* and *Ms Thyme* who both think they'll probably be able to make it. Left a message on *Mr Beef*'s answer-phone. I've already decided that the starter will be pumpkin soup, made with the inside of *Ms Pancake*'s Halloween pumpkin.

In practice I used an alternative, equivalent form of communication (phone rather than email) to achieve my goal. Circumstances external to the main event of this dinner party have dictated the starter (by coincidence, a Halloween pumpkin will be at hand).

Research Log 21.10.99 @ 6.51 p.m.

When *Ms Pancake* got home, she told me that 13th November was the day she's going to the theatre in Sunderland to see the 'The Rocky Horror Show' with *Ms Waffle*. Still, that should be OK.

I've now started this event and to go back and switch the date with the guests would be an additional hassle since by this time I regard *fix date and time* (A^3) as being completed. I felt that I would lose face, in Goffman's (1959) sense, if I did try to alter things since it would show incompetence in planning on my part (and therefore weaken my claims to be a mature and capable agent[4]). In the end I decide that *Ms Pancake*'s trip to the theatre will not impact on the main event (as will be seen, I had clearly not thought this through).

---

[4] I discuss the relation between planning competency and agency in my book *The Psychology of Action* (Smith, 2000, especially chapter 6).

Research Log 23.10.99 @ 2.25 p.m.

Mr Beef said he and *Ms Mint* could make the 13th. Bought a large pumpkin today. It was larger than what I would normally get but I'll use the flesh for a soup base, when I've carved it for *Ms Pancake*. It cost £3.99.

This confirmed the guest list and the main ingredient for the starter has now been purchased. The next step is to choose the menu (even though I am committed to pumpkin soup as a starter, I have not at this stage settled on a particular recipe for it).

Choosing the menu is important, since decisions made at this point will translate into a meta-plan to control much of the shopping, cooking and scheduling activities in the subsequent sub-episodes. I expand *define menu* (A^5) to the next level of detail in the hierarchy in Figure 5.3. My research notes reveal that searching for an acceptable pumpkin soup recipe was not as straightforward as might be expected.

Research Log 30.10.99 @ 10.56 a.m.

... Next I started hunting for a recipe. I looked in my lever-arch file and found that I had filed a booklet on squashes that I must have picked up at the supermarket a few years back. The main thing I noticed was that they use thyme and I made a mental note of that. Also they recommended white wine to be added into the stock – sounds good. Still, I thought that I would look round some more. I went down to my cook book collection and got out *The New Cranks Recipe Book* (Abensur, 1996). I looked in the index and found several entries for pumpkin (pie and tart) but couldn't see anything for soup. I therefore turned to one of my favourite books: *Jane Grigson's Vegetable Book* (Grigson 1980). She gives a recipe for a homely, basic farmer's soup, found in the Loire district of France. This is made with milk and I don't really fancy that. Another one she bases on *potage au potiron* from the Orléannais (Grigson, 1980, p. 419). This looks good. (The full text for this recipe is reproduced in Appendix 1.)

The recipes also provide important information relating to the preparatory shopping and cooking episodes: it may not be possible for me

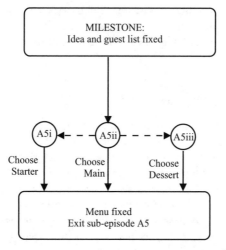

Figure 5.3 Network diagram for dinner party sub-episode A^5 (Define menu)

to buy some ingredients and some of the kitchen techniques may be too advanced for me. With respect to my dinner, I settled on a variation of the Grigson recipe.

Research Log 30.10.99 @ 10.56 a.m.

... I'll need about 2 lb of pumpkin flesh. I hope I'll get that since I have to leave enough in the pumpkin to keep the walls strong enough for carving into a Halloween lantern. Grigson's recipe uses leeks and turnips and I like that idea. I also found out from here that there would be no need to use any additional thickener; I had wondered about using a potato. When the soup has been blended and when the seasoning has been adjusted, she recommends serving with just a ladle of cream and a pinch of sugar. This suits me very well. I can make the base of the soup, blend it, and then freeze it. On the day, I merely have to defrost it, heat and serve. I shall omit seasoning until the final heating. My rationale for this is that it seems silly to put salt into a liquid that is about to be frozen, since that will lower its freezing point. I always do it this way, so I don't think I'll forget the seasoning on the day.

In thinking about the use of a potato for thickening and in making the decision not to season the base until defrosting, I draw upon my background knowledge of kitchen chemistry (see Chapter 3). I also satisfy myself that using this recipe will enable me to cook the soup well ahead and I thus have an eye to the reduction of stress in the *main dinner* (E^0)

Research Log 30.10.99 @ 10.56 a.m.

I feel pleased about this decision. Because this soup does not require much cream, that will give me the freedom to use more in the dessert, if I so desire. Also, by deciding on soup for the starter, I have the option of using pastry in either of the other courses. The fact that soup is hot means that I can opt for a cold dessert if I choose. I seem to have lots of options open to me. Once I've made the soup base and frozen it, I shall probably go ahead and fix the rest of the menu.

I shall postpone my description of cooking the soup base until the next section, since I now wish to pick up the story in my research log where I settle the remainder of the menu, even though this means that I take things out of strict chronological sequence.

Research Log 31.10.99 @ 1.00 p.m.

One possibility for dessert is chocolate chestnut *pavé* with Chantilly cream (see Willan, 1980, p. 70 and p. 425 for the recipes). I did that for friends last February. It's very rich but would be OK for this dinner party, I think. And it would be made and chilled ahead of time. The cream could be made at least a couple of hours ahead, too. So, if I did that, there would be nothing in the oven and I could do some sort of pastry dish for the main course. (The full text of Willan's recipes is reproduced in Appendix 3.)

I checked out the idea of the *pavé* with my partner and she agreed that it would be good. Moving on to the main course, I thought about a spinach roulade in Elliot's (1988) *Vegetarian Cookery* but decided against it; I also rejected Tovey's (1990) potato and mushroom flan. In the end a recipe for cheese and apple savoury strudel with spiced pickled pears in Smith's (1995) *Winter Collection* caught my attention. (The full text of these recipes is reproduced in Appendix 2.)

Because I had never cooked the strudel, I decided to try it out before the dinner party. In my research notes, it can be seen that I started to rehearse my plans for *The Home Stretch* (Episode D) as soon as the dish was chosen.

Research Log 31.10.99 @ 1.00 p.m.

... One further factor that needs to be checked out is whether I can assemble the strudel one day, keep it in the fridge, and then cook it the following day. If that works OK, I could assemble the strudel on Friday night. I could cook the spiced pears on Saturday afternoon and let them cool since it is recommended to eat them cold. I think there might be a case for making the chocolate chestnut *pavé* early and freezing it.

I put a mental marker down to remind myself that I have not made filo pastry for a year or two and I need to practise before the day. This brings out the skills aspect of dinner party preparation. With regard to my general plan, I seem to be satisfied that I can go ahead with these recipes, acknowledging that a trial must take place for the strudel.

Research Log 31.10.99 @ 2.57 p.m.

It now looks quite clear. I shall be on call looking after *Ms Pancake* on the Thursday before the dinner party. Therefore I must shop for the strudel, *pavé*, and wine on Wednesday evening. I must also make the *pavé* then. On Friday, I must prepare the strudel, assuming my previous trial worked. I also need to take the two cartons of soup base out of the freezer, last thing. On Saturday, I need to shop for last-minute items: cream for Chantilly and soup, bread rolls for the soup, and cheese and biscuits (if for any reason I am in Newcastle or Northumberland at the end of the week, I could buy some local cheeses – not possible in Sunderland). Then I have to assemble my table from the garage, pickle the pears, lay the table, and make the Chantilly cream. I think that's as much detail as I need to go into for now. So, the only thing that I have to do between now an Wednesday 10th November is to do a trial cooking of the savoury strudel. That's good.

At this point, I have moved into considerable detail in my advanced planning. The advantage of this is I am able to relax, knowing that I have little to do over the coming ten days. I turn now to the next episode, which is concerned with advanced preparations.

Episode B: Advanced Preparation

In this episode I deal with advanced cooking and freezing and the shopping necessary to facilitate this. In my case study, there was also the trial cooking of the savoury strudel, which was primarily an opportunity to practise cooking skills ahead of time. The advantage of cooking in advance is that it takes the pressure off the host when the guests are present and thus helps to keep stress levels down (I discuss this in the concluding section of this chapter in relation to Lawson's, 1998, and Tovey's, 1990, views on the subject). Within the advanced preparation in my case study, the following three things needed to be done (see Figure 5.4):

1. Supermarket shopping
2. Cooking and freezing the pumpkin soup
3. Trial cooking of the savoury strudel

With regard to the *supermarket shopping* (B^1) episode I first made a shopping list, working from the recipes chosen previously (in Episode A^5), and then went to the supermarket. The shopping proceeded in an unremarkable fashion until towards the end when I had to get help from one of the stackers to find the filo pastry. The only ingredient that I could not find was juniper berries (for the pickled pears).

I shall deal with the cooking of the pumpkin soup in some detail and I have listed events within the log covering this activity by approximate time of occurrence. As far as the trial cooking of the strudel is

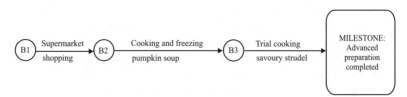

Figure 5.4 Network diagram for dinner party sub-episode B (Advanced preparation)

concerned, I shall merely summarise what happened. The cooking of the soup started with the carving of the pumpkin for Halloween.

Research Log 30.10.99

4.00 p.m.   *Ms Pancake* draws the zigzag for the top to come off.
4.20 p.m.   I start carving the top off with a kitchen knife.
4.37 p.m.   The lid has produced about 400 g of pumpkin flesh.
5.05 p.m.   I'm getting bored with scraping the flesh out of the pumpkin so I put on the radio and listen to *Jazz Record Requests*.

This is proving to be a much slower job than I had thought.

Research Log 30.10.99

5.25 pm.   I've got far too much bulk in this pumpkin flesh. Decide that I'll pressure-cook it. I finish up with about 2.3 kg. It will have to be done in about three loads.
5.30 p.m.   Had a visit from *Ms Eggplant* and *Ms Pancake* who came into the kitchen and complained that the jazz is too loud on the radio. Nuisance! Now the pressure cooker is drowning the jazz with white noise hiss. *Ms Pancake*'s friend has come. They say they want their tea in about three-quarters of an hour. I'm hungry but it's going to be too complicated to cook anything for *my* tea. I decide to have another sandwich.

I am now feeling the consequences of my previous spontaneous decision, at the supermarket, to pick out such a large pumpkin. Had I chosen a smaller one, I would not have to repeat the pressure-cooking cycle and I would have been able to make myself some tea.

Research Log 30.10.99

6.00 p.m.   The girls have decided they want their tea now. The ignition on the cooker has failed. I go to the garage and find a box of matches I keep by the barbecue equipment. Get the girls' pizza in the oven and put some water on to boil for the rest of their tea. Put the third load of pumpkin into the pressure cooker. Using matches to light the stove reminds me of my childhood.

It's very easy to get frazzled in the kitchen. My mood shifts in a negative direction when I turn the jazz down and I'm feeling a little fed-up because I won't have time for my tea. The preparation of the pumpkin is taking too long. In retrospect, I should have bought two smaller pumpkins: one to carve for the girls, and one for me to cook with. Of course, had I separated the Halloween event from my dinner party, there would have been no particular reason to choose a pumpkin recipe in the first place. I now see this as bad planning: I should have anticipated the negative consequences of the long preparation time.

Research Log 30.10.99

6.27 p.m.   Pause to write up this cooking log and have a rest. I've finished pressure-cooking the pumpkin now and it looks as though it will all fit into my big saucepan. I make a mental note that I must buy a big stockpot sometime. *Ms Eggplant* has come into the kitchen to cook her tea. I've finished the girls' tea and they have eaten it. I've just washed up the pots and pans. When I did the pressure-cooking, I didn't change the water between each steaming. The result is that I've got about a pint of nice-looking liquid, which I can use to start off my stock. I'm feeling a bit tired but there isn't much float[5] around this episode. I have to get the soup made and frozen before I go to bed tonight. Liquidising it will take more than one go, I'm sure.

The accumulation of stock water is an unintended consequence of pressure-cooking, this time a very positive one.

Research Log 30.10.99

7.00 p.m.   I've got the wine, pumpkin juice and water heating up in the pan with a bay leaf, small onion, carrot, celery stick and some thyme. This is for my stock. Now I'm frying some chopped leeks, onion and turnips in butter. Then add in the pumpkin and, finally, the sieved stock.
8.00 p.m.   Turned off the gas beneath the soup and left it to cool.

---

[5] Concept of 'float' is used in critical path analysis to spotlight flexible pockets of activity within an overall project design.

8.45 p.m. Sieved the liquid into another pan. Then liquidised the remaining bulk; it took two goes. Put the soup into two containers to cool (before I put them in the freezer). I've got about $4\frac{1}{2}$ pints. I then ate a bowl of leftover soup, with a piece of bread. It tasted OK. I must remember to add a little sugar with the seasoning and cream when I serve it on the day. Then I did a bit of washing-up. ... Got squared up and put everything away. Time is now 9.30 p.m. and I'm feeling quite tired.
11.00 p.m. Finally placed containers into the freezer.
Midnight Finished writing up these notes.

Apart from placing the containers in the freezer after cooling, the pumpkin soup episode ran from 4 p.m. to 9.30 p.m. (approximately $5\frac{1}{2}$ hours). As mentioned above, I grossly underestimated the time this would take.

The trial cooking of the strudel (Episode B[1]) stands tangential to the main dinner party episode. It can be regarded as an independent subplan to make sure that, when included in the dinner party episode, it will work smoothly. I shall not report it in detail, here. I made the strudel and stored it in the fridge, wrapped in foil, for about a day. This proved to be a mistake since some of the pastry had turned soggy and the outer layer stuck to the foil. However, all was not lost: I cooked it, we ate it, and it was very tasty. I decided to proceed with this dish but that it would have to be cooked on the day of the dinner party (not prepared ahead of time). It was just as well that I carried out this trial.

Episode C: Penultimate Chores

I have included this episode to cover the dinner party preparations that come after the completion of advanced shopping and cooking but before the activities which fall on the actual day of the dinner party. I deal with the jobs done on the day of the dinner party, prior to the arrival of the guests, separately (see Episode D). The penultimate chores may be regarded as a heterogeneous collection of activities, since they are marked by temporal, as opposed to conceptual, boundaries (see Figure 5.5). Within my case study, the following things were sorted out at this stage:

1. Review of the meta-plan
2. Bought local cheeses

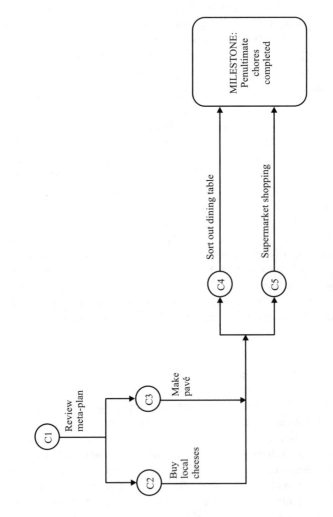

Figure 5.5 Network diagram for dinner part sub-episode C (Penultimate chores)

3. Made the chocolate chestnut *pavé*
4. Sorted out the dining table
5. Did supermarket shopping

On the 6th November I reviewed my plans.

Research Log 06.11.99 @ 2.18 p.m.

I modified my preparation plan this morning. My current idea is to make the *pavé* on Friday evening and to put up the table then. That will leave me to make the Chantilly cream and the strudel on the Saturday.

I checked in the garage to make sure that all the bits and pieces for my table were present and correct. In fact the dining table sub-episode (C^4) could be broken into the following three component activities, spread across the temporal boundaries of sub-episode C^0:

- C^{4i} Check that the bits and pieces are all present and correct in the garage.
- C^{4ii} Assemble the table.
- C^{4iii} Complete the first phase of laying the table (on the day before D-day).

I made a trip out of town to buy some local cheeses (C^2). It was now sufficiently close to the dinner party for me to make the chocolate chestnut *pavé* (C^3), since it could be kept in the fridge without any harm coming to it.

Research Log 10.11.99 @ 6.50 p.m.

I assemble the ingredients for the chocolate chestnut *pavé*. Normally I would melt the chocolate in the microwave but since it specified water to be added in I did it over a very low heat in a smallish saucepan. Took this off the heat. Gave the butter from the fridge two 10-second blasts in the microwave to soften it a bit prior to beating in the sugar.

7.15 p.m. After I had stirred the melted chocolate into the beaten butter and sugar mix, I started to incorporate the puréed

> chestnuts. I could not get rid of the lumps of chestnut so I decided to attack it with the hand-held electric beater. I finished it off with the wooden spoon and poured it into my loaf tin. The quantity was perfect and it filled the tin to the brim. I felt good about this.

This appeared to be a job well done. I had no anxiety about it storing well in the fridge. I now move on to cover some further chores.

> **Research Log 12.11.99 @ 7.00 p.m.**
>
> Earlier today, before I went shopping, I spent 35 minutes assembling my dinner table. This involved bringing the timber in from the garage and then putting it together bit by bit. I listened to some music while I did it and quite enjoyed myself. Went to the supermarket. Made last-minute shopping. Got everything. Left bread rolls to get tomorrow morning. When I came back I couldn't find my tablecloth at first. Then when I did, I put it on the table.

The assembly of the table (C^{4ii}) provides the first dramatic evidence that the event is about to take place: the stage is being set (Goffman, 1959, would refer to this as *front*). Up until now preparatory activities had involved shopping (outside the house) or cooking (in the kitchen).

> **Research Log 12.11.99 @ 7.00 p.m.**
>
> Laid out the cutlery and found a couple of flower vases. Put out some small side plates. Can't really do much more now. I'm conscious of the fact that I shall have a hectic day tomorrow since I have to drop *Ms Pancake* off somewhere out of Sunderland in the afternoon and then pick her up a couple of hours later. That will cut into my preparation time, so I need to try to get ahead. My hand feels sore from banging the table joints together. I should have gone back to the garage for a mallet. I hope that's not going to be a problem tomorrow.

In laying out the best cutlery and crockery (C^{4iii}), and by using flower vases on the table, I act in accordance with the template articulated by Warde and Martens (2000):

> Dinner parties were understood to be 'sit down meals' which happened in a dining room and around a dinner table that displayed the household's best tableware. (p. 57)

In retrospect, I felt at that point driven by the event. All the advanced preparations had been completed. I was totally committed to the dinner party and only something serious would warrant its cancellation; yet there was still much to be done.

Episode D: The Home Stretch

This episode started bright and early on the day of the dinner party (13.11.99). Because this day was hectic, I did not type up some of my hand-written notes until the following day (14.11.99). In this episode, many tasks which were conceptually distinct had to be completed. A flow diagram does not seem to be an appropriate format in which to model these heterogeneous events. I have therefore produced a time line, in Figure 5.6, to cover the following:

D1 Last-minute shopping
D2 Cooking:
    D2.i   Garlic and parsley breadcrumbs: (a) make; (b) wash processor
    D2.ii   Pickled pears: (a) find dish; (b) prepare pears; (c) put in oven; (d) wash dish
    D2.iii   Strudel: (a) filling; (b) assembly; (c) washing up
    D2.iv   Chantilly cream
    D2.v   Coffee
    D2.vi   Cheese board
D3 Revise guest list
D4 Extraneous activities:
    D4.i   Drive *Ms Pancake* to venue
    D4.ii   *Mr Broccoli's* lunch
    D4.iii   Collect *Ms Pancake*
    D4.iv   *Mr Broccoli* takes nap (fantasy)
    D4.v   *Mr Broccoli* rests in chair
D5 Scene-setting:
    D5.i   Sweep path
    D5.ii   Flowers for table
    D5.iii   Tidy up

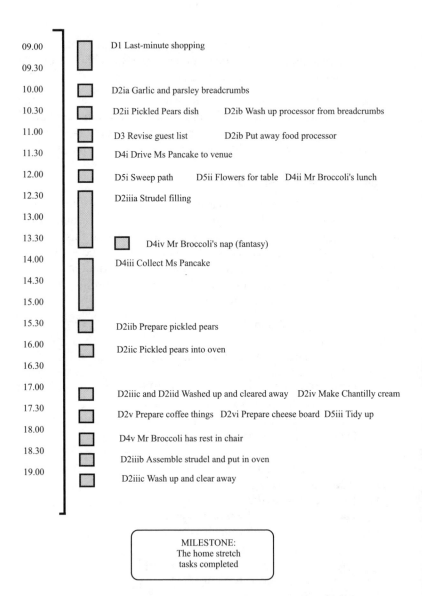

Figure 5.6 Sub-episode D (The home stretch): vertical timeline chart

First thing, I headed off to the supermarket and bought all the last-minute items. I pick up the story with the first cooking chore of the day (I have recorded events in the form of a timed log).

Research Log 13.11.99

10.20 a.m. Made the breadcrumbs with garlic and parsley (for the savoury strudel). *Ms Eggplant* came into the kitchen with some flowers, which we put in a vase. I then found a heavy casserole for the pickled pears. When I tried to put 8 of them into it they barely fitted. I then wished that I had chosen smaller pears (I had deliberately picked out some large ones).

Several unrelated sub-episodes are taking place more or less in parallel here. The timing and order between these is arbitrary (it doesn't matter whether I do the breadcrumbs before or after finding a casserole for the pears).

Research Log 13.11.99

10.40 a.m. Washed up the processor from the garlic bread-crumbs.

10.50 a.m. Received a phone call from *Ms Tarragon* advising me that something serious had happened, unexpectedly, to prevent her from coming tonight. I had a brief chat with *Ms Eggplant* about this and we thought about one or two people who we might ask at this late stage, in order to make up the numbers. In the end we chose two of our friends who I felt sure would not be offended by such a last-minute invitation. They were out but I left a message on their answer-phone.

I had planned to cook for 8 persons and I felt that it would be too complicated, at this late stage, to rearrange my cooking for the reduced party of 6 (the friends I had contacted at the last minute had another engagement and were not able to come). Visser (1991) comments on the difficulty of issuing last-minute invitations:

> a guest must not be asked too close to the date, because that looks as though he or she is really being asked to fill in for a preferred guest who has dropped out. Friends need to be very close and compliant if they are to be asked on short notice to fill a gap. (p.103)

> **Research Log 13.11.99**
>
> **11.00 a.m.**   *Ms Pancake* is still not out of bed and there seems to be lots of mess in the dining room, which needs to be tidied. Tricky. I decide to ignore those problems and, instead, put away the food processor.

I think I was putting away the food processor as a displacement activity, to avoid dealing with the mess in the dining room or with *Ms Pancake*.

> **Research Log 13.11.99**
>
> **Midday.**   Got back from dropping off *Ms Pancake*. Swept up some autumn leaves from the front path, then picked a few fuschias and some foliage for a couple of small flower vases I usually put onto the dining table. I arranged them as best I could and then made myself some lunch.
> **12.30 p.m.**   I started cooking the leek and celery component of the strudel filling. That takes quite some time, what with the apples, mozzarella, and so forth. One way or another it was 1.45 p.m. before I finished. I find it a bit puzzling to know where the time went. I was listening to *Any Questions* on the radio but it wasn't very interesting. I feel really tired now. I'd like to have a nap but I must leave in 10 minutes to pick up *Ms Pancake*.

The sweeping-up and the picking of flowers for the table are both tied into setting the scene in a dramaturgical sense (Goffman, 1959). I am moving into a low ebb at this point: I'm getting bored with some of the preparation and I'm feeling tired. Although I can think of a sub-plan to correct the situation (i.e. take a nap), another pressing external plan (i.e. pick up *Ms Pancake*) prevents me from putting it into effect.

> **Research Log 13.11.99**
>
> **3.45 p.m.**   Prepared the pickled pears. Having peeled them, they did all fit into the pot. I heated the cider vinegar (with the

brown sugar, peppercorns, cloves and crushed juniper berries) on top of the stove and then transferred the covered casserole dish to the oven at 4.00 p.m. *Ms Eggplant* said the smell of vinegar was very strong in the house, so I kept the kitchen door shut and opened a window while the pears cooked.

Things are going well at this point. It is a good feeling to know that I have one of the components of the main course under control.

Research Log 13.11.99

5.00 p.m. Washed up. Ground some coffee beans and put the coffee into my big cafetière so that it will be ready when needed. Made the Chantilly cream. Seemed OK.
5.30 p.m. Got my cheeses out of the fridge to bring them up to room temperature. Set them roughly on a cheese board. Found my cheese knife. Put some bottles of mineral water in the fridge to chill. Tidied up.

Of course, I could sort out the coffee and cheeses as and when they are required at the end of the meal. I think I do these jobs at this point in time in order to make myself feel good: I must be in control if I can get so far ahead.

Research Log 13.11.99

6.00 p.m. Having a rest. I'm going to have to make the strudel at 6.30 p.m. and I'm going to have to move quickly. Timing is all a bit tricky. It's at moments like this when I wish I'd opted for something that you just bang in the oven and forget about.

The cause of my anxiety is that my timing has to be very precise. The strudel needs to be placed in the oven directly it is finished and that should be as soon as the guests have arrived. Because it requires some concentration to make, I did not want to still be constructing it while welcoming the guests. So, the planned end-point of the strudel-making sub-episode was 6.55 p.m., no earlier and no later.

Research Log 13.11.99

6.25 p.m.   Melted butter ready for filo. Unwrapped filo and lay it between two wet teatowels. Worked quickly and assembled the strudel. Everything went very smoothly. Uncorked a bottle of red wine and poured a glass to have by me on the kitchen counter. Kept a close eye on the clock, since timing is fairly crucial now.

6.55 p.m.   Got the strudel in the oven. Moved very fast to get washed and cleared up from the strudel before the guests arrived.

It was important not just to get the strudel in the oven but also to clear up since I needed all my work surfaces and a clean sink for cooking and serving within the main dinner episode. I think I did it with about two minutes to spare.

Episode E: Main Dinner

The main dinner episode is broken into the cycle of cooking, serving, eating and clearing, course by course (starter, main, dessert). I have excluded the serving of cheese and coffee from this episode, placing it in the next sub-episode (see *End Game*, F^0, below). In Figure 5.7, I provide a prototypical representation of the main dinner, in flow diagram format. Because of the complexity of this flow diagram, I have labelled the sub-episodes consecutively from E^1 to E^{15}, without using auxiliary suffixes to distinguish the three courses.

My dinner party followed the prototypical pattern reasonably well, to start with. However, we had to cope with the arrival of visitors after the main course had been eaten (but before pudding had been served). Events post-coffee I have included in the next and final episode.

Our first guests arrived on time at 7.00 p.m. and the others soon followed them.

Research Log 13.11.99

We were all seated comfortably in the sitting-room area and the conversation roamed round a range of topics as might be expected for a group who had just come together for the first

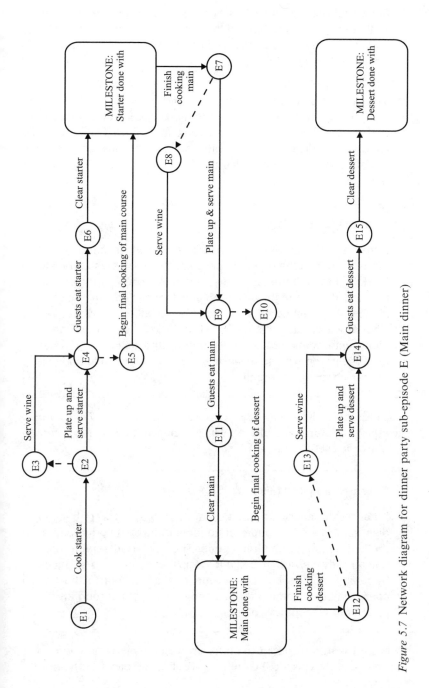

Figure 5.7 Network diagram for dinner party sub-episode E (Main dinner)

time. I felt happy about this and decided to get the soup on. At that very moment, I heard the kitchen timer go and this signalled that my strudel had been in the oven for 30 minutes. I departed to the kitchen.

Although I felt some anxiety about the demands of the forthcoming evening, I thought that my preparations had been sufficiently extensive: the meal should more or less cook itself now. I quite enjoyed retreating from the dining room into the kitchen. This felt as though it was my domain and reminded me of Goffman's (1959) concept of back stage.

Research Log 13.11.99

I checked the strudel. This was fine, not at all burnt, and I merely reduced the oven temperature (from UK Gas Mark 5 to Mark 2). I then lit the top burner under the soup pan (I was so pleased that I bought a bigger pan for the job). In between stirring and tasting this I placed a selection of white and wholemeal bread rolls in a bowl and took them to the table, along with some bottles of sparkling and still spring water from the fridge. The soup warmed up and I decided to add in a further spoonful of Kirsch.

The idea for the Kirsch had come from an article I saw in *The Guardian* newspaper (Saturday, 30.10.99) which included a recipe for pumpkin soup by the chef Raymond Blanc.

Research Log 13.11.99

I then asked everyone to sit up at the table and went back to dish up. I lobbed a couple of dobbles of butter into the pan at the last minute to finish the soup. Then I started serving up. I had already cleared myself a lot of space on our work surfaces by taking various containers and appliances out to the tiny conservatory adjoining the kitchen. So, I could spread all the plates out without any bother.

A lack of worktop space can crank up the stress level no end during this phase of the episode. I therefore give clearing spaces a top priority.

> **Research Log 13.11.99**
>
> I took the first two servings through and decided that this would take far too long. I therefore enlisted the help of *Mr Beef* to carry some of the other servings through for me. I then checked that everyone who was drinking wine had some and that those not drinking alcohol were also topped up with whatever they wanted. We sat down and had our soup.

This was an interesting social decision. As my guest, perhaps I should not have asked *Mr Beef* to act as a waiter. Still, I did need some help if the soup was not to get cold. I like to think that in asking him to do this I was paying him a compliment by treating him in a fashion that was closer to the way I would treat a member of my household.

> **Research Log 13.11.99**
>
> I felt a lot more relaxed now, since I was sure that the main course would be OK. I must have been talking a lot because I was the last to finish my soup. I made myself hurry up, since I knew that I should not leave the strudel in the oven for too long. *Ms Eggplant* cleared the soup dishes away and I got on with serving the main course.

I was very glad to have some help with clearing the dishes.

> **Research Log 13.11.99**
>
> I got the strudel out of the oven and decided to transfer it onto a large wooden board to serve it. I put some lettuce in a bowl, dripped in a few spots of olive oil and smidgen of balsamic vinegar and tossed the salad with my fingers. Then I cut a slice of strudel (it's shaped as a long roulade) for each plate. I put a little bit of salad beside the strudel and then placed a pickled pear onto the salad. The pickled pears looked great and they were cooked to perfection, in terms of their tenderness (they started very hard). I felt really pleased with the way this main course came together. I then took the servings out to my guests and we all ate the main course.

Just as everything appeared to be going according to plan, the neat structure of the anticipated dinner party unravelled. What follows was thoroughly enjoyable but it does emphasise the fact that huge deviations from prototypical episode structures may happen in practice.

Research Log 13.11.99

Around the time that we were finishing our main course there was a ring at the door and this signalled the return of *Ms Pancake* and her friend from their trip to the 'Rocky Horror Show'. They all came in, in costume, including *Ms Pancake*'s friend's parents (who we knew very well). *Ms Pancake* was dressed as 'Magenta', *Ms Waffle* and *Ms Watercress* were both 'Janet', and *Mr Mango* was 'The Criminologist'. *Ms Watercress* and *Ms Waffle* said that they would like a little supper; *Mr Mango* said he just wanted a glass of wine. At this point all notions of a regular seating plan went out the window. *Ms Eggplant* said she would vacate her seat at the end of the table and sort out some food for *Ms Pancake*, then sit in an easy-chair for a bit if necessary.

Eventually *Ms Pancake* found an extra chair or two from somewhere (a diagram setting out the changes to the seating arrangements is provided in Figure 5.8).

Research Log 13.11.99

I placed *Ms Watercress* in the middle of one side between *Ms Thyme* and *Mr Beef*. *Mr Mango* took the chair at the end of the table, vacated by *Ms Eggplant*. *Ms Pancake* took my seat. *Ms Waffle* sat on a corner at my end of the table next to *Ms Pancake*. When I needed to sit down I sat at the corner on the other side of *Ms Pancake*.

I sorted out some food for the new arrivals but I then had a scheduling problem to deal with, since my original guests were waiting for their pudding.

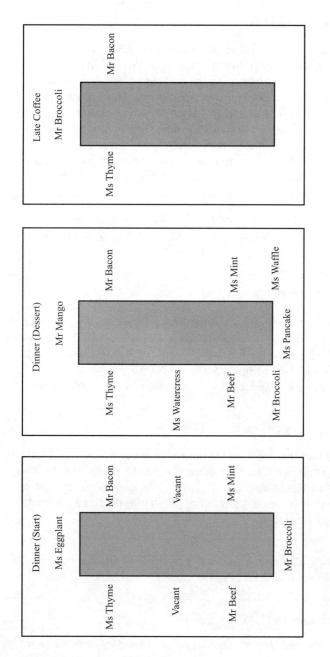

Note: The key to the dramatis personae is given earlier in the chapter.

Figure 5.8 Dinner party seating arrangements

> **Research Log 13.11.99**
>
> Back in the kitchen I had a debate with *Ms Eggplant* as to whether I should wait until the recent arrivals had caught up with everyone else before serving dessert. She was not in favour of this and felt that I should go ahead and serve. This I proceeded to do. At first I had a bit of a fright, since my *pavé* wouldn't turn out of the loaf tin. I got a knife round the sides and eventually it came out OK. Then I used a slice to cut slabs onto the plates. I tried for a thin sliver but it was difficult to get it off my slice without breaking it. I therefore dished up slightly chunkier wedges.

Pudding seemed to go well and I have taken it as the point of closure for the *Main Dinner* episode. The remainder of the event I construe as the *End Game*.

Episode F: End Game

This episode starts with the winding down of the dinner party, leading to farewells, and finally concludes with clearing up (the clearing up episode spilled over to the following morning). A flow diagram for this episode is presented in Figure 5.9.

The first thing to happen was the serving of coffee and cheese.

> **Research Log 13.11.99**
>
> After we had the dessert, I prepared a cheese board and took it in together with some crackers. Without doubt, the North-umberland Nettle and the Beamish cheeses were the ones that caught everyone's attention. I then served some coffee to those that wanted it.

In terms of planning, there was very little to do but relax at this stage of the event.

> **Research Log 13.11.99**
>
> *Mr Mango* and *Ms Watercress* left ahead of the close of proceedings. *Ms Pancake* and *Ms Waffle* went into another

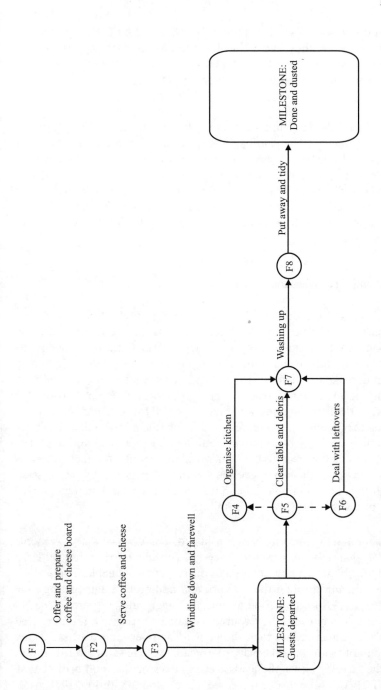

Figure 5.9 Network diagram for dinner party sub-episode F (End game).

room to watch a video, I think. *Ms Mint* and *Mr Beef* then took their leave; they had to get back to see to their cat. *Ms Eggplant* went to bed at about 1.00 a.m. At the end of the evening I was left chatting to *Ms Thyme* and *Mr Bacon*.

In fact, I did very little clearing up that night. This was partly due to the fact that *Ms Eggplant* had already done a large amount. The next morning I finished off clearing up in the dining room, took down my table and stowed it in the garage, put out the rubbish and, finally, finished off washing up and putting away. I move on now to consider general issues relating to the planning and the schedule of the dinner party as a whole, drawing upon my case study for illustrative purposes where appropriate.

Planning and Scheduling Issues

Lockyer and Gordon (1991, p. 5) argue that an effective plan will be explicit, intelligible, capable of accepting change and capable of being monitored. Project network techniques (PNTs), typically involving the use of diagrams such as those I have produced in Figures 5.1–5.9, may help to make the planning explicit and provide a basis for critical path analysis. So far, I have paid little attention to the interplay between the logic of the flow diagrams and time estimated for the completion of the constituent components represented within them. The industrial application of PNTs involves the calculation of the total time for the project and, where this exceeds the time available (either for the project as a whole or for the sub-episodes), scrutiny of critical activities to see if their time of execution can be shortened by using a different method or the problem solved by re-scheduling:

> Time and logic having been considered, it may be necessary – in some fortunate cases it is not necessary – to consider the resources required by the plan as it now stands and the resources available. This is done by moving through the network and adding up ('aggregating') the resources for each period of time. The aggregated resources ('loads') are compared with the resources available ('capacity'). If they exceed the resource ceiling then the network is re-examined to see if any manipulation can take place to 'spread' the load satisfactorily. If not, then clearly either the available resources or the total project time (TPT) or both must be increased. (Lockyer and Gordon, 1991, p. 5)

At first it may seem strange to apply industrial PNTs to a domestic dinner party. However, the consequences of getting the planning and scheduling wrong can be dire both for the cook and the guests. This has little to do with strict questions of culinary competence. Elizabeth David is acknowledged by many to be one of the greatest English food writers of the twentieth century, yet Chaney (1998), in her biography, indicates that scheduling problems were endemic with her:

> Elizabeth stayed with Doreen and her husband Colin Thornton for over three months, experimenting, cooking, writing. 'This was fine,' says Doreen, 'but what wasn't was that when we had people to dinner Liz would invariably say "I'll cook" and she wouldn't produce dinner until eleven o'clock at night. Once my stepfather was staying and it was awful. He needed to eat and Liz had hardly started by nine o'clock. She'd have spaghetti hanging all over the kitchen chairs to dry and everything in general disarray.' (p. 310)

For cooks who care about their guests and have respect for their use of time, the problem of delivering the dinner on schedule may generate much stress and anxiety. Lawson (1998), in her book *How to Eat*, provides the following recognition of how stressful cooking for friends or family can be:

> I once went to a dinner party a good friend of mine gave, and she was so anxious, she'd been up till three in the morning the night before making stocks. She said scarcely a word to any of us after opening the door, since she was in the middle of the first of about five courses. The food was spectacular: but she spent most of the evening ever more hysterical in the kitchen. At one point we could, as we stiltedly made conversation between ourselves, hear her crying. The fault wasn't her competence, but her conception: she felt that her dinner party must be a showcase for her culinary talents and that we must all be judging her. (pp. 330–1)

In passing, I note that Lawson's friend breaks one of the rules embedded within the dinner party template as articulated in Warde and Martens (2000), since she neglected her guests once they had arrived:

> Managing time and sociability were other important concerns for 'doing the job right'. Respondents talked about using the oven and

doing a lot of the preparation work prior to the event as ways of managing it in such a way that they were not in the kitchen too often or too long while guests were in the house. (Warde and Martens, 2000, pp. 57–8)

Lawson's (1998) strategy is to be quite ruthless. For example, if having a starter adds to the tension, then she would advocate scrapping it from the planned menu. Such a strategy may fly in the face of social expectations: there could be family or peer group pressure to provide one. I think that whereas issues relating to self-confidence would normally be associated with the management of the social interaction within the dinner party episode, Lawson's approach indicates that self-confidence may be important even in the planning stage. The unfortunate corollary is that those low in self-confidence or self-esteem may not be able to bring themselves to take such stress-reducing steps. Interestingly, the involvement of counselling in the psychology of food has, by and large, been in relation to problems surrounding eating disorders (see Chapter 4). There may, however, be some scope for an extension of this role into issues relating to ordinary home cooking.

Tovey (1990) is also concerned about planning in advance in order to avoid hassle on the night when entertaining at home. Again, he offers a number of simple rules for the home cook to follow:

It [home entertaining] only works properly if *you*, the host or hostess, are *relaxed*. This is why most of the dishes in this book can be prepared ahead of time, which is always such a boon when entertaining ... Never try, either, to have three hot courses, for instance. It's not necessary, and causes too much hassle. Serve at least one course cold. When having folk round in the evening, I often make up these cold platters, cover them with cling film and leave them somewhere cool until I need to serve them. Thus no last minute hassle. And *never*, *ever* do a completely new dish when you have folk coming round. This is a sure recipe for disaster. (p. 8) (emphasis in the original)

Tovey not only provides some simple rules to avoid hassle but also issues a caveat against attempting new dishes. This aspect of planning is designed to avoid slips, errors and mistakes in cooking (see Reason, 1990, for a wider discussion of human error). In terms of my dinner party, I carried out a practice cooking of the savoury strudel prior to the dinner in order to test for its viability as a component of the meal. The trial cooking revealed a major mistake (keeping the uncooked strudel in the fridge caused the pastry to go soggy). I felt that this could be rectified but at a cost: the strudel had to be assembled immediately prior to the arrival of the guests and thus contributed to a potential increase in stress at such a crucial time. Looking back, I made the right decision.

Both Tovey and Lawson draw attention to the way the construction of the menu may have an effect on stress levels. In planning my dinner party menu, I was looking not only for a balance of ingredients across courses but also for items that could be prepared well ahead, a day or two in advance, or a few hours before the dinner started. Any recipe or component that can be shifted out of the focal episode of the dinner party *per se* will help to reduce stress.

A more formal way of expressing the problem of scheduling for dinner party preparation is to use the concept of *float*. In order to illustrate how this may be done, I shall draw upon ideas set out in Lockyer and Gordon's (1991) book on critical path analysis (see, especially, their chapters 6 and 7), adapting them somewhat to suit my purposes. I start with a formal definition of float.

Any activity within the project or episode may be given the following temporal descriptors:

- Earliest Start Time (EST)
- Latest Start Time (LST)
- Earliest Finish Time (EFT)
- Latest Finish Time (LFT)
- Window (W)
- Duration (D)
- Float (F)

The Window (W) is the amount of time within which the activity can take place. If this exceeds Duration (D), then there is some Float (F) within the episode. A formal definition is as follows:

$$W = LFT - EST$$

and

$$F = W - D$$

In a situation where W equals D, there is no float and timing is crucial (in my dinner party, I felt that I was close to this situation when I assembled my strudel, and I was in it when I did the clearing up after putting the strudel in the oven and before receiving the guests). Total float is the amount by which an activity can be extended or delayed without affecting the total project time. It is important that any given activity not be delayed in such a way as to affect subsequent activities. This will happen where W is less than D, and Lockyer and Gordon (1991) refer to this as negative float. Negative float is what stresses the cook or, in Elizabeth David's case (see above), keeps the guests waiting for unnecessarily lengthy periods of time.

In principle, it would be possible to provide an estimate for every job or activity that is required in order to execute the dinner party plan. In industrial production this may be done with some accuracy but to go through such a procedure for a domestic dinner party would seem a trifle heavy-handed. In terms of my own dinner party, it is obvious that I could not have done everything within the two or three hours the guests sat at the table.

At the start of this section, I broached the topic of spreading the load in connection with PNTs used in industry. The total person-hours for each task is plotted out per time period as a histogram. The estimated work requirements can then be compared with the maximum resource available over the same time scale. Where there are peaks (i.e. the estimated person-hours exceed those available for the task), attempts can be made to shift some of the activities into the troughs (i.e. periods where there is some slack in the system with more person-hours available than it is estimated will be used up). Where a schedule is so tight that it is impossible to spread the load in this fashion, a more drastic solution must be sought in terms of revising the project goals or finding alternative strategies to overcome the points of overload. Lawson's strategy of scrapping a starter illustrates this approach.

Moving away from the topic of loading and scheduling, another interesting aspect of planning is the compilation of the guest list. The invitation list may be of great interest from a social psychological point of view. Decisions will have to be made as to who will get on with whom, whether to try to obtain an homogeneous group where consensual values and opinions will be maximised or whether to opt for a more heterogeneous assembly in the hope that the proceedings will be more lively. Because I am here more concerned with food and cooking, my treatment of this aspect of the planning activity will be brief (see Visser, 1991, for a fuller discussion, especially her chapter 3). From a nutritional standpoint, the choice of guests may affect the menu, especially if any are known to have strong dislikes or restrictive diets. It is possible that issues relating to guest list and menu planning may be dealt with in parallel on some occasions. If the hosts wish to build the main course around a particularly good item of game or fish that they have been promised, for example, this could result in the *menu-driven* disqualification of vegetarians from a possible guest list. On the other hand, the primary commitment may be to gather together a particular group of people (e.g. close work colleagues), in which case it would be *dishes* which might be subjected to *guest-list driven* disqualification. In the case of my dinner party, because I am a vegetarian and I was the cook, I excluded from consideration any meat, poultry or fish dishes.

The main planning and scheduling issues concern spreading the load for shopping, pre-cooking and general chores relating to preparation on the day. In particular this will reduce the likelihood of stress for the cook in the main dinner event. Apart from this, some consideration will have to be given to planning the menu and the guest list; these may affect one another. The menu, once planned, will determine the specific tasks that need to be accomplished at particular points in time in the dinner party schedule, considered as a whole.

Conclusion

I shall start by placing my dinner party episode in a slightly broader context. It has to be acknowledged that I am writing about the situation for middle-class dinners in affluent Western societies. Goody (1982) reminds us that what is on the menu may well be dictated by circumstances:

> Famine often brings its own cuisine, based upon a selection of foods that are not ordinarily consumed. In towns, animals such as cats and rats enter into the repertoire from which in normal times they are excluded. The most extreme instances include the flesh of horses and men. (p. 59)

With regard to my dinner party, we were fortunate in not being driven to such extremes. However, while we had a nice dinner with plenty to eat, I do not feel that the event could be construed as an unreasonable display of affluence. I present a full costing for the dinner in Appendix 4. For eight persons I spent £42.29 (£5.29 per head), excluding wine. At the time of writing, the rules for the UK television cookery competition *Master Chef* allow contestants a budget of £35 to cover a three-course meal for four persons (i.e. £8.75 per head). My local pub offers a two-course meal at the carvery restaurant for £5.99 per head.

Of course, my menu, avoiding expensive cuts of meat, possibly leans towards what Bourdieu might expect from one high in cultural, as opposed to economic, capital.

In the next chapter, I move away from home entertainment to consider eating out.

6

Eating Out in a Small Way (Idiographic Observation)

My approach to eating out, in this chapter, is similar in many respects to the one I adopted in Chapter 3 when I reported the episode of preparing and eating a simple lunch comprising a boiled egg on toast. The topic in this chapter shifts from my kitchen at home to the wider social setting implied by the notion of 'eating out'. Warde and Martens (2000) draw attention to the fact that the variety of venues available for eating is large and because of this it is difficult to find a generic term to cover them all:

> Thus we have, among others, cafés, restaurants, steakhouses, diners, brasseries, bistros, pizzerias, kebab-houses, grill rooms, coffee bars, teashops, ice cream parlours, food courts, snack bars, refreshment rooms, transport cafes and service stations, buffets and canteens. There are commercial places to eat which are not primarily devoted to food provision, like the tavern, the pub, the wine bar, the hotel, the in-store restaurant, the boarding house and the motel. (p. 21)

In the end, Warde and Martens (2000) go for the term 'eating out place' in order to solve their problems of nomenclature. Because, in the previous chapter, I have described a dinner party, I shall steer away from the more formal setting of restaurant dinners in the present chapter. My selection of venue was adventitious: it depended on whether I was in the mood for research, whether I was going to an eating out place, and even whether I had my notepad or palmtop computer to hand. The following *Eating Out* (EO) events provide the basis for my analysis (I give them an EO number for ease of reference):

- EO1: Self-service lunch in a vegetarian restaurant in central London
- EO2: An afternoon snack in the food hall of a small central London shopping mall

- EO3: Breakfast in the dining room of a central London hotel
- EO4: Lunch in a riverside pub in Sunderland
- EO5: Lunch in a cafeteria in a central Sunderland store

Warde and Martens (2000, pp. 54–5) report that, for their sample, most people expressed the strongly held attitude that eating out was a social activity to be done in the company of others (although this view was not held so strongly by Londoners and those living alone). There were two reasons why I decided not to record episodes where I was eating with friends, relatives or work colleagues. Firstly, I felt that my being embedded within a dyadic or small group meal would distract me from the business of recording the event for the purposes of my research. Secondly, I thought that I would be tempted to focus exclusively on the social psychological aspects of the interaction; this would have the effect of pushing the salience of food, as a topic, into the background. Although vaguely supported by these two reasons, I readily admit that my decision was somewhat arbitrary and I look forward to conducting further studies in the future where I participate in eating out as a member of a small group or dyad. For the purposes of this chapter, I eat solo.

In making my records of these eating episodes and, also, in reporting them here, I have been mindful of Condor's (1997, p. 117) observation that critical psychologists, while advocating reflexivity 'do not seem keen to implicate themselves fully either in the data or their analysis'. She also suggests that they may tamper with their data in an unduly manipulative fashion:

> The author then takes on the task of editing, re-packaging and re-sequencing these accounts in order to form a new narrative, the researcher's story. (p. 123)

I am conscious of the fact that, in the previous chapter on my dinner party, I felt obliged to edit and prune my research notes to a considerable extent (my rationale for this being the word-count budgeted for the chapter). I shall resist the temptation to do this to the research notes which form the basis of the present chapter. Condor (1997) describes the texts typically produced by critical psychologists as monovocal meta-narratives. I shall achieve mine by presenting my notes, section by section, for each eating out episode. I shall generate my meta-narrative partly through annotation and partly by providing discussion and comment at the end of each section.

EO1: Self-Service Lunch at a Vegetarian Restaurant in Central London

The field notes for this episode were generated in two phases. In the first instance I made some brief hand-written notes, scribbled on a small notepad during and immediately after lunch (see Figure 6.1). I then returned to my hotel room and typed up a much fuller version on my palmtop computer within approximately one hour of the end of the episode.

Typed field notes:
I approached the restaurant from a narrow lane. I don't really know why I chose to start with this place, or to start today.[1] I am in London for a meeting and I feel that I ought to be making a start with my participant-observation records. I had already decided to take no audio-visual recording apparatus with me since I felt that would be too intrusive.[2] I have my palmtop computer in my breast pocket and a little notebook in my side pocket.[3]

And now I've entered the door and barely noticed that I've done so.[4] It's changed since I was last here, some years ago. I can't get my bearings. There are a lot of sandwiches to take out and pre-wrapped stuff. But is that true? I'm really sitting in my hotel room, some 2 hours later, writing up how I remember it.[5] I have a few jottings on my notepad to help me (see Figure 6.1). I can't really remember about the

---

[1] While an admission to such fuzzy planning might be an embarrassment to a mainstream psychologist, I feel that my gesture of damning self-disclosure may add some strength to my claim to be a critical social psychologist (see my discussion of Condor, 1997, above).

[2] Even a small camcorder, when pointed in the direction of other diners, would arouse suspicion and could have an effect on their behaviour. Choosing not to video does not mean that I shall not observe. If anything, the decision forces me to acknowledge my position as a researcher-voyeur.

[3] These are the tools for the production of data in the form of text (field notes). The palmtop and the notebook are props which, in different guise, might support the fiction that I was an intrepid reporter or perhaps a novelist or playwright doing background research for a café scene.

[4] Part of me thinks that I should turn into this perfect human being with superb powers of concentration and excellent observation skills whenever I switch into research mode. Of course that doesn't happen. In everyday conversations I often drift off into a reverie and lose the gist of what the other person is saying or my mind wanders off into some daydream when I'm driving and I can't recall the details of my route. Although I do try to pay attention in research, there is no reason to expect perfection. Here I have the embarrassment of not noticing that the start of the first research episode of my current project had, in fact, begun.

[5] I find it very difficult to be honest about time perspective in field notes. The only way I can capture how it felt at the time of the primary episode is to think myself back into the episode and write in the present tense: this offers great scope for conveying the misleading impression that the notes were being written as the primary episode unfolded.

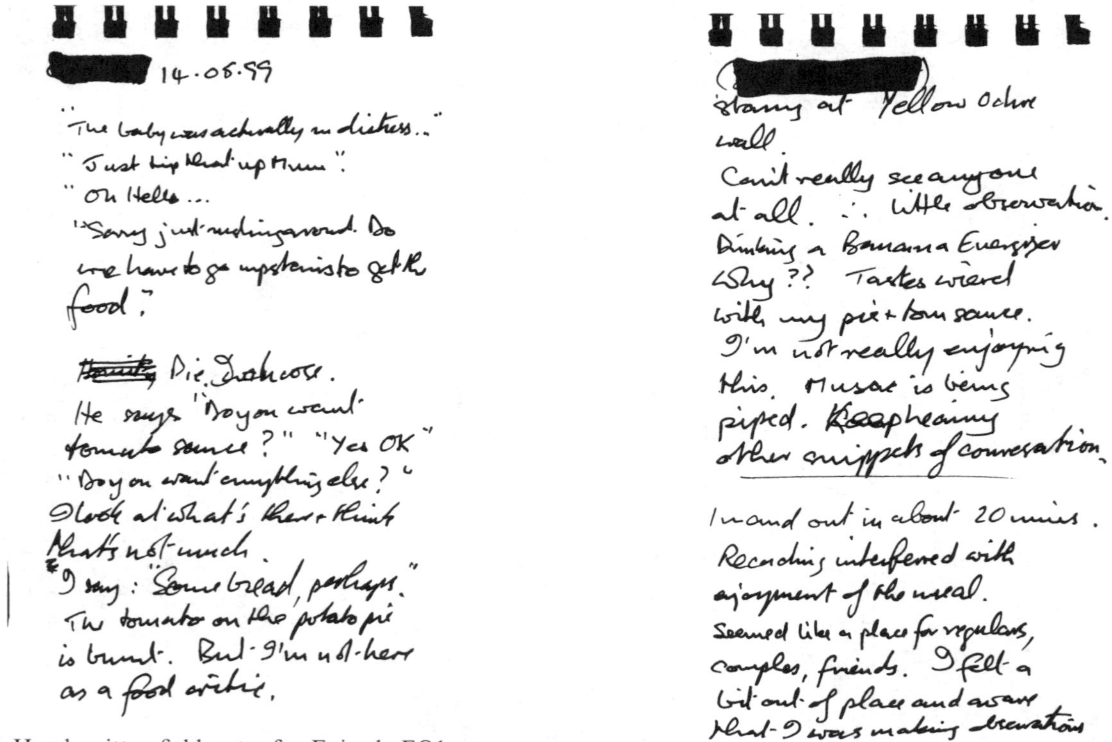

[redacted] 14.08.99

"The baby was actually in distress.."
"Just tip that up then".
"Oh Hello...
"Sorry just reading around. Do we have to go upstairs to get the food".

~~Haunty~~ Pie Dishcore.
He says "Do you want tomato sauce?" "Yes OK"
"Do you want anything else?"
I look at what's there + think that's not much.
I say: "Some bread, perhaps."
The tomato on the potato pie is burnt. But I'm not here as a food critic.

([redacted])
staring at Yellow Ochre wall.
Can't really see anyone at all. ∴ little observation.
Drinking a Banana Energizer Why?? Tastes weird with my pie + tom sauce.
I'm not really enjoying this. Musac is being piped. ~~Keep~~ hearing other snippets of conversation.

In and out in about 20 mins.
Recording interfered with enjoyment of the meal.
Seemed like a place for regulars, couples, friends. I felt a bit out of place and aware that I was making observations

Figure 6.1 Hand-written field notes for Episode EO1

sandwiches. I do remember that I was rather confused. I just had a chance to glance at some dishes on display beneath their labels on the serving counter, and then the woman in front was gone and this young man was asking me what I wanted.

He had dark hair, and a dark complexion; a handsome man, not too aggressive or surly. I was panicking. I had to make a decision, yet I couldn't see anything conventional like a menu. I kept thinking that I ought to be remembering what was going on because this was a research episode; and this guy wasn't helping me out. I noticed the dish in the middle, directly in front of me and I remembered that I had had it before. Indeed, it was in one of my cook books at home. I decided that it would do.

'I'll have the pie,' I said.

He got a dish, turned to me and asked 'Do you want tomato sauce with it?'

'Yes,' I said. I looked at this tiny bowl of pie. It had tomato sauce splodged over half of it. It didn't look enough. I guess I must have looked dissatisfied.

'Do you want anything else?' he said.

'Yes,' I said, 'Something. Do you have any bread?' He reached for tongs and deftly picked up a very modest morsel of bread (neither loaf, nor roll). I had had in mind something altogether more substantial when I had thought about it on the train coming down from Sunderland this morning.

He took my pensiveness for acquiescence, satisfaction, or perhaps the manifestation of learning difficulties, and said 'You pay over there,' gesturing to the other counter.

I took my stainless steel circular tray to the counter. At first I thought that the tray might have been a rather trendy eating utensil. I realised that it was not when I grasped the local norms for size of portion operating in this establishment. As I turned to make my way to the second counter, I noticed that there was a rack full of drinks. I thought about water but didn't want a full bottle. I therefore started looking at what I had assumed to be smaller plastic glasses of fruit juice. There was nothing simple of that nature: rather, the likes of elderflower cordial and mango smoothies seemed to be the norm. All the time customers were performing complex dances between tills and counters on this busy Friday lunch period. I felt like a novice, and I felt old. There were certainly no other men of my age in the establishment. Everyone else seemed to know what they were doing. In the end I picked up a 'Banana Energizer' and took it to the till.

'Aren't you having any salad?' said the woman behind the till.

By then I was fed up. I didn't want to balance my tray and help myself to a tiny bowl of salad from yet another counter. 'No,' was my terse reply.[6]

'That'll be £4.35,' she said. I gave her a fiver and waited for my change, thinking how glad I was that I didn't have to pay for lunch in London every day of the week.

'Can I take this downstairs?' I asked.

As she said 'Yes, of course', I wondered why I had asked her in the first place.

I descended the narrow steep stairs and quickly noted that most of the tables were occupied. I went for a bar-stool against the wall counter. I felt pleased that I had found a seat and that I hadn't spilt my dinner over anyone. I quickly got my notebook out and started writing. Eating could wait a bit.

'The baby was actually in distress...,' said the older woman at the nearest table. 'Just tip that up Mum....' I hadn't a clue what the daughter meant.[7]

A young man entered and greeted a young woman already seated: 'Oh, Hello. Sorry, just been rushing around. Do we have to go upstairs to get the food?'

As I'm writing up from my notes after the event, it occurs to me that that should have made me feel more relaxed, since this man obviously didn't know how the place worked either. But this doesn't register at the time, because I feel the need to have a bite of my pie, and to start noting down what happened to me when I ordered. I'm going to think myself back into the present tense now, as if I'm at the restaurant.[8]

This potato isn't bad. It's mashed quite smoothly and the tomato sauce tastes nice with it. I'm just using my fork, US-style. Wait a minute, one of the sliced tomatoes on the top of the potato pie is burnt. Shall I leave it? I'd better not or I won't be able to say how it tastes.

---

[6] The fact that I was in a bad mood may well have coloured the way I wrote up this episode. In mainstream psychology the researcher's mood state is not usually an issue and can be assumed to be calm and neutral by default. As a critical social psychologist, I'm afraid you get me as I am, warts and all.

[7] I seem to be turning myself into a tape recorder. In terms of writing up, I am beginning to adopt the authorial voice of a conventional novelist.

[8] Once again, the temporal framing of the research episode and the reporting is becoming problematic. It is at this point in the real episode that I paused to make notes on the opening phase of the episode concerned with ordering my meal. This phase has just been reported in my typed-up field notes. I then flag up to the reader the fact that, from the spatio-temporal position of typing up my field notes in my hotel, I am about to recreate the primary episode using first-person, present-tense conventions.

It's OK, but then I will eat burnt toast at home if necessary. Am I meant to be doing this? I'm not here as a food critic, I'm here as a psychologist![9]

I'd better describe what I can see as I sit facing the restaurant wall. The answer is simple: a fairly strong colour (I think we called it yellow ochre when I was at school). The wall is about 12 inches maximum from my face and exhausts my field of view.[10] I can see a few bedraggled flowers to the extreme left of field. As for the other diners, I can't see anyone, unless I turn round in my seat and stare down (I'm on a high bar-stool). I don't want to do that because I'm not planning to do any Garfinkelling today.[11] So, I'm not really observing much at all. I'll try a piece of bread. It's nice and fresh but I would normally drink some water at this stage. Why on earth did I buy this ridiculous 'Banana Energizer'? I'm having a swig of the banana drink. That tastes revolting with the potato pie and the tomato sauce. I'm not enjoying this.

Several people have left and others have come in. It's all happened too fast for me to say anything about it.[12] Musac is being piped and that certainly isn't helping. I finish my food and leave. I should say that I was in and out within 20 minutes.

I sat down on a bench in the courtyard nearby. I felt inadequate as a psychologist and as a participant observer. Surely, I should have made a better job of that. But why should I? And what would count as doing a 'better' job? Apart from that, I was annoyed because, had I not designated this lunch as a research episode, I feel sure that I would have poked my nose into the restaurant only to move on somewhere else. I felt that my research had spoiled my lunch.

Comments on EO1

Several facets of this research episode would be regarded as problematic from the standpoint of mainstream observational methodology. For example, when the episode started I was barely paying attention to what was going on. Furthermore, I allowed my feelings to show through in my report. I was in a bad mood and I was annoyed that my research had played a part in spoiling my lunch (it got cold).

---

[9] Yet another crisis of confidence. I'm judging the food: is this psychology?
[10] I think I'm trying to be a camcorder here.
[11] For a discussion of ethnomethodology, see Garfinkel (1967).
[12] I'm running into a lot of problems. Because there is no video record I can't replay or slow down the speed of the recorded event for a more detailed examination. Because I'm so fed up with my meal, I'm not paying as close attention to my surrounds as I should.

The unreliability of my memory is a factor to be borne in mind when assessing the status of my data, if not its integrity. An example of this occurred when I could not remember if sandwiches were displayed for sale. Admittedly, getting this particular fact right does not seem terribly important, in retrospect. However, there is nothing in the methodology, *per se*, that guides me to make that meta-judgement. A Freudian might well have me free-associating cling-film with condoms; tomato sauce with blood; and the size of portions with matters I would prefer not to talk about here, thank you very much. My point is that what I dismiss as peripheral to what I take to be a (superficially atheoretical?) observational report might assume central importance were I to create an account which was grounded within the psychoanalytic discourse.

It was also difficult for me to handle time in this report. Some of my reporting occurred within the episode, as happened when I made notes with pencil and paper about the start of the lunch, for example. However, those events were in the past at the time I was writing. Some aspects of the episode I did not write up until afterwards, in my hotel room. I flagged this up in my account by admitting where I was and saying that I was going to pretend that it was happening in the here and now. I achieved this by deliberately adopting the first-person present tense in the text of my report at those junctures.

Far from producing an objective account, I was forced to make rhetorical choices at every turn as I fashioned the narrative of my lunchtime story. The points at which I broke frame from the primary tale (to explain that I was, in fact, sitting in my hotel) gave the narrative a meta-fictional air (see Waugh, 1984, for a discussion of metafiction). My disorientation at the restaurant was exacerbated by the fact that I was occupying two roles: diner and researcher. My bad experience as a diner caused my mood to plummet and this may have impacted on my ability to execute the researcher role with efficiency and skill. I am pleased to say that I was in a happier frame of mind in the next episode, which I report below.

EO2: Afternoon Snack in the Food Court of a Small Shopping Mall in Central London

A variety of small shops were represented in this mall, including several chain-stores typical of most UK malls at the time of writing. The food court was on the top floor.

Typed field notes:
I need a bite to eat because my brother and I have decided not to have a meal this evening when we meet. Up to the first-floor food court. Reminds me of the food court at Gateshead Metrocentre. I notice: Singapore Sam, Spudulike, Seattle Coffee Co, Arkwrights Traditional Fish & Chips, McDonalds, Delifrance, KFC, and Rollover Hot Dogs. I make a circuit before going to one of the counters. I ask for the equivalent of a cafetière with cold milk. She suggests a filter coffee. I agree.

'What size?' she says. I point to a cup on the counter. She tells me how much to pay.

'Can you give me a piece of carrot cake?' I say.

'Sure,' and she puts a slice on the plate. I pay her.[13]

There is a large cup for tips containing coins positioned at the point of sale where change is returned to the customer. She gives me 30p change and, for some reason, I put it in the cup.

'You'll get a fork for your cake where you pick up your coffee at the end of the counter,' she said. Maybe she wouldn't have told me if I hadn't given her the tip. As I walk down to collect my coffee, I feel annoyed about the business of the tip. I ask the second woman who has been pouring the coffee for the milk and she gestures to the jug. I pour my milk. She hadn't seen me give the tip; I wonder if she would have poured the milk for me if she had?[14]

Once again, I'm on my own and many of the tables for four are taken. I opt for a bar-stool at a counter. This time it is not up against a wall and I am able to look out onto two of the food stalls and a small dining area somewhat off the main hall. I try a piece of carrot cake. It looks vaguely like the real thing, but it tastes a bit dry round the edges. I assume it's been standing for too long. The coffee is in a double paper cup. No doubt the double cup is to prevent burnt fingers, but it is nowhere near as attractive a solution as the corrugation round the upper portion of the coffee cup I had on the train this morning. Is this observation? It's reporting stream of consciousness and associations.[15]

---

[13] I am aware that I have adopted the stylistic conventions used in fiction writing to report this dialogue, thereby invoking the metaphor of researcher as novelist.

[14] This speculation takes me far beyond the data as given. This is not something that worries me, although I can see that it would if I was a behaviourist. Interestingly, these thoughts would not have been picked up by any discursive psychologist who, by coincidence, happened to be lurking with a surreptitious microphone and tape-recorder. An ethogenic psychologist might have uncovered my musings had he or she approached me to collect my account of the ordering sub-episode (see Harré and Secord, 1972, for a discussion of ethogenic methodology and the collection of accounts).

[15] It is partly through the stream of consciousness that this reported and temporarily bounded episode (EO2) is tied into the broader spatio-temporal matrix. Here the coffee cup serves to link my present situation to the prior episode on the train.

I hated drinking warm milk from Bakelite beakers at break-time at school in the 1950s. The beakers were re-usable and us kids used to chew the tops, so you drunk your milk through a serrated edge formed by the collective gnashers of all your chums.[16] Nothing like that here. I wonder whether I should be suppressing such associations in the interest of psychological research. But then if I did, that would be dishonest.

I'm swigging the coffee. I make better at home. And I'm already wishing that I had plumped for another vendor. I just thought that the other vendor's[17] pastry might give me indigestion (although what the carrot cake will do is anyone's guess). There are some very good coffee houses in Soho and that's just over the road, down Wardour Street. I did think about that, but remembering last month's nail bomb made me nervous.

They wrapped my carrot cake in a sheet of non-clinging cling-film (would that be plastic or polythene?). I feel embarrassed with myself about stumbling over such nomenclature, given that I once did some training in chemical engineering. Anyway, I'm having difficulty cutting the cake with the fork because the plastic keeps getting in the way. The plate is very small and, being paper, has little mass to keep itself steady. I don't want to use my fingers in case I decide to switch to typing into my palmtop instead of writing my notes in my notebook. This carrot cake is really sticky. I open my mouth very wide in order to pass the forkful in without getting sticky stuff on my beard and moustache. The arrangement of my facial muscles and jaw triggers double mental associations: being at the dentist and belting out bass notes (the *jah* syllable of the last Hallelu-*jah* in the Hallelujah chorus, for example). I like the icing on the carrot cake. As a generic item, I always have. Mind you, I'm no slouch when it comes to butter-icing myself.[18]

It's very busy in here; lots of tourists. I feel as if I'm looking out of a window. If I describe that to you, it will be as if you are watching a television screen.[19]

---

[16] The links go even further afield in time and space, as I delve more deeply into autobiographical associations.

[17] I'm using this awkward style of description in order to preserve anonymity, although this might be going beyond what is strictly required by the ethical guidelines of the British Psychological Society relating to the way psychological research should be conducted.

[18] Huge amounts of gratuitous autobiographical material have been blended into my field notes here.

[19] This meta-comment implies that I am going to try to become a human camcorder at this point.

It's now 10.30 p.m. I didn't finish these notes earlier because I met with some of my relatives. I'll now think myself back to the afternoon coffee episode.[20]

People keep strolling past, from left to right and from right to left. I observe a little altercation about wrong change, at the counter opposite me, between the guy who is serving and a young woman customer. The woman wins.

One whole family is leaving in front of me. I never even noticed they were there. Some observation, this.[21] A blonde woman strides through my field of vision to go to one of the food counters nearby. I keep trying to see what she has ordered. I guess I feel that I ought to write it down. But why is it important for me to know what she's got? It isn't really. Still, if I keep looking over at her she is going to start wondering what I'm up to. She's walked off with some coffee – out of field. The security man struts about. A couple in their 30s sit and relax at a table. They share a coffee, smile a lot and talk. They look like tourists.

I'm now beginning to notice lots of little interactions taking place between the staff who work at the food court. At first I didn't see them, possibly because I thought I should be watching the punters. I can hear some back-stage altercations over at one of the counters. Next door, a woman behind the counter is giving another woman worker a drink and a pill (it seems as though this woman has a headache – she keeps holding her head). Then along comes a customer and the two women instantly end their interaction. I watch the man walk off with his spud and cottage cheese.

And I then walk away, go down the escalator, and out into the sunshine of a busy London street.

Comments on EO2

After what I felt to be the debacle of my lunch (see EO1, above), I approached this episode rested and in a much calmer state of mind. It seemed to me that, as social episodes go, an afternoon snack would be a relatively straightforward affair and that it ought not to present too many problems from a research standpoint. In fact, this event

---

[20] This is another example of frame-breaking within the narrative of the field notes.
[21] I find it almost impossible to shake off my positivist undergraduate training which convinces me that if I only had a video record of this event it would reveal something amazingly interesting. As I make this annotation, I draw on Condor (1997) for the courage to put some distance between myself and the academic fables on which I was raised.

caused me to think hard about some difficult issues surrounding participant and non-participant observation. The details of my analysis may be found in the annotation to the field notes; here, I shall concentrate on broader matters.

Part of the problem thrown up by this episode was the worrying question of how to make sense of who I was while I was doing the research. Sampson (1989) describes and criticises the Western concept of the person (and self) which underpins positivist North American psychology. In this, the person is seen as a bounded centre of awareness, emotion, judgement and action:

> In concept, the individual is adopted as the primary reality, the ontological base from which issues the remainder, including society and social relations ... the critical theorists argue, however, that the reality is quite different. The concept describes a fictitious character, the bourgeois individual, whose integrated wholeness, unique individuality and status as a subject with actual powers to shape events has become null and void. (Sampson, 1989, p. 3)

He makes the point that there is an essential penetration of society and the individual:

> Society constitutes and inhabits the very core of whatever passes for personhood: each is interpenetrated by its other. (p. 4).

The intrusion of societal norms into my state of being arises where I experience anxiety over my observation of the blonde woman buying her coffee. At that point, it seemed to me that the more I pursued my research goal of observation, the more likely it was that my behaviour might be misconstrued as a gauche attempt at flirtation or, more seriously, some form of harassment. Taken to extremes, I could imagine the research episode being prematurely terminated with security being called to escort me off the premises. I did not therefore feel able to observe the scene with the neutrality of a value-free social scientist. Social and normative constraints were all-pervasive and on this occasion they placed limits on where and how I directed my gaze.

I am also aware of perturbations to my sense of self as my subjective dramaturgical frames keep shifting, often willy-nilly. Sometimes, in a Goffmanesque fashion, it is as if I am in the audience, looking onto the stage. Yet my function is not so much to sit back and enjoy the play as to endeavour to scribble down the script in real time. The weirdness is that the stage expands and contracts: sometimes to engulf me and sometimes to exclude me. Thus I alternate between being part of the play and being outside its frame. Although this can happen under my control (I can distance myself to take in the broad picture) it also happens to me in a fashion that is untouched by my volition.

I think what may be happening is that I am shifting between behavioural and hermeneutical observation. In the penultimate paragraph of EO2, I state that I am starting to notice interactions which are taking place among the staff of the food court. The food court at first appears as something of a blooming buzzing confusion. Gradually I impose some order on the scene. Possibly by chunking disparate stimuli into small meaningful wholes, I build up a picture of the layout and begin to grasp the *un*changing nature of much of what I see. This then forms the backdrop against which change (i.e. events) may be noticed. Having bracketed off a lot of the physical scene as 'done' or 'sussed', I then begin to notice what the staff are doing. Where the object of my observation is hermeneutically arid, I delve into autobiographical memory to generate points of interest. For example, taking a bite of carrot cake may not be a sub-episode that over-brims with plot. In my field notes, I use this scene as a vehicle to give away some information about my interest in music as well as the religious culture that surrounded me when I was young. In this fashion I bestow surplus meaning on the carrot cake vignette. When I feel guilty about doing that (in my role as researcher) I scuttle into behaviourism: 'people keep strolling past, from left to right and from right to left'. It is the shift into a behaviourist mode of being that may have caused my unease about my personal identity and sense of self during the episode as a whole. Baumeister (1990) suggests that something similar to this may occur in the steps leading a person to suicide. He refers to this process as cognitive deconstruction and describes it as follows:

Deconstructed ('low-level') awareness means being aware of self and action in concrete, short-term ways, focusing on movements and sensations and thinking only of proximal immediate tasks and goals. The essence of cognitive deconstruction is the removal of higher meanings from awareness. (p. 92)

At the moments when I enter a phase of cognitive deconstruction, there will be less of a distinction between myself and my surroundings. At the risk of sounding like a 1960s hippy, I would become at one with the mall. Paradoxically, it is my behaviourist training which seems to lead me away from my tightly bounded sense of self (the identity which Sampson, 1989, might describe as my bourgeois individuality) into a more environmentally interpenetrative mode of being.

EO3: English Breakfast in a Central London Hotel

The next episode occurred in a more formal setting. I had to wait to be seated at a table, and although I went to a breakfast bar to serve myself, waiters and waitresses were in attendance throughout the episode.

Typed field notes:
I'm walking into the restaurant. It's more or less empty, breakfast has just started. The guy in the mustard jacket is talking to another employee (black jacket). Sounds like Mustard Jacket has rank over Black Jacket.[22]

'Table for one?'

'Yes, please.'

'Your room number?'[23]

I give him my number and then I'm ushered left down to a corner table. It's got a good view of the room, which pleases me.[24] He asks me to sign a billing slip.

'Tea or coffee? Can I bring you some toast?'

'Coffee would be nice, and some toast.'

'Would you like white or brown toast?'

I'm thinking of the opulence of the setting and this choice between white or brown toast. I contrast my situation with that implied by the newspaper headline I glanced at before coming down to breakfast: 'Nato accused of huge blunder as refugees are slaughtered'.

'White, please. And do I go up to get my breakfast?'[25]

Mustard Jacket points to where I get the stuff and walks back to his desk. Young woman in white tunic and black tights, carrying a stack of plates, cuts across my path as I reach to get a tray from a pile.

'You don't need a tray,' said with Eastern European accent (what do *I* know?).

I turn and go to take a plate. Tunic Jacket taps the pile of plates with her hand and points to another pile at the other end of the counter. I work out that this is a reference to plate temperature and that I need

---

[22] I seem to have used physical descriptions of clothes as a vehicle to enable me to index the major players in this episode.

[23] Once again, I adopt the guise of researcher as novelist in generating my field notes (as opposed to the discursive psychologist's tendency towards researcher as playwright in the production of transcript).

[24] My vantage point in previous episodes (EO1 and EO2) was poor.

[25] Warde and Martens (2000) refer to the hotel dining room as a site for social control and discipline. I clearly need guidance as to the liturgy and stage directions for this performance: the waiter is in control.

a hot plate if I am having the cooked English breakfast. I smile at her, without understanding the words she speaks, and move down to the start of the cooked-breakfast counter. Tunic Jacket is very nimble on her feet, since she miraculously appears in front of me on the serving side of the counter and starts turning up the heat on a mini cooker under a frying pan with about six eggs in it. She gets a spoon and starts ladling the hot fat over the eggs. Tunic Jacket stares intently at the eggs and keeps on ladling. I begin to feel anxious about my egg. It's going to be hard-fried! She obviously doesn't know how to fry an English breakfast egg. The male chef comes out and stands behind her. His hands tweak her waist and there is some wriggling of hips beneath the tunic. They seem intimately comfortable with one another. I don't make the attribution of male harassment at work, but I guess others might. Chef's Hat takes charge of the eggs, and serves mine to me on a plate. I then pile on hash browns, mushrooms, baked beans and tomatoes. I think I overcompensate for not having any of the bacon or sausages. I take my breakfast back to my table. I see that they have put out my toast and coffee on the table next to me but by then I am sitting down, so I move them across to where I am.

As I cut off a bit of hash brown and position a few baked beans on top of it, in a reasonably adroit fashion with my knife, I notice the sounds in the room. Lots of china sounds (plates, and so forth). Some non-English exchanges between the hotel staff. And then a North American voice cuts through. I lock on to it.

'Someone told her not to eat anything white,' said the elderly female in red sweater.

'And does it help?' said her brown-jumpered partner at the table to my right.

'She looks so healthy,' replied Red Jumper.

I am eating a mushroom; it has mass and density and yields its flavour with reluctance. Can I say that as a psychologist? Sounds more like food-critic-speak.

'Ooh! That tom*a*to was delicious,' said Red Jumper.

I have opened up my palmtop so that people will think I'm a businessman and not be bothered by my making notes in my pad with my pen.[26] I briefly think about this ridiculous subterfuge from the Goffmanesque standpoint of impression management.

I'm back into the baked beans – they've gone cold. The act of observation and recording affects the temperature of one's food (variation on Heisenberg). There is one rather hyper-efficient older female

---

[26] This is pathetic.

waitress who keeps taking people's plates. Mine went within seconds of my finishing up the last mushroom.

The room has a high old-fashioned ornate ceiling. All round the walls are long rectangular mirrors positioned A4 portrait-wise. This has the effect of making the room seem much larger and gives it an airy feel. I turn to my toast which has been sitting in the rack for some while. Of course, it is now stone cold. I try to apply some rather stiff butter to it and then take a spoonful of marmalade from the pot. At first I put the spoon back in the pot. Then I wonder if there could be an etiquette relating to this. I decide to imagine that there is and I reach out and move the spoon out of the pot and lay it down on the plate upon which the pot stands. I then think about the implications of what I have just done and wonder whether I might not be completely round the twist!

Back to the toast; it tastes cold and unpalatable. I pause to think about this breakfast. I feel sure that I could have cooked all the items better at home, and would have used superior ingredients. Setting aside the fact that some spoilage was my own fault due to letting the food get cold (and the coffee), I think about the charge of £14.95 for the full breakfast. I guess the bulk of that goes to pay Mustard Jacket, Black Jacket, Tunic Jacket and Co., the expenses of this prime Oxford Street site, the upkeep of this lovely, ornate room, and the remainder to the shareholders of the hotel company. This is taking me beyond observation. My mind is wandering. Is this permissible in data collection? Who is to make up such a rule? Perhaps data collection in psychology is a ritual. In that case I can't do anything about it single-handed; I don't have the power or authority to change a ritual.[27]

Comments on EO3

From a dramaturgical point of view, I felt that there were some interesting issues concerning the role I occupied as a guest and the roles of Tunic Jacket and Chef's Hat. When Tunic Jacket was over-cooking the egg, I did not feel able to interfere since chefs are supposed to know what they are doing and, in any case, no particular egg had been given to me at that point. Maybe if Tunic Jacket had been a young English girl I would have said something like 'That's enough, you can take it out now'. But I could barely understand Tunic Jacket's English and I couldn't see a way to successfully negotiate my way through a 'Don't Overcook My Egg' sub-episode. When Chef's Hat

---

[27] See Rothenbuhler (1998) for a discussion of this societal aspect of ritual.

caressed Tunic Jacket's waist, I felt that this was behaviour which, as a guest, I should not have witnessed. One interpretation would be that Chef's Hat and Tunic Jacket, in their canoodling, showed a disregard (or even a contempt) for me. Another interpretation would be to construe the behaviour as occurring in a region which could be described as ambiguously backstage. They were behind a serving counter and cooking does often take place out-of-sight in hotel kitchens. Thus the activity of cooking eggs, behind a counter, may have been interpreted as taking place behind a symbolic backstage curtain. I'm not suggesting that Chef's Hat or Tunic Jacket thought about it in this Goffmanesque fashion. In passing, I would like to point out that, had I been making an audio tape of this encounter, the transcript would have been remarkably sparse: small pickings for the discursive psychologist.

Condor (1997) warns that positivist academic fables picked up in undergraduate study may still reverberate in the minds of critical psychologists much later in their careers. It is sometimes said that, while a Protestant can become an atheist, the only alternative for a Catholic who loses belief is to become a lapsed Catholic. I sometimes wonder if the best status that a recalcitrant experimentalist can aspire to is that of a lapsed positivist. I was clearly bothered by the fact that I wasn't doing straight observation in this episode, and that is revealed especially in my comments at the end.

I think that any attempt to return to the fold of the mainstream, for someone who has read the critical literature and who by and large agrees with its thrust, is likely to be doomed to failure. As Tom Wolfe said, 'You can't go home again' (a line given to him by Ella Winter – see her autobiography: Winter, 1963). I would be most reluctant to return to the mainstream by embracing wholeheartedly the analysis of variance. I have no desire to talk to you about the intricacies of a three-way interaction thrown up by a sheaf of questionnaire data on hotel breakfasts. That having been said, working out what to put in its place is by no means an easy task.

EO4: Lunchtime Sandwich at a Riverside Pub in Sunderland

Whereas the previous three episodes took place in London, this one happened where I live in Sunderland. I drove down to a pub by the river for my lunch. I had eaten there before but not for about a year. I was a tad on the early side and the staff were still getting ready for the lunchtime trade.

Typed field notes:
Enter the pub. It's very quiet. First I go to the loo.[28] Then into the bar. The barmaid is writing up the lunch menu on the blackboard.

'I won't be long.'

'That's OK.' I use the time to get out my notebook. The chef is fiddling about behind the servery.[29]

'What can I get you?'

'I think I want a sandwich of some sort.'

'Right, well, the sandwiches are up on the board there.' She gestures to a board on the wall behind the servery, not the board upon which she has just been writing. The only possibility for a vegetarian is cheese.

'I'll have a cheese sandwich.'

'Do you want white bread, brown bread, or a crusty roll?'

'I'll have brown bread, please.' This said quickly but with some internal vacillation.

'Do you want anything to drink?'

'Have you got an alcohol-free beer?'

'Uh, huh.'

'I'll have one then.'

I have been typing for about ten minutes on my palmtop and I'm still writing up the start of this episode.[30]

The barmaid gives me my drink. The glass is too small and so I have to keep sipping it down in order to get rid of the bottle.

'That'll be £2.60.' I give her a five-pound note.

'Excellent,' she says. 'I'll bring your sandwich over to you.' She leaves me and goes over to sit with a young man at a spare table. She is writing some stuff on some forms. It sounds as though she is interviewing him for a job. I go over to her:

'Excuse me, I think I'll sit outside.'

'OK. I'll bring it out to you.'

---

[28] For the curious, I recommend Middlemist *et al.* (1976) for an account of a dodgy experiment conducted in a gents' toilet, and Koocher (1977) for a serious discussion of the ethics of using observational techniques in such places. I regard my visit to the loo as a private affair and I shall say nothing further about it in this context.

[29] Episodes have a start time. I had arrived at the pub thinking that my lunch was starting. The behaviour of the staff indicated that, as far as they were concerned, lunch in the pub had not yet started. This provides a simple illustration of the social nature of the episode and the fact that its timing has to be co-ordinated in the public domain. There is a moral dimension to the timing of this episode: if my definition of the start time is right, then the staff owe me an apology; if theirs is taken to be correct, they do not. Of course, the bar staff were not to know that they were holding up the start of my research episode, too.

[30] This is another example of the time lag between reporting and the occurrence of the activity. In this case, the reporting is taking up time within the primary episode.

I choose a small garden-style white plastic table out on the quay-side. There is a couple at a table nearby. And then two men (probably in their 30s) sit down at another table. The barmaid brings me my cheese sandwich, on a plate with knife and fork. There is a nice helping of salad on the side. The sandwich is made with a really generous cut of big crusty brown bread. Lots of cheese and mayonnaise in the middle. I sit and watch the river and the little fishing boats. There's a cold east wind coming up the river and now that the sun has gone in, it is not so pleasant. Another man has sat down at one of the tables and is reading the paper. A wasp hovers over my cheese sandwich. I can hear two seagulls squawking above me. They have now flown away.

I'm now typing this up at the university library. I had to make a decision as to whether to come straight here to type up or whether to call in at the flat-pack furniture store to order a small cabinet for my daughter's room. The recommendation to write up as soon as possible after the event is a good one, but research has to take its place among the stream of everyday life events. So I went to the shop. I got lost in it and couldn't find my way out of the kitchen section. I keep getting a mild after-taste of the cheese sandwich. To be more accurate, I think it is the burnt crust of the brown bread that I'm picking up. It is not an unpleasant sensation (no regurgitation, or anything like that). So, maybe it is legitimate to include this within the lunch episode. Getting lost in this store reminds me of rats running mazes for food rewards; I read about this when I was an undergraduate. I've already had my food, though. Eventually I find what I'm looking for, order it, arrange delivery, and pay for it. I'll think myself back to the riverside pub now.[31]

A mobile phone goes off (the male person of the couple). I hate that. Three more lads have joined the guy reading the newspaper. My cheese sandwich tastes great. I like the coleslaw on the side and there is lots of cress in the salad, which is nice. Across the river, I can see a timber yard. I'm also watching the tiny cars going over the bridge. I'm finishing up my salad. I may regret this because I often like to eat things in parallel so that I have a bit of everything left right up to the last moment! This is so much nicer than having lunch in London. The sun's

---

[31] The description of lunch seems to have broadened out to include the secondary episode of buying the flat-pack furniture but this has only occurred because of the way it impacted on the reporting of the lunch episode. The reporting, originally contained within the primary lunch episode, has now moved to a separate episode with its own location at the university library.

come out again and I can feel it warming my back where previously the wind had chilled it. This sandwich needs a lot of chewing. The brown bread is very tasty. I'm finding it very hard to decide when to finish this episode. I could simply sit and stare at the river flowing by for a bit. Decide not to. Get in the car and pick up the train of thought about buying flat-pack furniture.

Comments on EO4

I find it extremely difficult to work out whether my lunch would have gone differently had I not declared it to myself as a research episode. I think I would still have gone to the same place. I would probably have eaten my cheese sandwich more quickly. Also, I might have been a bit more careless and messy; as it was, I tried to keep my hands clean so that I could type into my palmtop computer. I would certainly not have thought about the episode in the way that I did, although I might well have spent some time thinking about writing this book, but that is different. My guess is that things would have been more contemplative (watching the river go by, and so on).

EO5: Lunch at an In-Store Cafeteria in Sunderland City Centre

Earlier in the morning I had been reading Kearney (1994) on Husserl and I resolved to see if I could bring some of the phenomenological ideas to bear in my observations. Walking into the city centre from the library, I passed a small Italian café and I would have liked to have made that the venue for my observations, but unfortunately I had to go to the bank first and that was across town. I had to walk behind about four different sets of young couples who were smoking cigarettes and I briefly thought about the small levels of concentration needed to detect some odours. I didn't like this, given that I was about to have lunch. I had already noticed hunger pangs in my stomach while I was sitting in the library. Had I had a balloon in my stomach connected up to a measuring device, I expect contractions could have been recorded. I shall stop my preamble and come to my observational notes. As usual, I have written these up from the paper-and-pencil notes recorded at the time.[32]

Typed field notes:
I looked at the menu on the board near the entrance of the in-store restaurant. There is a vegetarian section and I decide that I will have

---

[32] These were typed about one hour after the primary lunch episode had finished.

the 'broccoli bake' for £4.10. I go to the queue and get a tray. The restaurant is not very busy. I see a plate of broccoli and tomato quiche with salad for £3.85 and decide to get this, on the grounds that if I am making notes, there will be no hot food to get cold.[33] I think of the several occasions previously where that has happened. However, I do buy a mug of coffee. The server passes me two containers of milk. I thank her and pay for the food. I move on to collect cutlery. It's wet and a bit grimy but I decide to go along with it. I also collect sachets of salt and pepper. I settle down at a side table, looking into the middle of the room. I take my plate and coffee off the tray. Then I unwrap the cling-film from the plate, get out my notebook and also open up Kearney (1994) at the Heidegger chapter.[34] I keep Kearney open by laying my tray across the top of the pages.

Without thinking I've taken a whopping bite of quiche. I did this totally with no regard for my research. I felt hungry and, for a moment, forgot what I was about.[35] Anyway, I've regained control. The quiche tastes nicer than I thought it would even though the pastry is rather limp. In general the quiche tastes excessively salty. The broccoli in the quiche is the last thing to remain after chewing. It feels quite stringy. I half wonder whether the broccoli might be spinach in disguise: that would account for the stringiness. Any appeal to taste as an arbiter of the truth in this matter seems doomed to failure. Visually, it is the case that there is something green in the quiche, of that I am certain. I can't see any tomato though. I'm getting nowhere on this; I'll assume it's broccoli. Take a swig of coffee. That's nice and hot and it tastes of coffee. It usefully takes away the taste of the green-stuff-that-might-be-broccoli.

There are quite a few families with kids in here. I know the Catholic school is off today since my daughter's friend is having an extra day tagged on to her half-term holiday. The lettuce and cucumber are very salty. Even so, I put the salt from the sachet over the whole plate. I think I've just seen the office manager from my school at the university sitting on the opposite side of the restaurant; I hope she doesn't see me.

The pepper has just hit the back of my tongue, followed by a little burp. The potato in the potato salad is very firm and the mayonnaise is

---

[33] This is something that I have learned to do over the course of the research project. I now explicitly acknowledge that the research interferes with lunch and I take the strategic decision to minimise its effects on this occasion.

[34] This ruse was designed to make it look as though I was taking notes from the book and not making notes about the people in the restaurant. I put it down to reading too many Sherlock Holmes stories when I was a boy.

[35] A rather similar example of absent-mindedness occurred at the start of episode EO1 (see above).

a bit sharp. I think the potato is nearly under-cooked and I can tell that mainly by the taste on my tongue. I try some pasta spirals in a spicy sauce – yum! Can't remember the spice. Bit of hotness in there somewhere. Now I try two forkfuls of coleslaw. We never had that at home and I can't say that I like it now very much.[36] There's a grandmother feeding a little baby with a bottle at the opposite table. It reminds me of when I used to do that, but it was quite some time ago, when my daughter was a baby. I've now mixed some potato with the quiche and put a forkful in my mouth. The quiche swamped out the taste of the potato.

There's quite a revolting colour of yellow on the wall opposite me. The restaurant is a barn-like shape within the store and is located next to Ladies Underwear and Cooking Utensils. I wonder about the juxtaposition of the various departments next to the restaurant. I suppose that brassiere and brazier are near homophones and both could be confused with the term brasserie by a visiting Martian.[37] I've just noticed a piece of fresh parsley as a garnish on the plate by the quiche. I break off a bit and put it in my mouth. As soon as I bite into it I get a powerful blast of parsley up my nose. Wow! I'm going for another bit about the same size straight away. In it goes. Still pretty good but not so strong.[38]

I now take some tomato and coleslaw. The tomato tastes insipid beside the coleslaw. The skin of the tomato hangs round the front of my teeth like a bit of plastic, after everything else has been swallowed. The office manager is leaving and it turns out that one of my ex-bosses has also been in the restaurant. They have both gone now and they didn't speak to me. All the same, I found it unnerving. Here I am trying to be at one with my quiche salad and Husserl, embracing a phenomenological meditation, only to be put off my stroke by a couple of university colleagues. Still, I feel more relaxed now that they have gone.

I ought to try this stuff on imagination that Husserl advocates. I've got a bit of quiche on my plate and it looks pale yellow. I've just thought of it as the darker yellow which is on the wall. Now I've put the quiche on top of a bright green piece of lettuce. The yellow certainly looks more vibrant. Now I'll try and imagine that it's blue. I can't perceive it as blue but I can just about *think* of it as blue. Now for a taste. I'll try to think of it as strawberry. No. Couldn't manage that one. I could get into the texture of a strawberry mousse from the quiche but then they do have reasonably similar textures. I'm going to have to stop recording now.

---

[36] In retrospect, I find it difficult to know what to make of this comment, given that I appeared to enjoy the coleslaw in episode EO4 (see above).

[37] Should I be thinking along such frivolous lines in my role as researcher/observer?

[38] This reminds me of the study reported in Woodworth and Schlosberg (1954) on the adaptation to rubber smells (see Chapter 3).

I have to eat up and get back to the university, and, in any case, my coffee's going cold.

Comments on EO5

Pollio *et al.* (1997) comment on the fact that what we experience is inextricably bound up with the culture in which we are embedded and the sociolinguistic community of which we are a part. Although culture may be regarded as an organising structure for our experience, it is not a causal force:

> For one person, going to a local shopping mall may be experienced as an adventure (such as hunting for unadvertised sales); for another, it may be experienced as a laborious chore. The reference of the experience (i.e., going to the mall) and its alternative meanings (adventure or chore) are but two of many culturally given possibilities. Understanding the meaning of some experience requires us to describe the intentional stance (or situated perspective) of the event from the point of view of the experiencing person. (p. 8)

Pollio *et al.*'s (1997) example of going to the mall applies equally to going to the in-store restaurant. It seems to me likely that I had a very different experience of having lunch there compared to the other customers, although I have no direct evidence as to what their subjective experience was like. For example, it is unlikely that anyone else in this Sunderland city store would have recently been reading about Husserl or would have resolved to carry out phenomenological experiments in the course of their lunch. Incidentally, I have to admit that I enjoyed conducting these somewhat trivial experiments in phenomenology; they were good fun (a more serious experimental comparison between perceptual and imaginary tastes in chemosensation is provided by Schifferstein, 1997).

I can only guess at the intentional stances of some of the other customers. The university couple that fell under my gaze seemed more intent on their own private conversation than on observing what the other people were doing (and thus differed from me in that respect). For the grandmother, the focus was on feeding the baby, and her own lunch seemed to hover somewhat in the background. In this regard, eating lunch may have taken a more peripheral position than in my own case, since I did pause from time to time to concentrate on the food. Of course, I am only assuming she was the child's grandmother and I made that assumption on the basis of a somewhat casual observation of her behaviour and an estimation of her age. In sum, I feel convinced that my experience of lunch was atypical, compared with that of the other customers. The question arises as to whether that should bother me as a social scientist. I don't think that it should, unduly. The problem would not be solved by my entering the restaurant with a clipboard, pencil and observation chart organised around a set of pre-ordained research categories. For the sake of argument, imagine that I used a specially adapted version of Bales's (1950) Interaction Profile Analysis (IPA). This would still leave my intentional stance as atypical, since it is highly unlikely that anyone else would share that stance in that particular lunchtime setting (very few, if any, would be familiar with IPA).

One of the reasons my experience in the restaurant was so idiosyncratic was that I brought with me my stock of academic knowledge (I can't help the fact that I have read what I have read). This was more salient to me than it otherwise might have been, given the fact that I had defined this particular lunch as a research episode. In writing up my notes I could not help making the association between taking the second bite of parsley and what Woodworth and Schlosberg (1954) said about adapting to the smell of rubber. I start with an event located squarely in mundane reality (biting parsley in the restaurant) only to be swept back into the textual world of food psychology by a process of involuntary associations. The power of the culture of academic psychology has me in its grip as I eat my lunch. Like a person with an obsessive disorder, I am at the mercy of these mental associations.

Conclusion

Pollio *et al.* (1997), reflecting on the stream of consciousness, note that the categories of time, body, world and social order are continuously changing:

> First-person experience does not yield to ordinary categories and concepts nearly as well as that of technical third person description, and it is no wonder that psychology more frequently chose the third – rather than the first – person view as appropriate to its disciplinary task. Unfortunately, psychology must also confront first-person experience, and when this attempt is made, we are forced to deal with phenomena that yield unambiguous organization and structure only when the flow of experience is stopped. (p. 27)

In reporting my experiences of eating out in the five venues, I have moved between first- and third-person descriptions of experience. The first-person descriptions have been volatile. In EO1 (vegetarian restaurant in central London) I was fed-up, flustered and annoyed and this provided anything but a neutral backdrop to the reporting. In EO2 (afternoon snack in the food court) the cardboard coffee cup triggered an association with 1950s Bakelite beakers and swirled me into autobiographical reminiscence. In EO3 (English breakfast) international events (bombing in Bosnia) intruded into the calm world of the stately, old-fashioned hotel dining room, through a chance perception of a newspaper headline. In EO4 (riverside pub lunch) it is the flow of my reporting, not the flow of the original episode, that is disrupted by other events in a busy day. Descriptions of the taste of my cheese sandwich become intermingled with accounts of getting lost in a flat-pack furniture store.

There were some occasions where I used third-person descriptions of the events that took place within the episodes but these tended to be where I was merely documenting what was happening as if I were a tape recorder. For example, in EO1 (vegetarian restaurant in central London): '*The baby was actually in distress . . .*' *said the older woman at the nearest table.* When I attempt to make an objective description of the physical environment, I fail to resist sliding back into the first-person and thereby open the door to subjective associations. The following example, again from EO1, illustrates this point:

> I'd better describe what I can see as I sit facing the restaurant wall. The answer is simple: a fairly strong colour (I think we called it yellow ochre when I was at school). The wall is about 12 inches maximum from my face and exhausts my field of view. I can see a few bedraggled flowers to the extreme left of field. (Typed field notes from EO1, see above)

In this extract, even the description of the colour of the wall comes with an autobiographical association. To classify flowers as 'bedraggled' is not to place them in an objective category, it involves a value judgement on my part.

Phenomenologists sometimes use the technique of bracketing: it involves the suspension of any preconceptions of what is real or not real about the experience in question. This is a very slippery technique:

> Bracketing refers to an attempt to identify and correct interpretations in which the phenomenological perspective has been coopted

by incompatible suppositions. An interpretation premised on Freud-ian dynamics provides one such example. Other examples include an interpreter's applying his or her own standards of what constitutes an important or unimportant experience, judging a participant's reflections as illogical because they do not conform to some pre-established norm, or arguing that the 'real' experience is not being described because the participant's reflections do not mesh with an imposed theoretical framework. (Pollio *et al.*, 1997, p. 48)

I can think of one example where I may have bracketed off the use of Freudian defence mechanisms as an aid to interpreting some of my behaviour in EO1 (vegetarian restaurant in central London). I was trying to work out why I got upset about my age, since this does not normally worry me. I wondered whether my feeling tired and confused (in what was a rather stressful busy London restaurant) could have triggered me to regress to a more childlike ego state. I was also, retro-spectively, puzzled by the fact that I asked the cashier if I could take my lunch downstairs. Although in one sense this could be regarded as a request for information, in another it could be seen as tantamount to asking teacher for permission. However, I decided to bracket off the use of Freudian defence mechanisms in my reporting of the episode. I am not entirely convinced that this was necessary, since I have read some Freud and Freudian concepts truly are a component of my world picture. However, I can see that the phenomenological technique of bracketing would be helpful were I to imply in my description that somebody else was showing regression.

Eating out locally, especially at good venues, may sometimes inspire people to try new dishes at home or to replicate items that they have ordered while at a restaurant (admittedly, that does not apply strongly to the venues I have discussed in this chapter). Two sources of infor-mation which help to expand the cook's horizons and then to translate a desired dish into a practical reality in the kitchen are cook books and magazine articles relating to food. It is to a consideration of these sources that I now turn.

7

Food Discourse
(Magazines and Cook Books)

Introduction

In this chapter I cover women's magazines, and cook books. In keeping with my idiographic tendencies, I shall avoid breadth of coverage in favour of a focused treatment of a small sample of material. The obvious problem with this strategy is that the choice of material tends to be somewhat arbitrary and the narrowness of the database limits the confidence with which the generalisation of findings may be made to the superordinate class (e.g. from one women's magazine to all women's magazines). All this means is that the more idiographic the approach, the less it can serve nomothetic functions. I think that it is important to note that this problem rears its head whenever any form of sampling from the wider pool takes place: even in nomothetic studies. For example, Warde (1997) provides a content analysis of food-related items appearing in 80 issues of women's magazines (5 weekly and 5 monthly titles across two time periods) and yet he still deems it necessary to urge caution when interpreting his findings on the grounds that the sample size was comparatively small.

The choosing of my material is embedded within the flow of my everyday life and I do not suddenly cease to be a person just because I am reading a magazine for research purposes. This situation is not dissimilar to the way the eating out episodes that I reported in Chapter 6 sometimes became entangled in other events occurring to me at the time (for example, reporting my riverside lunch became intertwined with buying flat-pack furniture). I shall, where appropriate, allow my analysis of food talk in this chapter to reflect this fact and my reading of the material will sometimes take on the feel of phenomenologically oriented participant observations. One consequence of this approach is to distance myself from both content analysis and discourse analysis.

When I come to consider cookery books, in the latter half of the chapter, I shall focus mainly on the ideas the authors set forth in their prefaces. The examination of prefaces has been found to be a useful strategy to adopt in the analysis of social psychology texts, in recent years, especially by deconstructionists (see Stainton Rogers *et al.*, 1995; Stringer, 1990).

In examining the prefaces of cook books, I shall explore the extent to which the goals of the authors relate to some of the broader social and personal food-related themes I have covered in this book. However, I start the chapter by considering three recently published women's magazines.

Women's Magazines

In this section I examine one issue each of *Elle*, *Cosmopolitan* and *Good Housekeeping*. Warde (1997) suggests that, in relation to food, women's magazines have multiple functions: they provide the reader with daydreams through visual imagery, they offer practical advice through recipes and so forth, and they give the reader the opportunity to expand their knowledge about food-related matters. I shall bear these points in mind as I approach my material.

Elle (September 2000)

I'm sitting on a seat at Newcastle airport, waiting to meet someone off a flight. Driving over from Sunderland I kept worrying about how I would ever be able to make a rational decision regarding what magazines to analyse for this chapter. When I arrived at the airport about ten minutes ago I decided to go into the newsagents and buy something on a whim, to get me started. Warde (1997) had used *Cosmopolitan* for one of his 1991 samples. I tried to find this in the racks of magazines but without success. I then caught sight of *Elle* magazine and remembered, with some excitement, that I had looked at several issues of the French edition of *Elle* in relation to my criticism of Barthes's claim about the magazine's endorsement of fancy recipes in the 1950s (see Chapter 2). I decided to buy it.

I have now returned from the airport and I am sitting at my desk with the September 2000 UK edition of *Elle* before me. It is wrapped in a see-through plastic bag. In black letters on pink I am informed that there is a 40-page front-row fashion guide included. Maybe not what I really wanted. The price is £2.70. Given that I was charged

£1.05 for a cup of coffee at the airport, maybe this is not too bad, although, on second thoughts, I recently bought my daughter supper for £2.50 at the local fish and chip shop. I mustn't pre-judge: *Elle* magazine may be every bit as good as a plate of cod and chips.

I decide to cut open the plastic bag. There are two enclosures: the *Elle* fashion supplement (mentioned above), together with a fashion mail-order catalogue. My feeling is that I can safely put these aside, although I plan to go through them later on just to make sure there are no food items. The main headline on the cover page reads 'Exclusive! Sarah Jessica Parker on dirty sex, kissing girls & true love'. Already I'm beginning to wonder about the wisdom of this research strategy but I guess there's no turning back now. I am unsure as to how to proceed, since the bulk of the magazine seems to be devoted to fashion photographs. I decide to find the contents page and check out any obvious food features. Later I can go back to the beginning and turn through, methodically, page by page. The most relevant features are as follows:

- 'I like my man in an apron: men were made to cook, says Maggie O'Farrell. Which is just as well, as she most certainly wasn't' (p. 165)
- 'Food for thought: how to eat healthily even when you're on the go – we peek at three girl's dietary diaries to see what they tuck into' (p. 360)
- 'And you can cook in it, too: no longer the room that design forgot, the kitchen is officially coolest. We meet four seriously stylish girls who have taken theirs to hot heights' (p. 370)
- 'Rock the boat: beautiful people and gorgeous bites on board a boat cruising past London's coolest sights – ELLE sure does know how to throw a barbecue' (p. 382)
- 'Food & drink: Smart cookie Allegra McEvedy's cool kebabs: hot voddies; the Bloomsbury Set goes organic; plus the perfect way to throw a party' (p. 387)

I'll deal with each one of these features, in turn.

*'I like my man in an apron' (*Elle*, September 2000, pp. 165–6)*
This is an article covering two pages with about three-quarters of the space being devoted to the text. It is illustrated with a couple of nicely created photos of gingerbread folk. The first photo is of a gingerbread man wearing a little apron, and in the second photo he is pictured holding hands with an apronless gingerbread woman. I got quite a

surprise when I read this article, since it was nothing like the articles I had read in the 1950s French edition of *Elle* that I referred to in Chapter 2. O'Farrell, the author, delivers a lively and amusing polemic in which she claims zero skill in culinary matters and asserts that men, on the other hand, are much better cooks and are much more at home in the kitchen. Although she likes eating out, she regards day to day food as fuel[1] and couldn't care less about food or cooking:

> I am convinced that, historically, society has laid the role of chief cook at the wrong door. How much happier we would all have been over the past few centuries if men had been the main food preparers in families. This so-called new trend of men starting to cook is just society righting itself, putting the people who really care in charge. (O'Farrell, 2000, p. 166)

She acknowledges that the traditional gender roles operated in her parents' generation but argues that the image for female cooks is currently problematic. In the UK, Delia Smith is too much hard work (see my recipe in Chapter 5), Nigella Lawson is too perfect to be a viable role model (see my discussion of stress in Chapter 5) and for many women the root of all evil stems from Mrs Beeton's extraordinarily demanding advice (see my discussion of breastfeeding in Chapter 1, for example). On the other hand, she thinks that the lads in contemporary UK culture can have a lot of fun with Jamie Oliver, and can create food that is sexy, if not pornographic, with Nigel Slater.

The style of O'Farrell's article is upbeat and 'in your face'. She comes out with shock-horror taboo attitudes (woman can't cook and won't cook). Of course, the article does not square with reality. As I mentioned in my preface, recent studies are failing to uncover the assumed shift in gender roles in the kitchen that should have been triggered by 1970s feminism. Still, I can't imagine a women's magazine carrying such an article back in the 1970s, let alone the 1950s.

'Food for thought: how to eat healthily even when you're on the go'
(Elle, September 2000, pp. 360–4)
This article is spread over four pages. The main argument is presented in roughly one page of text. There is then an analysis of three food diaries and these take up about two pages. There is one full-page colour photograph of a pile of healthy fruit and vegetables stacked

---

[1] This reminds me of Fox and Cameron's (1961) description of the body as a slow combustion stove using carbohydrate as its fuel (see Chapter 3).

precariously, one upon another (half a melon, lettuce, red pepper, broccoli, aubergine, carrot, apple), topped off with a burger. The thrust of the article has a contemporary ring to it. Busy city women have become Americanised in their eating habits and no longer eat well-balanced meals. They are tempted by fast-food solutions; they don't eat breakfast and, instead, opt for high-calorie snacks, taking lunch on the run. Some girls, especially models, are too tall and skinny; others (not the models) are unhealthily overweight. The positive advice given, towards the end of the article, is very straightforward and focuses on buying and cooking fresh food, instead of indulging in the unhealthy products and ingredients. A varied low-fat diet is advised if the problem is that the person is overweight. The article concludes with an analysis of the food diaries recorded by three women: a food stylist, a model and an athlete.

Although this article was written about women, for women, it could easily be applied to busy men, too. I found the article interesting in relation to matters I discussed in my previous book, *The Psychology of Action*. It seemed to me that problems in diet are being construed as intimately connected with difficulties surrounding time management, planning and the balance between work, home and leisure activities. If anything, stress is given a more prominent place in this article than body image.

Interestingly, all three women who completed the food diaries say that they never weigh themselves. Two of them acknowledge that they sometimes adjust their diets, depending on how their clothes seem to fit. If the clothes feel too tight, they respond with a range of simple strategies such as cutting out fatty foods, eating smaller portions, or going to the gym. This can be related to the cybernetic feedback model for ordinary dieting that I referred to in Chapter 4.

'And you can cook in it, too: no longer the room that design forgot, the kitchen is officially coolest' (Elle, September 2000, pp. 370–5)
This article targets singletons (single people) with high disposable incomes and no children. Because there is less pressure on such people to worry about the practicalities of feeding families and so forth, they can afford to make a design statement through the appearance of their kitchens. The article provides photographs and short descriptions of four women and their kitchens: two designers, a film director and a music teacher. The article starts by pointing out that people often potter about in the kitchen, cook, make phone calls and listen to music there. I do all of that, so I read on with great interest (even though I'm not female, not a singleton, and don't really have a high disposable

income). A collage of about 4–5 photographs is provided for each of the kitchens, alongside the text comprising a short personal statement from each of the four women. By flicking over these photos I get a quick first impression as to whether I like the designs or not. Two of them are a bit too 'girlie' for my taste but the others look great. I had planned to do something on kitchen ergonomics for this book but, one way or another, it seemed to get squeezed out. Thinking of the kitchen as a work of art, as well as a site for applied ergonomics, seems like a good idea. I can't help making comparisons with my own kitchen as I look at these photos. I think this is going to depress me. I know my DIY skills are not good enough to achieve results like these. Furthermore, a glance at some of the equipment suggests that I could not afford this sort of thing, anyway. Apart from that, I think I'd have a lot of trouble thinking up the design ideas. I've just been downstairs to make myself some lunch and, of course, I'm now looking at all the unused spaces, the poor utilisation of storage cabinets, the potential for hanging pots from rails, and so on. I've just remembered that I have a copy of Conran's (1996) kitchen book. Already, I've started leafing through it and I'm positively drooling over all the wonderful photographs. I'll be reaching for my tape-measure soon. I must regain control and get back to the magazine.

*'Rock the boat: beautiful people and gorgeous bites on board a boat cruising past London's coolest sights' (*Elle*, September 2000, pp. 382–5)* This article is spread over four pages. Approximately two pages contain collages of photographs, mixing shots of the barbecue food with shots of the young and beautiful partygoers. One page is a text description of the event and one page is devoted to recipes. Given that the text description is written for young women, I suppose it's not surprising that I have difficulty in getting to grips with it. The prose style doesn't make it easy for me. Here are a couple of examples of the sort of thing I mean:

- 'One model, with limbs long enough to make a giraffe look stocky, slinks past and helps herself to a skewer of tandoori chicken with mustard-seed raita' (p. 383)
- 'One bloke, almost too handsome to look at lopes past ... he has the sort of lips you could fall asleep on' (p. 383)

Time to press on, swiftly, I feel.

By way of contrast the page containing about half-a-dozen recipes presents clear culinary information in a down-to-earth fashion. The recipes have an adventurous ring to them. One is for baby corn tossed in chilli-coriander butter. Another is for sweet potato chips with jerk seasoning and sour cream and chive dip. I've not come across jerk seasoning before but this may be because I'm a vegetarian. Davidson (1999) says that jerky is a name for dried meat and that the practice of drying meat was widespread among American Indians and pioneering colonists.

In modern times jerky occupies a niche in the nostalgic realm of 'trail foods'. (p. 418)

Apart from clear recipe instructions, there is a bulleted list of suggestions and recommendations for successful barbecuing. The advice ranges from marinating meat for 24 hours prior to cooking, to keeping a water spray bottle to hand. All the information seemed eminently sensible and some of it I had seen in books devoted exclusively to the topic of barbecues.

'Food & drink: Smart cookie Allegra McEvedy's cool kebabs'
*(*Elle, *September 2000, p. 387)*
Elle's regular chef provides a recipe and instructions to cook Mediterranean vegetable kebabs in the oven (brochettes). She also tells the reader how to prepare a wild rice salad and pistou, which may be served with the brochettes. The article includes a couple of photographs of the food; reading it makes my mouth water. I'm seriously tempted to cook McEvedy's kebabs outside on the barbecue when we next have some friends round.

General comments
I was surprised by how interesting I found these articles (I realise that this may be construed as deeply patronising and for this I apologise). Some of the multiple functions served by women's magazines alluded to by Warde (see above) were present in this issue of *Elle*. Women's conventional attitudes to cooking were challenged in the article on men in the kitchen. Advice on healthy eating seemed sensible and easy to follow. The section on kitchen design was inspiring and there was plenty of information about where to find goods, stockists, and so forth. If readers could not afford the more expensive solutions, there were many examples where the women in the case studies confessed to buying second-hand items or finding bargains at markets. The dream image of the young and beautiful was pedalled powerfully in the article covering the party on the boat. Providing that was not taken too seriously, the instructional advice both on barbecue techniques and

recipes could easily be transferred to a more humble occasion at the reader's home in the yard or garden (assuming that they had access to such facilities). I now move on to consider *Cosmopolitan*.

Cosmopolitan (September 2000)

Many pages in this magazine are devoted to fashion photographs of beautiful models wearing beautiful clothes. This is similar to *Elle*, although there seems to be proportionately more text in this issue of *Cosmopolitan* than I detected in *Elle*. The first thing to strike me is the prominence given to matters of a sexual nature in *Cosmopolitan*. For example, 'My Day as a Dominatrix' purports to be an account of what happened when one of the *Cosmopolitan* reporters went undercover for the day as a dominatrix to 'whip men into shape with the leather girls'. Photographs show her (in fetishistic clothing) apparently enjoying herself as she goes about her business. 'Hollywood's Secret School of Oral Sex' is, as you've probably guessed, all about a class in oral sex. Not too much food information is conveyed in this article, although in response to one of the pupil's questions the reader is informed that semen ejaculate contains about six calories (p. 60): a really useful piece of information if ever there was one.[2] There is also an article about what sort of underwear a woman should wear if she wants to turn a man on sexually: three women reveal their thoughts on the matter and the views of their boyfriends are also reported. In 'Introducing Moreplay', the emphasis is on how to extend the period of sexual ecstasy as long as possible with 'afterplay' techniques. In one of these, 'getting kinky in the kitchen' (p. 122), the woman blindfolds the man and has him guess what foods she feeds him. In terms of the psychology of food I suppose this could, at a stretch, be related to taste discrimination experiments à la Woodworth and Schlosberg (1954). After reading about all that, I had to pop down to the kitchen and make myself a nice cup of cocoa. Apart from a very short article relating to a Feng Shui cook book, there was only one feature in the whole magazine devoted exclusively to food and recipes.

The feature was seasonal and dealt with what food and drinks to provide for gatherings on hot summer nights (perhaps on the patio, a roof terrace or in the garden). Although the article speaks of 'sophisticated summer dining' in the header, the three recipes are all for bite-sized canapés: chilli and lime prawns; salmon tartare; chicken and

---

[2] It seemed highly irresponsible to me that there was no explicit discussion in this article of safe-sex issues and the possibility of HIV transmission from unprotected fellatio.

rocket crostini. The cooking times varied between 3 and 10 minutes per dish and the preparation times between 10 and 15 minutes. The instructions were clear and direct. More advice was given on how to supplement the main recipes by putting out bowls filled with olives, dips, or nuts, for example. My impression was that the main recipes were designed to create an air of sophistication but without the use of sophisticated kitchen skills. The emphasis was on quick dishes that would involve minimum effort.

Both *Elle* and *Cosmopolitan* appear to target young female singletons with high disposable incomes. I therefore decided to turn to *Good Housekeeping* (another one of the titles covered by Warde, 1997) which seemed more suited to the family situation.

Good Housekeeping (September 2000)

Even though much more textual material is included in this magazine than in either *Elle* or *Cosmopolitan*, there is still plenty of space devoted to fashion, especially in the first half of the magazine. In one article the issue about fashion being for real people (as opposed to the ideal feminine form) was taken up directly. Many of the models appearing in this magazine seemed older than those in either *Elle* or *Cosmopolitan*. This would make sense if it were assumed that the targeted readership is also older.

Whereas in *Elle* the feature on kitchen design was set forward as a strong artistic statement for the readers and, as such, may have connected to their ideal images and dreams, *Good Housekeeping* contains an article on kitchen design that has a more practical orientation. For example, floor plans are included and some useful layouts are given to cover most kitchen shapes. The technical aspects of design are dealt with in a serious fashion with matters such as the kitchen triangle[3] being made explicit in each layout plan. The *Good Housekeeping* article concludes with 4–5 small photos of sample kitchens, grouped into price ranges: budget, mid-priced, upper end, and dream kitchens.

My personal response to reading the *Good Housekeeping* article on kitchens was that I felt more unhappy with myself and with my own kitchen than I did as a result of reading the *Elle* article. I think that I could persuade myself that I could not possibly achieve a kitchen equivalent to the ones dreamed up by the talented young women

---

[3] Conran (1996, p. 122) explains that the kitchen triangle is drawn between cooker, sink and refrigerator and the line between the three should not measure more than 6 metres (20 feet), with the component legs of the triangle ranging between 3.5 metres (12 feet) and 8 metres (26 feet).

designers or film directors in *Elle*. Because *Good Housekeeping* set out details for a family kitchen on a tight budget, I had less of an excuse to dismiss their ideas as unattainable dreams. I turn now to the food recipes. There were several articles dealing with food:

- 'A week's menu for the way we live now' (pp. 160–8)
- 'Everything you need to know about mushrooms' (pp. 172–8)
- 'Masterclass: blackberry and apple jam' (pp. 181–2)
- 'Leslie's cookery school: roast chicken' (p. 184)
- 'Dessert for September' (p. 187)
- 'What's in season' (p. 189)
- 'Food news' (pp. 189–90)
- 'Small kitchen gadgets' (p. 202)
- 'Fulfil a dream: improve your cooking skills' (p. 212)

Just glancing at the above makes me realise that there is too much material to deal with here, so I have not included items which appear to be more generally concerned with consumer issues (e.g. 'What's going on at the supermarket'). I have also excluded several advertisements that feature recipes as part of their copy. I shall also leave out the last four pieces on the above list: the article on improving cooking skills mainly provides information on holiday cooking courses; that on gadgets contains brief reviews of nine items (garlic press, grater, etc.); food news sets out ideas for making up children's school lunch boxes; and the article on what's in season singles out various foods such as plums which are fresh for the time of the year. With regard to the first five articles, I shall take each one in turn, as I did with the material from *Elle* magazine (see above).

'A week's menu for the way we live now' (Good Housekeeping, *September 2000, pp. 160–8)*
This article reflects closely the trends revealed by the sociological surveys in terms of shifting patterns of food preparation and styles of consumption in contemporary Britain. This is emphasised in the title, since it is not simply a menu for the week but a menu 'for the way we live now'. The article starts with a double spread of seven photographs showing the finished dishes for each of the days, Monday through Sunday. A column running down the left page at the start of the article provides the following message of reassurance and rationale for the choice of menu:

> There's no need to reach for a ready-meal when time is short – we've created seven easy-cook suppers that are a mix of old favourites and

new combinations. They're full of flavour and flexible enough to serve up at different times to suit your busy lifestyle. (p. 160)

This could be interpreted as the *Good Housekeeping* Institute fighting a rearguard action against the inevitable drift towards the widespread use of ready-meals in British households: once everyone is buying ready-meals there will no longer be a rationale for magazines dealing with cookery skills and advice. Alternatively, it can be seen as providing a solution to the contemporary lifestyle problems experienced by many busy family providers. The article summarises some of the major trends in the nation's eating habits on the opening double-page spread. I think it is fair to interpret the content of the article as providing a creative response to problems thrown up by these trends. For example, it acknowledges that sales of fast food are booming and that more people are eating alone (since 85 per cent of ready-meals are individual portions). It agrees that commensality is on the way out and makes the point that 43 per cent of all adults eat in front of the TV. Only a third of families still eat a meal together each day and, perhaps as a result, snacking has become a substitute for regular meals. Finally, people seem to be eating out much more often than they did in the 1980s (see *Good Housekeeping*, September 2000, p. 161). I have already touched on many of these issues, especially in my Preface and Chapters 1, 2 and 6.

The following dishes are suggested for the week's menu:

- Thai noodles with prawns (Monday)
- Chorizo sausage and chickpea stew (Tuesday)
- Chicken fajitas (Wednesday)
- Garlic cheese pizza (Thursday)
- Smoked bacon pappardelle (Friday)
- Seared salmon with lime dressing (Saturday)
- Glazed duck with rosemary and garlic (Sunday)

Warde (1997) has described the shift in British cooking from its traditional roots (and the phase of experimentation of the 1960s) to the 'routinization of the exotic' in the early 1990s (p. 61). I think that the *Good Housekeeping* week's menu confirms that the exotic has, indeed, been routinized: there is not one dish amongst the seven that I would regard as traditional British fare. This menu recommends one prepared dish per meal per day only and this, in itself, provides a contrast to Beeton's (1861/1982) menus for plain family dinners, which frequently comprised three courses. She provides two separate week's menus for each month. I have selected dishes from these

September menus (excluding surplus courses and simplifying the ingredients/accompaniments somewhat) in order to provide a yard-stick by way of comparison for an imaginary but equivalent week's menu drawn from the mid-nineteenth century:

- Cold beef and salad (Monday)
- Boiled fowles and parsley-and-butter, with French beans (Tuesday)
- Boiled round of beef, carrots, turnips, and suet dumplings (Wednesday)
- Roast hare, gravy, mashed potatoes (Thursday)
- Bubble and squeak, made from cold beef (Friday)
- Irish stew (Saturday)
- Roast beef, Yorkshire pudding, horseradish sauce, French beans and potatoes (Sunday)
  (Drawn from menus presented in Beeton, 1861/1982, p. 942)

I feel that this provides a stark illustration of the extent to which the family menu has changed over the years, in the UK.

Returning to the *Good Housekeeping* week's menu, information in preparation and cooking times is provided for all the dishes. Preparation ranges from 5 to 20 minutes and cooking times range from 5 minutes to 1 hour (for the glazed duck) although apart from Thursday's pizza, which is 30 minutes, the remaining cooking times are all 15 minutes or less. An interesting feature of each recipe was a boxed instruction for what to do if the cook has to feed a latecomer. For example, in the case of Tuesday's stew the cook should 'microwave one portion of the stew on High for $1\frac{1}{2}$ min in a 900W oven' (p. 163). This addresses the fact that work and leisure activities may prevent an individual family member joining the others at mealtimes. A small red square containing a short comment is positioned at the edge of the photographs for each day's dish. Sunday's comment (for the duck) says: 'One-pot roasting means you won't spend Sunday morning stuck in the kitchen' (p. 168). Once again the emphasis is on saving time to accommodate a busy lifestyle. All recipes state the calories, fat and carbohydrate values per serving. They start with a conventional list of ingredients and quantities and then provide clear instructions as a numbered series of steps.

'Everything you need to know about mushrooms' (Good Housekeeping, September 2000, pp. 172–8)
The article starts with a warning about picking wild mushrooms and recommends supervision by an expert. The article is timely, since

September is a good month for wild mushrooms in the UK. After a general introduction to varieties of wild and cultivated mushrooms, together with advice on sources, storage and preparation, there follows a selection of illustrated recipes:

- Wild mushroom and chicken pie
- Wild mushroom risotto
- Wild mushroom sauté
- Chestnut mushroom gratin
- Warm oyster mushroom and spinach salad
- Wild mushroom and monkfish parcels

The same format as is used for the week's menu recipes (see above) is applied to these dishes. Again there is an emphasis on speed of preparation. For example, the wild mushroom and chicken pie receives a time budget of 15 minutes' preparation, 15 minutes' chilling (for the pastry), and 30 minutes' cooking. This speedy execution is achieved partly by using bought puff pastry (and cooking it in the oven separately from the pie) and partly by buying cooked chicken which is added into the pan of mushrooms and warmed through towards the end of the cooking cycle.

'Masterclass: blackberry and apple jam' (Good Housekeeping, *September 2000, pp. 181–2)*
Once again, the choice of blackberries is seasonal for September in the UK. The first page of the article is devoted to a large photograph of two jam-jars full of blackberry and apple jam. The instructions are set out on the second page, with six numbered steps each illustrated with a photograph. There are also several 'tips' given in a column to the left of the main instructional photographs. For example, the cook is advised to put four saucers in the fridge to chill prior to starting so that they may be used in the test phase to see if the jam has reached setting point (jam cooled on a cold saucer should, when set, produce a wrinkly skin when a spoon is run through it). The instructions seemed clear and comprehensive.

'Leslie's cookery school: roast chicken' (Good Housekeeping, *September 2000, p. 184)*
In this article, National Magazine's executive chef, Leslie Murrain, explains how to cook roast chicken. The article follows the standard recipe layout for the magazine and includes three photographs, each with a short message in a red box:

- 'Succulent and tasty: a whole chicken roasted to perfection'
- 'Thyme adds extra flavour'
- 'A gingery marinade turns roast chicken into an oriental dish' (p. 184)

Having covered the basics of traditional roast chicken, a plan for conversion into an exotic dish is included with instructions for the sweet ginger marinade. Also included are some safety points (e.g. use separate boards for raw and cooked meat) and a guide to defrosting and reheating chicken. The main recipe is specified as 6 numbered steps.

'Dessert for September: Plum and cardamom fool' (Good Housekeeping, *September 2000, p. 187)*
This feature is contained in one right-hand page, the bulk of the space being devoted to one photograph of two glasses of fool against a pink (plum) background. Succinct instructions appear at the foot of the page. This fool uses Greek yoghurt and bought fresh custard instead of the more usual process of whipping double cream. Davidson (1999) explains that in the seventeenth century, Norfolk fool was made as a custard and, in fact, contained no fruit. He states that although eggs were used in some fruit fools in the eighteenth century, the practice has now disappeared (p. 313). A full-page advertisement for a low-fat custard lies on the page facing the feature on dessert. The use of bought custard, like the use of pre-cooked chicken in the recipe for wild mushroom and chicken pie (see above), saves the cook time and, once again, indicates that the editors of the magazine are sensitive to the demands of the reader's busy lifestyle.

General comments
Returning to Warde's (1997) description of the function of women's magazines (see above), I think that without doubt *Good Housekeeping* provides far more practical advice on cooking than the other magazines and also provides the reader with greater opportunity to expand their knowledge on food-related matters. The difference between the serious food articles/recipes in *Good Housekeeping* and those in cook books lies more in presentation and graphical layout than in content. It is to a consideration of cook books that I now turn.

Cook Books

I shall start with one of the classic English authors of the nineteenth century, Eliza Acton, and then move on to consider Escoffier, taking in

Mrs Beeton en route. I sample the twentieth century by taking the Roux brothers and Raymond Blanc as professional restaurateurs, together with Cracknell and Kaufmann as authors of serious texts for chefs in college training. Towards the end of this section I consider Nigel Slater, Jane Grigson and Nigella Lawson, all of whom provide cook books for the domestic cook. Clearly, my selection represents the tip of the iceberg.

Eliza Acton, in her book *Modern Cookery for Private Families* (Acton, 1845/1993), aims to combat waste of food and disease caused by ignorance or mismanagement on the part of the cook. This is to be achieved by imparting a better knowledge of first principles to the domestic cook. Her concern with the relation between health and food, and its scientific basis, gives her writing a contemporary relevance despite the passing of some 150 years:

> The influence of diet upon health is indeed a subject of far deeper importance than it would usually appear to be considered, if we may judge by the profound indifference with which it is commonly treated. It has occupied, it is true, the earnest attention of many eminent men of science, several of whom have recently investigated it with the most patient and laborious research the results of which they have made known to the world in their writings, accompanied, in some instances, by information of the highest value as to the most profitable and nutritious modes of preparing various kinds of viands. (p. 1)

Although Acton is writing for the middle-class reader, she claims not to be addressing the establishments of the wealthy. She advises that the food served to busy and exhausted people at the end of the day should be simple and light. She steers away from 'elegant superfluities or luxurious novelties' (p. 1) and concentrates instead on the basics of fruit, vegetables and bread. At one point, she does indeed provide something that might well stand for her mission statement:

> Merely to please the eye by such fanciful and elaborate decorations as distinguish many modern dinners, or to flatter the palate by the production of new and inticing dainties, ought not to be the *principal* aim, at least, of any work on cookery. 'Eat, – to live' should be the motto, by the spirit of which all writers upon it should be guided. (p. 2, emphasis in the original)

She also asks the question: 'Why should not all classes participate in the benefit to be derived from nourishment calculated to sustain healthfully the powers of life?' (p. 2). There is a close similarity between her stance and that of Barthes (see my discussion in Chapter 2). She also goes on to ponder why the English should be more ignorant of culinary skill and knowledge than their continental neighbours. It could be argued that the English had to wait until the 1960s before this call was really heeded.

It is often asserted that Mrs Beeton (who first published her *Book of Household Management* in 1861) plagiarised many recipes from Eliza Acton (see, for example, Elizabeth Ray's introduction to the 1993 edition of Acton's *Modern Cookery*). Jane Grigson (1977) does not dwell upon this aspect of Mrs Beeton's writing but rather draws attention to the way her book reflects the anxiety of the new middle class, 'balanced between wealth and insolvency, and always at pains to keep up appearances' (p. 3). In Chapter 2, I discussed Bourdieu's (1984) work on class and diet and I feel that, by and large, Mrs Beeton was addressing those possessing economic, as opposed to cultural, capital. One factor that spurred her to write her book was an anxiety that the available venues for eating out were tempting the middle-class menfolk away from their homes:

Men are now so well served out of doors, – at their clubs, well-ordered taverns, and dining-houses, that in order to compete with the attractions of these places, a mistress must be thoroughly acquainted with the theory and practice of cookery, as well as be perfectly conversant with all the other arts of making and keeping a comfortable home. (Beeton, 1861/1982, p. iii)

Setting aside the stark picture of patriarchy conjured by this quotation, there is a contemporary ring to the fear that eating out may destroy family commensality.

In some of the more luxurious hotels, eating out in the nineteenth century and early twentieth must have been quite an experience: this was the time Escoffier was working at the Savoy, the Ritz and the Carlton. It was with some surprise that I discovered that Escoffier (1921/1979) addresses the issue of fast food:

The art of cookery depends on the psychological state of society for the way it manifests itself; it follows closely the dictates of society without being able to separate itself from its impact. Where the steady, even pace of life is not troubled by any preoccupations, where the future seems assured and safe from the vagaries of fortune, the art of cookery always flourishes because it contributes to one of the most agreeable of the pleasures given to man to enjoy.

On the other hand, when life is hectic and where the countless cares of business and industry worry the spirit of man, good living can only play a minor role. More often the need to eat appears to those caught in the throes of business, as no longer a pleasurable occasion but an unnecessary chore. They consider the time spent in eating as wasted and what they demand above all else from those whose duty it is to cater for them is not to be kept waiting. (p. xi)

Here, the great French chef places the art of cookery in the context of prevailing social conditions and, also, the extent to which individuals may be experiencing stress in their daily lives. I discussed Maslow's (1968) theory of personality in Chapter 1. Escoffier's observation seems to marry well with Maslow's notion of self-actualisation, since when times are hard people will just want to fill their bellies; they will not be in a position to appreciate the higher pleasures of gourmet satisfaction. Apart from this, Escoffier's *Guide Culinaire*, while written primarily for professional chefs, is also designed to help the keen amateur cook. To aspire to cook at the standard set by Escoffier is to reach toward the higher levels of self-actualisation through the perfection of kitchen skills, the development of the imagination, and the refinement of sensory judgement.

Although Escoffier (1921/1979) predicted that cookery would become more scientific (see Chapter 3 for a discussion of kitchen chemistry) he was adamant that it would continue to be an art and, in that regard, closely regulated and regimented fast-food outlets (such as McDonald's) would not be what he had in mind:

Simplicity of presentation will be taken to its ultimate limits but at the same time nutritive and tasty values of dishes will be increased. We will make them lighter and more easily digestible for delicate stomachs. (p. xii)

This suggests an anticipation of nouvelle cuisine. The Roux brothers, two professionally trained French chefs, are often associated with this cuisine in the UK. They opened their first restaurant in England in 1967. Speaking of nouvelle cuisine, they too acknowledge that due to mechanisation and automation people use less energy at work and thus use fewer calories; the result being a dislike of heavy food and thickened sauces. However, they set themselves apart from nouvelle cuisine:

Neither of us, therefore, believe in a nouvelle cuisine. Rather, we believe in the 'cuisine of today', which, like all fashions, is constantly changing, but is firmly rooted in the past. (Roux and Roux, 1983, p. 18)

Cracknell and Kaufmann were the (English) translators of Escoffier's *Le Guide Culinaire* and they have recently produced the third edition of their text for chefs working in the catering industry (or students taking relevant courses at college). They acknowledge that the result of nouvelle cuisine has sometimes been to over-emphasise the garnishing and decoration of food and agree that the size of the portions has sometimes been too small (Cracknell and Kaufmann, 1999, p. 3). They recognise the growing importance and impact of ethnic cuisines in the UK, the greater concerns with nutrition, diet and health, as well as technological advances such as the widespread introduction of cooking by microwaves:

In these days of the global kitchen, customers expect to be offered a wide choice of dishes and many of them like to know that those they choose are felt to be beneficial to their health and well being. (p. ix)

Whereas the Roux brothers were professionally trained French chefs, Raymond Blanc (who also set up successful restaurants in England), although French, was self-taught. I feel that he is thus a more credible role model for the untutored home cook:

What I may lack from not having had a master to guide me, I have gained in enjoying the freedom to indulge my curiosity. (Blanc, 1988, p. 9)

This sense of exploration is likely to strike a chord with any home cook seeking self-actualisation in the kitchen. Having provided some good advice on how to give a successful dinner party (which is very similar to the advice offered by Tovey, 1990 – see Chapter 5), Blanc concludes his introduction as follows:

And so, to work. The whole process should be easy and fun, from planning to shopping and cooking. Your efforts will be well rewarded by the smiles of delight and admiration on the faces of your guests. Congratulations! (Blanc, 1988, p. 11)

So many chefs and cookery writers seem to be at pains to indicate how to achieve that sense of satisfaction and the reward that comes from both the taste of the food and the appreciation shown by the guests. Many do this not only by showing how to master the techniques required for the preparation of the various dishes but also by encouraging the cook to attain a peaceful state of mind and to avoid behaviours that will lead to stress.

I think that there is a danger that the stress-and-hassle card may be over-played. Of course, people who are in danger of becoming frazzled and stressed should take steps not to set themselves up for too demanding tasks in the kitchen. However, sometimes a really complicated recipe that presents the cook with lots of culinary problems to solve is just what is required. I remember in the late 1980s, before I became a vegetarian, cooking a couple of complicated recipes for friends, which were taken from the masters, as it were. One was for lamb and peppers (*noisettes d'agneau fondantes aux deux poivrons*, from Roux and Roux, 1983, pp. 193–4). The other was for salmon and cucumber salad (*tartare de saumon sauvage a la croque de concombres*, from Blanc, 1988, pp. 61–2). The whole point about doing recipes such as these was not to save time but to pass large chunks of the weekend in a challenging but enjoyable fashion. As an activity it took my mind off work and helped me to relax. Indeed, when I was planning the fish dish, I remember reading an article in the food section of a weekend newspaper about a small shop in a village in Scotland which stocked fresh, locally caught salmon. I then drove from my home on the Northeast coast of England, across the country to the Solway Firth on the West Coast of Scotland to the shop in order to buy the salmon. I can see how this might be dismissed as a very silly expedition. However, I had a lovely time and thoroughly enjoyed my adventure. Although there are some very good books on fast home cooking now available, this is not necessarily what people want.

One of the better books in the UK fast-food genre is Slater's (1992) *Real Fast Food*:

Most of the recipes are based on fresh food with as little as possible done to it. There are no complicated procedures, no dithering around with affected arrangements on over-sized plates, and no effete garnishes. It is a set of straightforward recipes for fast food with bold flavours, cooked in minutes and served without pretension. (p. 7)

Slater's food is very tasty and he provides a no-nonsense solution for busy (or lazy) people who like food but can't devote much time to it. However, as an antidote to the current trend, I offer the opening paragraph from Grigson's (1971) *Good Things*:

This is not a manual of cookery, but a book about enjoying food. Few of the recipes in it will contribute much to the repertoire of those who like to produce dinner for 6 in 30 minutes flat. I think food, its quality, its origins, its preparation, is something to be studied and thought about in the same way as any other aspect of human existence. (p. 9)

She goes on to say that anyone who likes to eat can soon learn to cook well. I think that this spirit has been carried on more recently by Lawson (1998) in her book *How to Eat*:

Cooking is not about just joining the dots, following one recipe slavishly and then moving on to the next. It's about developing an understanding of food, a sense of assurance in the kitchen, about the simple desire to make yourself something to eat. And in cooking, as in writing, you must please yourself to please others. (p. viii)

Lawson does include a chapter on fast food in her book but it is sandwiched between a chapter on cooking for one or two persons and a chapter dealing with the weekend lunch; it therefore seems to be placed in perspective and does not assume a prime position in her scheme of things.

Concluding Comments

I am conscious of an asymmetry between the section on women's magazines and the section on cookery books. I had no problem in making an arbitrary selection of magazines to examine in this chapter since I don't normally read them and had very little idea as to what to expect. With the cookery books, the situation was different. I was conscious of ignoring many writers whom I admire, and on several occasions where I chose one particular author, in order to make a specific point, I could easily have chosen others for the same purpose. Another difference in my treatment is that with regard to the magazines, I did feel that I was approaching them from an analytic standpoint, even though I did not explicitly use discourse analysis. However, I approached the cook books much in the same way that I would use texts in psychology or any of the other academic disciplines.

One theme that featured strongly in the magazine articles was the lack of time available for food preparation, given the pace of contemporary living. Much advice was therefore given on the preparation of fast food at home. It was also not uncommon for the articles to be concerned with diets that would contribute to health and fitness. With the relentless presentations of bodies beautiful, page after page throughout the magazines, it is hardly surprising that some degree of sensitivity to calorific and fat content should be a feature of the chosen recipes.

The cook book authors also provided instructions for the production of speedy meals, along with sound advice for the reduction of stress in the kitchen. An interesting research topic for the future might be to examine the extent to which readers follow such advice as they go about their everyday cooking.

8

Conclusion

Booth (2000), in an editorial reflecting upon the first twenty years of the academic journal *Appetite*, makes a strong plea for an interdisciplinary approach to food research. Speaking of the varied input from the disciplines and the professions he says:

> These diverse and interdisciplinary research interests signalled the inclusive ambition of the Journal [i.e. *Appetite*]. Food and drink choices and intakes depend totally on the brain and the body, entirely on society and culture, and completely on the mind and behaviour. (p. 1)

Appraising progress in this direction, Booth notes that multidisciplinary research groups tend to revert back to a narrow discipline base, be it physiological, sociological or historical. I have drawn upon work from several disciplines beyond the boundaries of psychology and upon more than one paradigm within the subject, in the course of this book. This may be a relatively uncommon approach for a single author to take: multidisciplinarity tends to be achieved through multiple authorship or through the creative juxtaposition of disparate contributions in journals (such as *Appetite*) or in edited books (such as Murcott's, 1998, *The Nation's Diet*). Regarding the latter, editors have the opportunity to provide some degree of synthesis in order to create interdisciplinarity from the multidisciplinary contributions, especially in their introductory or concluding remarks.

In Chapter 4, encouraged by Malson's (1998) example, I sought interdisciplinarity or its paradigmatic equivalent by intertwining the biomedical and feminist discourses on eating disorders with the (therapeutic) discourse of control. Malson (1998) speaks of discourses, rather than disciplines or paradigms. Langenhove and Harré (1999a, 1999b) regard paradigms as conversations and are thus able to bring to bear a rhetorical perspective on scientific texts, their authors, their audience or readership and the community of scholars signing up to any particular disciplinary perspective. I regard terms such as discourse, paradigm, or conversation as interchangeable in this context and feel that all have much in common with the earlier notion of a Wittgensteinian language game.

Because multidisciplinary and paradigmatic discourses feature so strongly in this book, I shall begin by summarising their contribution to the text, chapter by chapter, with the help of the discourse matrix I present in Table 8.1. I then move beyond the concerns of particular discourses to consider the textual world of food psychology that is created by this and other texts within academic psychology. I do this by developing a framework based upon Ricoeur's hermeneutics. I conclude with a brief personal comment on future directions for research into the psychology of food. I turn now to a summary of the way the major discourses have featured in the preceeding chapters.

Discourse Matrix

In Table 8.1, I provide a matrix to indicate the extent to which the main discourses I have used (rows) contribute to the academic conversation in each of the chapters (columns). I represent the strength of the contribution using ticks (the more ticks, the greater the importance).

The discourse matrix in Table 8.1 provides only a rough-and-ready map of the conversational flows in this book. I have made some arbitrary decisions in compiling the list of discourses. For example, it could be argued that the *feminist* discourse be subsumed within the category of the *post-positivist*. There is some overlap between the *psychoanalytic* and the *feminist* categories, as there is between the *mainstream* in psychology and the *biomedical*. Technically speaking, I should not have segregated the *sociological* (or the *post-positivist* psychological) from its parent category the *social scientific*. The *idiographic*, in this context, is closely linked to the *autobiographical*, since many of the experiences I report in the case studies are my own. It is not my purpose to strain for a clean-cut classification system for these discourses. In the hurly-burly of the conversations running through my manuscript a fuzzy matrix will do fine to highlight the interdisciplinary and multidisciplinary features of my text and to indicate where differing paradigmatic perspectives have been given weight, on a chapter-by-chapter basis.

In my preface, I start with the account of eating a tomato sandwich. Thus I give pride of place to the *idiographic* report of experience. I then respond to the *sociological* discourse of household surveys relating to gendered kitchen activities by using an *autobiographical* discourse

Table 8.1 The location of discourses within the text

Discourses/conversations	Preface	1 Introduction	2 Non-biolog.	3 Hunger etc.	4 Disorders	5 Dinner party	6 Eating out	7 Food disc.
				Chapters				
Mainstream psychology	✓	✓✓		✓✓	✓	✓		
Post-positivist psychology	✓	✓✓		✓			✓✓	✓
Social scientific (econ., anthrop., etc.)		✓	✓✓			✓		
Sociological	✓	✓			✓	✓	✓	✓
Psychoanalytic (esp. Freud and Klein)			✓✓✓		✓✓			
Feminist (incl. Lacan)		✓			✓✓✓			✓
Biomedical (and organic chemistry)		✓		✓✓✓	✓✓✓			
Control (industrial/cybernetic)					✓✓✓	✓✓		
Foodie (writers/chefs)	✓✓✓	✓		✓		✓	✓	✓✓✓
Autobiographical	✓✓	✓	✓	✓	✓	✓✓	✓✓✓	✓✓
Idiographic (and experiential)				✓✓	✓✓	✓✓✓		✓

Key: ✓✓✓ = major contribution to chapter; ✓✓ = significant contribution; ✓ = minor contribution.

to explain my interest in food, cooking and shopping. From time to time the *sociological* discourse resurfaces as the *autobiographical* gathers momentum (for example, I pause to mention that I read Oakley, 1972). I then speak of my academic background. Although this is technically *autobiographical*, I feel that the discourse is shot through with components drawn from *mainstream* and *post-positivist* psychology. In the course of this part of my preface I state the rationale for writing the book. In terms of the current discussion, this may be expressed as a response to my inability to translate between the *mainstream* psychological discourse on food, on the one hand, and my *autobiographical* discourse, on the other. I also signal that I shall look to the *post-positivist* discourse to close the gap, insofar as I generate new material in the course of writing the book. I then single out the *idiographic* discourse, citing Allport (1962) and the more recent advocates, Smith, J.A. *et al.* (1995c), as being the voice within the *post-positivist* cacophony[1] that will best serve my purpose.

The first substantial topic I tackle in Chapter 1 is breastfeeding. I start on firm ground within the *mainstream* by talking about sucking reflexes. Both Eibl-Eibesfelt's (1970) and Booth's (1994) treatment of babies sucking at their mother's breast seem a bit dull to me and so I draw upon the *foodie* discourse of Mrs Beeton (1861/1982), with her comments on porter and flatulence, to liven things up.

The transmission of the HIV virus through the mother's milk introduces a serious note to the chapter. It is not possible to proceed very far with this topic solely on the basis of the *mainstream* psychological discourse. *Sociological* evidence concerning the effectiveness of dietary supplements to raise milk production in mothers in Third World countries is discussed in relation to concerns about the safety of feeding voiced within the *biomedical* discourse. At this point I pursue a subsidiary argument within Palmer's *feminist* discourse on the topic concerning fathers and bottle-feeding. This heralds a return of the *autobiographical*, as I argue that fathers do not necessarily participate in bottle-feeding for their own emotional satisfaction.

There is little within the *mainstream* discourse to contribute to the topic of children and table manners, although it is not hard to imagine how an account based upon learning theory and the use of positive or negative reinforcement might be fashioned. The discursive study of the Australian families seems to be voiced within the *post-positivist* discourse, supplemented by the *feminist* and the *sociological*. With

---

[1] Post-positivist psychology, as a discourse, contains many dialects (see Smith *et al.*, 1995a and 1995b).

regard to food neophobia, Lowe *et al.* (1998) provide an interesting contribution from the *mainstream* based upon an extension of social learning theory.

The work on food attitudes and choices tends to be of mixed disciplinary and paradigmatic origin. Some of the surveys (e.g. reported in Lyman, 1989) may have used the questionnaire scales characteristic of *mainstream* psychology. However, surveys covering large population categories may be best placed within the *sociological* discourse (remember the US Armed Forces personnel and pickled pig's trotters). Some qualitative methods are clearly *post-positivist* (e.g. Wiggins *et al.*'s, 2001, analysis of mealtime conversations) while others seem closer to the *mainstream* (e.g. Stratton and Bromley's, 1999, coding of belief statements about family food choices).

The treatment of famine draws heavily upon the *social scientific* (especially Sen's, 1981, economic analysis) and *sociological* discourses. I bring in the *mainstream* discourse by pointing to concepts such as locus of control (Rotter, 1966), belief in a just world (Lerner, 1980), and inter-group co-operation (Sherif, 1966). The work on poverty and malnutrition is also marked by the absence of any significant contribution from the psychological discourses, being mainly served by the *sociological* and *biomedical*. I related this to the *mainstream* by reference to Maslow's (1968) hierarchy of needs (although not everyone would regard Maslow as a mainstream psychologist). In order to discuss the relation between malnutrition and the unequal distribution of resources in society, I moved into the *post-positivist* discourse of critical psychology.

Although, in Chapter 1, I intended to showcase the contribution of *mainstream* psychology, it did not work out that way in practice, since many different discourses were voiced. The mix of voices in the conversational text of Chapters 2 and 3 is more homogeneous in character.

My exploration of non-biological perspectives on food (Chapter 2) was a trifle disappointing, given that I had hoped to place a greater distance between my own *post-positivist* position and that of the *mainstream* and the *biomedical* discourses. Firstly, I could not take Klein's *psychoanalytic* talk seriously. Secondly, I had problems with Lévi-Strauss, Douglas and Barthes, all of whom I regard, for present purposes, as voices within the *social scientific* discourse. The simplicity of Lévi-Strauss's cultural triangle breaks down as it becomes a tetrahedron: the primary triad (cooked; raw; rotten) does not sit happily with the secondary (air; water; oil). The neatness of Douglas's formula for a meal $(A + 2B)$ unravels upon close examination. Barthes's semiotic analysis of cookery articles (specifically those appearing in

Elle magazine) is poorly done. Towards the end of Chapter 2, I draw heavily on Warde's (1997) *sociological* discourse and I find this to be very helpful.

Moving on to Chapter 3, I trace some of the early work on hunger which is fashioned from a discourse located at the intersection of the *mainstream* psychological and the *biomedical*. The *mainstream* survives into the treatment of taste and smell, especially in relation to psycho-physical studies, but as the topic shifts to digestion and cooking, it gives way to the *biomedical* (incorporating the discourse of organic chemistry). With regard to kitchen chemistry, there is an input from the *foodie* discourse (this contribution could have been enlarged to a considerable extent).

In Chapter 3, the voices entering into the sections dealing with hunger, flavour, digestion and kitchen chemistry are, for the most part, harmonious with one another. The intrusion of the *idiographic* at the end of the chapter does unsettle things and brings with it hints of the *post-positivist* and the *autobiographical*.

In Chapter 4 (eating disorders) there is a minor presence of the *autobiographical* discourse but this features in the negative sense that I am unable to relate the more serious matters, dealt with in the chapter, to my life experience. The *feminist* (incorporating the *psychoanalytic*) and the *biomedical* discourses, together with the (therapeutic) discourse of *control* provide the focus for this chapter. Some of the background features of anorexia nervosa come from the *mainstream* and the *sociological* discourses.

I introduce Chapter 5 with the *sociological* discourse, drawing on Warde and Martens's (2000) work on dinner parties. I then switch to the case study which uses the *idiographic*, supplemented by the discourse of *control* (especially the industrial and cybernetic aspects). The analysis of the dinner party episode also owes a debt to the early *post-positivist* discourse of 1970s's ethogenic analysis (see Harré and Secord, 1972). When I come to consider planning and scheduling, towards the end of the chapter, I am able draw upon the *foodie* discourse, too.

Chapter 6, on eating out, starts with the *sociological* and then moves to the *idiographic*. Issues relating to the tension between the *post-positivist* and the *mainstream* are constantly simmering throughout the chapter. For example, I responded to Condor's (1997) demand for greater reflexivity by incorporating an *autobiographical* stream into my *idiographic* reports. From a rhetorical standpoint, this gives the style of my observational material a very different look and feel from that which might be expected in *mainstream* laboratory reports. The *autobiographical* penetrates my meta-commentary when I acknowledge that my undergraduate training interferes with my ability to throw myself completely into a *post-positivist* mode of observation. *Autobiographical* considerations also intrude in a more mundane fashion when, for example, I postpone writing up my field notes while I go to buy flat-pack furniture.

A major component of Chapter 7 is the *foodie* discourse, whether taken from cook books or magazine articles. This is supported in part by the *sociological* (e.g. Warde's, 1997, analysis) and partly by the *autobiographical* (e.g. the state of my kitchen). I intend to consider how food texts, in general, may be construed from the standpoint of hermeneutics. Before I do that, I shall provide a brief introduction to the topic.

Preliminary Introduction to Hermeneutics

Kearney (1994) points out that Ricoeur takes hermeneutics beyond the boundaries of the original use of the term covered by the specialist science of biblical exegesis; he also notes that progress in this direction had already been made by Dilthey, prior to Ricoeur:

> Dilthey raised the problem of how the historical and human sciences (Geisteswissenschaften) could acquire a method of interpretation different to the positivism of the natural sciences (Naturwissenschaften). How, he asked, could a specifically human science be founded in the face of the methodological hegemony of empirical objectivity. (Kearney, 1994, p. 99)

Given that I have had recourse to the discourse of both the natural and the human sciences (see above), there would appear to be some potential in pursuing this turn in the development of hermeneutics; I need a superordinate discourse which in some way encompasses these two disparate language games. Dilthey argued that a reader gains an understanding of the text through empathetic identification with the experience of the author, thus reaching out across the spatio-temporal gap that separates the two. As a reader, 'I transcend my present historical situation in order to relive the privileged life-experience of the author's original subjectivity' (Kearney, 1994, p. 99). Ricoeur felt that by making subjectivity the key to understanding, Dilthey had produced a romantic hermeneutics and this is something he wished to correct:

But I believe that the hermeneutical circle is not correctly under-stood when it is presented, first, as a circle between two subjectiv-ities, that of the reader and that of the author; and second, as the projection of the subjectivity of the reader into the reading itself. (Ricoeur, 1981, p. 178)

Kearney (1994) argues that the problem with romantic hermeneutics is that it treats interpretation solely from an epistemological stand-point. Ricoeur attempts to solve this problem by linking interpretation to the reader's mode of being, thus introducing an ontological dimen-sion into the process:

The appropriation of the reference is no longer modelled on the fusion of consciousnesses, on empathy or sympathy. The emergence of the sense and the reference of a text in language is the coming to language of a world and not the recognition of another person ... If appropriation is the counterpart of disclosure, then the role of subjectivity must not be described in terms of projection. I should prefer to say that the reader understands himself in front of the text, in front of the world of the work ... Thus the hermeneutical circle is not repudiated but displaced from a subjectivistic level to an onto-logical plane. The circle is between my mode of being – beyond the knowledge which I may have of it – and the mode opened up and disclosed by the text as the world of the work. (Ricoeur, 1981, p.178)

Ricoeur allows that there will be many detours in interpretation; he opts for the long route where progress may be hampered or deflected by language, myth, the unconscious, ideology and so forth. Kearney (1994) stresses that taking the long route means that Ricoeur has to embrace the challenge of rival interpretations:

The conflict of interpretations is for Ricoeur a logical consequence of the symbolic nature of language. Because signs can have more than one meaning, they often say more than they appear to say at first sight. The ostensible meaning of a word frequently conceals another meaning which surpasses it. It is this typically equivocal or multivocal character of symbolic language which calls for the deciphering activity of the interpreter. (Kearney, 1994, p.101)

Ricoeur's ideas move at lightning speed from the word and the creative tension of the metaphor, through the sentence as the largest unit of analysis to be found in conventional linguistics, to texts, works and discourses. He develops his hermeneutics in such a flexible way as to be able to talk about poetry, narrative, fiction, history and science, drawing on a common set of fundamental principles. He tends to operate primarily at the level of the text and sees the text as having much in common with the Wittgensteinian notion of a language game.

Ricoeur's hermeneutics is designed to deal with multiple and competing interpretations; it is honed to operate at the interstices of disparate discourses. I find myself ineluctably drawn to it. The approach to language and semiotics, together with the acceptance of multiple interpretations of the text, aligns the approach closely to discursive psychology. However, the insistence that discourse is always *about* something brings to the fore questions concerning possible modes of existence that are difficult to voice within discursive psychology. In a way, this is comforting for those who feel uneasy with the extreme relativist stance taken by some of the discursive psychologists. There is something in Ricoeur for the deconstructionists, too:

> Fully cognisant of the propensities of consciousness to contrive premature solutions, Ricoeur conjoins 1) the project of phenomenological hermeneutics and 2) the critique of 'false consciousness' advanced by the three 'masters of suspicion' – Marx, Freud and Neitzsche. (Kearney, 1994, p. 104)

This ensures some common ground between Ricoeur and the postmodernist stance in psychology (e.g. Stainton Rogers *et al.*, 1995), given that he dismisses philosophical claims to absolute knowledge as false myths. Furthermore, I think that the hermeneutics of suspicion has something in common with the sociology of scientific knowledge and this establishes yet another strong link to discursive psychology (e.g. Potter, 1996). I shall expand my treatment of Ricoeur's ideas in the following section but, for the moment, I feel that I have taken matters far enough for the purposes of this brief introduction.

Food Texts and Hermeneutics

In Figure 8.1, I present a diagrammatic representation of 'The textual world of food psychology'. I shall start by providing a brief orientation to this diagram, before going on to consider its several parts in some detail. The 'Reader' is represented at top-centre in Figure 8.1, with the 'Food text' (this book, for example) immediately below. Beneath the 'Food text' lies 'The textual world of food psychology'

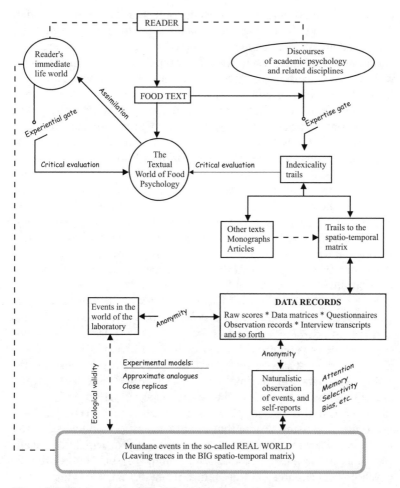

Figure 8.1 The textual world of food psychology

(in the centre circle on the diagram); I shall have more to say about this abstract conception, in due course. The 'Reader' may bring two aspects of his or her experience and knowledge to bear upon the 'Food text': the 'Reader's immediate life world' (top, left) and familiarity with the 'Discourses of academic psychology and related disciplines' (top, right). Lack of experience or lack of academic knowledge (represented by the two gates, in the diagram) will inhibit the critical evaluation of 'The textual world of food psychology' (centre, circle). Given the background academic knowledge, a reader will be able to place any particular food text within the broader context of 'The textual world of food psychology' by noting and sometimes pursuing the 'Indexicality trails' that are offered through citations of the academic literature. This is normally facilitated using the bibliographic information contained within the text, perhaps through the use of footnotes or otherwise in the form of a list of references placed at the end of the book or paper. Although some 'Indexicality trails' will simply lead to 'Other texts, monographs, articles', others will point to events outside the text; these will be 'Trails to the spatio-temporal matrix'[2] (centre-right of Figure 8.1, moving down). 'Data records' may lead to the 'Naturalistic observations of events, and self-reports' and hence on to the 'Mundane events in the so-called Real World'. Another way to get there is via 'Events in the world of the laboratory'. This will suffice as a preliminary orientation to Figure 8.1 and the textual world of food psychology. I shall use Ricoeur's (1981) hermeneutical perspective as a framework from which to develop my ideas and I shall draw primarily upon the material I covered in Chapter 3 (hunger, taste, etc.) by way of illustration.

Ricoeur's (1981) theory of discourse draws on the epistemological consequences of de Saussure's distinction between language (*langue*) and speech (*parole*). The former is a system of codes and is outside time, the latter is an event located within the here and now. Ricoeur associates discourse with speech act theory (see Austin, 1962; Searle, 1969). He thinks that the link between speaker and discourse is largely established through the use of indexicals, especially the use of personal pronouns (in this respect there is a similarity with Harré's, 1983, position). In passing, I note that the practice of providing assurances of anonymity and confidentiality to research participants typically functions as an institutionalised weakening of such indexicality in psychological research. Towards the bottom of Figure 8.1, I have indicated that this may prevent trails from the academic literature reaching the events in the real world upon which they were based and I have done this by breaking the connections on the diagram (see 'Anonymity').

Ricoeur (1981) goes beyond speech act theory to relate discourse to life-worlds:

> Discourse is an event in yet a third way: the signs of language refer only to other signs in the interior of the same system so that language no more has a world than it has a time and a subject, whereas discourse is always about something. Discourse refers to a world

---

[2] Following Harré (1983) this refers to the occurrence of events in time and space.

which it claims to describe, express or represent. The event, in this third sense, is the advent of a world in language [langage] by means of discourse. (p. 133)

Ricoeur introduces the notion of a 'work' to deal with extended sequences of discourse (longer than a sentence) which have a characteristic form or literary genre (such as a poem or a story) and which have a particular style. Language is thus seen as the raw material to be knocked into whatever shape is demanded by the stylistic and codification rules necessary for the production of a work of a particular genre. A student of creative writing might learn the rules governing the production of Spenserian or Shakespearean sonnets, for example. In an analogous fashion, a student of cognitive social psychology will learn the rules governing the production of Likert or Thurstone attitude questionnaires.

Ricoeur argues that texts, once separated from the mental intentions of their authors, become freed from the limits of ostensive reference:

For us, the world is the ensemble of references opened up by the texts. Thus we speak about the 'world' of Greece, not to designate any more what were the situations for those who lived them, but to designate the non-situational references which outlive the effacement of the first and which henceforth are offered as possible modes of being, as symbolic dimensions of being-in-the-world. (Ricouer, 1981, p. 202)

In Figure 8.1, I have applied this idea to 'The textual world of food psychology' (as circled, roughly in the centre of the diagram). This book, as you read it, may contribute to such a world for you. In Chapter 3, I drew heavily on texts located within the biomedical discourse and, in relation to digestion, to biochemical texts (e.g. Fox and Cameron, 1961). Such texts generate for me the 'world' of my internal body, in an analogous fashion to the way the 'world' of Greece might be generated through a reading of classical Greek literature or the 'world' of Elizabethan England might be generated from a reading of Shakespeare.

My reading of the biochemical texts was supplemented by fragments of autobiographical experience. The first job I took when I left school was as a trainee chemical engineer in a fertiliser factory. Part of my job was to take samples of materials from various points in the manufacturing process and deliver them to the chemistry lab for analysis. I became friendly with some of the young men and women who worked in the lab and, through hanging out with them, I built up an image of the world of the chemistry lab. I still retain a sense of this world, today, albeit in a rather hazy fashion. Thus, the world of human digestion, for me, is a world conjured up from reading the texts I have cited in Chapter 3, supplemented obliquely by my recollections of the real world of 1960s' industrial chemistry labs.

The extent to which psychologist readers, in general, will be able to flesh out the meaning of biochemical or physiological texts through their own laboratory experience may be relatively limited. It is impossible to provide a clear estimate of this, but one way to address the problem would be to assume that with regard to members of the British Psychological Society, only those psychologists who are members of the Division of Neuropsychology will have had direct experience of biochemical laboratory life. If this is done, the ratio of the membership of this Division to the membership of the Society as a whole will provide an approximate indication of the proportion of UK psychologists able to relate reported experiments in neuropsychology to relevant facets of their autobiographical experience. By my calculation, the membership figures published in the 1999 *Annual Report* of the Society indicate that only approximately 1.7 per cent of the total membership are neuropsychologists, as defined by divisional membership. Even if this computational strategy is felt to produce too conservative an estimate, the proportion would still be very small were the figure of 1.7 per cent to be doubled or trebled. On the basis of this estimate, the biochemical world of digestion will remain, for most, a *textual* world rather like the world of Greece to which I alluded, above. By way of contrast, I suspect that there will be no equivalent experiential barrier, for most readers, in relating the phenomenological description of my lunch, in Chapter 3, to their immediate life world (and even vegans might be able to relate to my descriptions of toast and the noises of kitchen and garden).

'The textual world of food psychology' may thus be critically evaluated on the basis of autobiographical experience in the 'Reader's immediate life world' and the latter may become changed by the former (since it is assimilated into the reader's knowledge base). An example of this, in relation to the foodie discourse, occurred in my description of lunch, in Chapter 3, when I rested the toast vertically instead of horizontally; I did this after I had assimilated the idea from the textual world of Delia Smith's cookery techniques (visual and printed).

Many of the 'Indexicality trails' within mainstream psychology will run to ground as 'Events in the world of the laboratory'. Obviously, events do really happen in psychology labs; they are called experiments.

However, it is convenient to separate out the world of the laboratory from the world of everyday life. Apart from anything else, there are often questions raised about the extent to which an experimental analogue possesses ecological validity. Experimental psychologists may sometimes go to great lengths to generate interesting analogues between 'Events in the world of the laboratory' and 'Mundane events in the so-called Real World'. For example, Visser *et al.* (2000) develop a procedure to test tasting sensitivity in very young children (as young as three years old). They approach this task by turning the experimental procedure into something of a theatrical experience:

> The test was introduced to the child by telling the story about an old goblin, who makes drinks for the baby goblins. It was told that by mistake a little goblin, who wanted to assist in making the drinks, had put water in some of the bottles instead of 'goblin drinks'. The experimenter asked the child to help him find the goblin drinks again by tasting two liquids. (p. 170)

This is an extremely interesting ploy. The research is conducted from within the mainstream experimental paradigm of psychophysics. As such, it is reasonable to assume that a realist perspective obtains (as opposed to the relativism that might be expected from investigations conducted within a discursive paradigm, for example). The excursion into the world of 'goblins' moves the child into fantasy or what Lewin describes as 'irreality' (see Lewin, 1936/1966, for an account of irreality in the context of his topological theory of the life space). Some aspects of the laboratory analogue are taken to be strictly equivalent to their real world equivalents (i.e. the operation of taste detection thresholds, in this experiment), while assumptions of reality are suspended with respect to others (e.g. the existence of goblins). The methodological credentials for taking this step are presented by the experimenters in the form of test–retest reliability statistics. As might be expected, there is no discussion of these credentials from a narratological standpoint (see Murray, 1995, for a discussion of narratology). Setting aside the details of this particular illustration, critical and post-positivist psychology is, in the main, dismissive of knowledge generated from 'Events in the world of the laboratory'.

Other trails may lead directly (e.g. from naturalistic observation studies) or indirectly (e.g. from self-reports through questionnaire or interview) to 'Mundane events in the so-called Real World' (see bottom of Figure 8.1). There may be many issues clouding the collection of

data in this regard: the reliability of memory; concentration and attention; selectivity in observations and in memories reported; questions of
biased reporting, and so forth. Furthermore, it may be a moot point as
to whether trails which claim to map directly into the real world
actually do so. For example, a discursive psychologist might use a
transcript from a focus group: it could be argued that the conversation
produced in the focus group shares some of the artificiality of the world
of the psychological laboratory and should not be regarded as a
naturally occurring conversation.

I decided to include phenomenological case studies and idiographic
investigations in this book because I think that they offer a more direct
path to critical evaluation against the reader's immediate life world
than do the more structured nomothetic investigations of mainstream
psychology, based upon experiment and survey. I also believe that, at
the end of the day, even the most tortuous 'Indexicality trail' will be
evaluated in the last resort against the 'Reader's immediate life world'.

Future Directions

I concluded my preface with a quotation from Smith, J.A. *et al.*
(1995c) in which they called for more idiographic projects that would
provide detailed descriptions of individual human beings and their
psychological functioning. I have made a start in this direction in the
reports of my lunch at home (Chapter 3) and the dinner party
(Chapter 5). Although I shifted between participant and non-
participant observation during the eating-out episodes (Chapter 6),
I feel that the descriptions were generated within the idiographic spirit.
The tension between this approach and the dominant mainstream
methodologies prompted Allport (1962) to suggest a change in
terminology:

> It would serve no good purpose here to review the long-standing
> debate between partisans of the nomothetic and idiographic meth-
> ods, between champions of explanation and understanding. Indeed,
> to insure more rapid progress I think it best to avoid traditional
> terms altogether. For the purposes of our present discussion I shall
> speak of 'dimensional' and 'morphogenic' procedures. (p. 409)

Allport's use of the term 'morphogenic' reflects his interest in the
existential outlook and its emphasis on 'the individual as a unique

being-in-the-world whose system of meanings and value-orientations are not precisely like anyone else's' (pp. 414–15). I have made scant use of the existentialist ideas put forward by Sartre, for example, and in this regard I differ from Allport. However, I have drawn on hermeneutics (and, to a limited extent, on phenomenology). Kearney (1994) suggests that Sartre's existentialism and Ricoeur's hermeneutics are both built upon phenomenological foundations and so this difference may not amount to much, in the end. Bringing Allport's methods into alignment with hermeneutics and other contemporary approaches within critical social psychology (that term being interpreted broadly) could result in the development of a neomorphogenic perspective more closely attuned to the discursive spirit of the times.

Allport argues that there is a case for studying the individual as opposed to the commonalities across individuals. He aligns himself with John Stuart Mill's distinction between the study of mind-in-general and the operation of psychological laws within individual characters. Similarly, he draws upon Dilthey's distinction between 'explanatory' and 'understanding' psychology. This distinction brings him more closely in touch with contemporary post-positivist psychology with its ties to the linguistic turn in philosophy, interpretive sociology, and hermeneutics. Of particular relevance to food research, he resists the temptation to base human psychology upon generalisations drawn from lower animals:

> The human system, unlike all others, possesses a degree of openness to the world, a degree of foresight and self-awareness, a flexibility and binding of functions and goals that present a unique structural challenge far more insistent than that presented by any other living system. (Allport, 1962, pp. 406–7)

Allport (1962) was at pains to state that the morphogenic approach did not necessarily have to be practised in its extreme form. Indeed, he listed several techniques which he classified as semi-morphogenic. For example, he included the Q-sort and repertory grid as examples of quantitative techniques which serve social constructionist ends. This stance has been echoed recently in critical social psychology (see Stainton Rogers et al., 1995).

Within mainstream psychology, it is not uncommon for the Theory of Reasoned Action[3] (TRA) to be used in food-related research, especially where this is concerned with people's intentions (e.g. Paisley

---

[3] See Ajzen and Fishbein (1980) for a full account of this theory.

et al., 1995; Grogan *et al.*, 1997). This approach may be regarded as the epitome of nomothetic research: it typically involves collecting paper-and-pencil questionnaire data from large samples and results are reported as properties of the population as a whole (often this will be in the form of correlations between the theoretical variables, such as attitude, social expectation and intention).

Measurements of the variables in TRA research tend to be made using (e.g. 7-point) rating scales. Allport did not reject the use of rating scales out of hand and so there is a prima facie case for the TRA research paradigm to be regarded as quasi-neomorphogenic. I have previously argued that the TRA may be interpreted from a post-positivist perspective (see J.L. Smith, 1999, 2000). With regard to the measurement of attitudes, in particular, I feel that research based upon expectancy-value rating scales may be construed as an exercise in attitudinal semantics (see J.L. Smith, 1996).

Allport (1962) notes that scientific psychologists strain for general-isations that will apply to all humankind or to identifiable sections of the population:

> We recognize the single case as a useful source of hunches – and that is about all ... We tolerate the single case only as a take-off point. (p. 406)

As a future research development, I would like to see this situation reversed (at least to some extent). In other words, instead of using the single case study in pilot work for the main nomothetic study, a small-to-medium-scale nomothetic study would become the pilot for a more extensive neomorphogenic investigation. I shall illustrate how this might be done, taking a study by Grogan *et al.* (1997) as my nomothetic starting point.

Grogan *et al.* (1997) used the theory of planned behaviour to explore gender differences in attitudes towards eating sweet snacks. They found that men's intentions were only predicted significantly by attitudes whereas women's were also predicted by perceived social pressure. The study is nomothetic, since it is based upon the responses of 65 women and 64 men. I particularly like the way the researchers report mean ratings and Standard Deviations (SDs) for their variables. I think a table of means packs a good nomothetic punch.

One of the tables was concerned with the reported frequency with which men and women ate various snacks. For example, for chocolate biscuits men scored a mean of 2.98 and women a mean of 3.14. There was no significant difference between these scores and an SD of just under 1.5 was reported for both groups. Using the operational definitions for the various points on the rating scale (as reported in their methodology section), a rating of 3 might be translated into the linguistic statement: 'I eat chocolate biscuits about once a week.' Someone scoring two SDs below the mean might say: 'I hardly ever touch the things, perhaps one a month!' On the other hand someone scoring two SDs above would be more likely to say: 'I eat chocolate biscuits at least twice a day – Mmm ...' The liberties taken in translating from operational definition to hypothetical speech are entirely mine: this is not the sort of thing Grogan *et al.* (1997) get up to.

In the nomothetic study, there is a symmetry between the high and low scorers, about the mean, and this is expressed statistically in SDs. A neomorphogenic study might start by using the nomothetic questionnaire as a screening device to get at those individuals occupying the more extreme reaches of the distribution as defined by the SD. Thus, I might want to talk to both someone who eats chocolate biscuits several times a day and to someone who hardly ever touches them. At this point, the contrasting respondents may be treated even-handedly in terms of neomorphogenic methodology (both may be interviewed or invited to participate in small group discussions and the data subjected to discursive analysis or something of a similar nature). However, this equivalence is unlikely to go on for long, since there is not going to be much future in observing the null-activity of the low scorer not having anything to do with chocolate biscuits. On the other hand, there may be lots for the researcher to do in order to track the profusion of chocolate biscuit episodes spattered through the high scorer's everyday life: the planning, the shopping, the possible attempts at restraint, the social settings, the mental associations, the smells, the mouthfeels, the range of brands consumed, the disquisitions on quality in chocolate biscuits, the discussions, the anticipations, the surfeit, the frustration of finding the cupboard bare, the brushing of teeth and the visit to the dentist. A plethora of neomorphogenic research opportunities may spring from a single nomothetic finding.

Of course, it is possible to break down quantitative data in order to carry out a more focused nomothetic analysis but that is not the same as making the switch from nomothetic screening to neomorphogenic case studies. An example of the nomothetic subdivision of samples is provided by Paisley *et al.* (1995) who examined and reported TRA correlations between attitude and intentions to eat more healthily in relation to nine food categories (e.g. reduce cakes and biscuits and fried foods; increase fruit and vegetable consumption). The researchers reported the correlations for low, medium and high-fat consumption groups (and also perceived consumption). The research remained nomothetic in character, since the correlational analysis for the sub-groups was identical to that carried out on the total sample. I acknowledge that breaking a sample down into sub-groups facilitates further statistical investigation through analysis of variance techniques, but that, once again, is a nomothetic tool.

I have already indicated that neomorphogenic methodology has some affinity with discourse analysis. Although I find the discursive approach to food research as exemplified by Wiggins *et al.* (2001) extremely interesting, I prefer to retain links with the earlier ethogenic techniques involving the negotiation of accounts. In my previous book, *The Psychology of Action* (J.L. Smith, 2000), I suggest that the use of accounting methodology makes little sense if the researcher holds to a strongly relativist position on language (such as that put forward by Edwards and Potter, 1992). In rejecting the hard discursive line, I free myself up to subject the primary discourse to further interrogation and negotiation. Although this might involve the researcher interrogating the participant, there is no reason why such interrogation should not manifest itself as the *post hoc* self-reflection of subjective reports. The annotation I provided for the 'Eating-out' field notes in Chapter 6 is not far removed from what I have in mind. The negotiation of accounts also has much in common with the T-group techniques developed by Kurt Lewin in the 1940s (see P.B. Smith, 1980, for a description of these techniques). Incidentally, I think it's a shame that experiential social psychology has fallen into abeyance since the 1970s, at least in the UK. Perhaps it is time for a resurgence of interest; neomorphogenic research into food-related activities could act as a catalyst in this regard.

My investigation into food discourse looked as though it might take on the cast of a neomorphogenic case study when I spotted a copy of *Elle* magazine at Newcastle airport. However, I soon adopted a more conventional approach to my analysis of the magazines and cook books. This was partly due to the fact that the reading of these magazines was done directly for the purpose of the analysis and did not occur naturally as episodes in the context of the unfolding narrative of my life story. This contrasts with what happened in the eating-out episodes (reported in Chapter 6) where, although I argued that designating my meals as research episodes affected the way I experienced them, the meals were naturally-occurring. I needed to eat at the time and probably would have done so at most of the venues I chose, whether or not I was in research mode. My need to read women's magazines was driven, I argue, primarily from a reserch motive.

In sum, I feel that there is scope for taking food-related episodes, as they occur in the flow of quotidian events in the person's life world, as a topic for further study. Adopting this strategy would result in a relatively holistic approach to the psychology of food and this is something I would welcome.

Once again, I'm seated in my kitchen eating lunch. It's well over a year since I ate the tomato-and-basil sandwich that I described at the start of my preface. On this chilly December day I'm having a microwaved winter vegetable soup, bought recently from the supermarket. As I take a spoonful of the mediocre broth, I notice a box of fresh cranberries lying on the worktop. They remind me that I need to make some cranberry-and-orange relish for the Christmas season. I toy with the idea of doing lunch for friends on Boxing Day. We could have a little party, as we did last year. When I start to think about what to cook and whom to invite, I find myself reaching for notepad and pencil. Having written this book, I cannot be sure whether I am merely sketching out my plans or starting my next neomorphogenic case study: Christmas food, now there's a topic. I set these thoughts to one side and resolve to end this book, right now.

Appendices

Appendix 1: Recipe for *Potage au Potiron* (Pumpkin Soup)

Extract taken from Grigson (1980, p. 419), with permission.

Pumpkin Soups
Simplest of all are the farmer's soups in the Berry and Vendômois districts of France, around the Loire and the Loir. Ideal for a winter's night, all the ingredients close at hand. This kind of homely dish often carries the older name of '*soupe*' rather than the later and more elegant *potage* ...

For a more elaborate soup, follow this recipe for *potage au potiron* from the Orléannais. Cook slowly in butter the white parts of two or three leeks, a large onion, chopped, and a couple of small turnips, diced. Add the cubed flesh of a 1 kg (2 lb) slice of pumpkin and cook for ten minutes longer. Moisten with 2 litres ($3\frac{1}{2}$ pt) stock or water and season. Simmer for 45 minutes, then sieve through the *mouli-légumes*. Correct the seasoning, add a pinch of sugar and a ladleful of cream. (Italics in the original)

Appendix 2: Recipe for Gorgonzola Cheese and Apple Strudel with Spiced Pickled Pears

Extract taken from Smith, D. (1995, pp. 106–7), with permission.

Serves 6.
Here is a recipe that provides something really stylish for vegetarian entertaining. Serve the strudel with the pickled pears. It's a brilliant combination of crisp pastry, melting cheese and the sharpness of the pears.

12 oz (350 g) young leeks weighed after trimming (this will be about $1\frac{1}{2}$ lb/700 g bought weight)
8 oz (225 g) prepared weight of celery (reserve the leaves)
1 small Bramley apple

1 small Cox's apple
8 oz (225 g) Mozzarella, cut in $\frac{1}{2}$-inch (1-cm) cubes
12 spring onions, white parts only, chopped
1 × $3\frac{1}{2}$ oz (100 g) pack ready-chopped walnuts
3 tablespoons chopped parsley, flat-leaf or curly
1 oz (25 g) white bread, crust removed
2 medium cloves garlic, peeled
10 sheets of frozen filo pastry, 18 × 10 inches (45 × 25.5 cm), thawed
6 oz (175 g) Gorgonzola piccante, cut in $\frac{1}{2}$-inch (1-cm) cubes
4 oz (110 g) butter
Salt and freshly milled black pepper

You will also need a large flat baking sheet approximately 16 × 12 inches (40 × 30 cm). Pre-heat oven to gas mark 5, 375°F (190°C).

First of all prepare the leeks by trimming and discarding the outer layers, then slice each one vertically almost in half and wash them under a cold running tap, fanning them out to get rid of any grit and dust. Then dry them in a cloth and cut them into $\frac{1}{2}$-inch (1-cm) pieces. Now wash and chop the celery into slightly smaller pieces.

Then melt $1\frac{1}{2}$ oz (40 g) of the butter in a frying pan 9 inches (23 cm) in diameter. Keeping the heat at medium, sauté the leeks and celery for about 7–8 minutes until just tinged brown, stir them and keep them on the move to stop them catching at the edges. Then tip them into a large bowl and while they are cooling you can deal with the other ingredients.

The apples need to be cored and chopped into $\frac{1}{2}$-inch (1-cm) pieces, leaving the skins on, then as soon as the leeks and celery have cooled, add the apples, diced Mozzarella, spring onions, walnuts and 1 tablespoon of chopped parsley. Season everything well and stir to mix it all together.

Now you need to make a breadcrumb mixture and to do this, place the bread, garlic, the rest of the parsley and reserved celery leaves in a food processor. Switch it on and blend until everything is smooth. If you don't have a food processor, grate the bread, and chop everything else finely and mix together.

Next take a large clean tea-cloth and dampen it under cold water, lay it out on a work surface, then carefully unwrap the filo pastry sheets and lay them on the damp cloth, folding it over. It is important to keep the pastry sheets in the cloth to prevent them drying out.

It is quite complicated to explain how to assemble a strudel, but to actually *do* it is very easy and only takes a few minutes.

Place a buttered baking sheet on a work surface. Because the filo sheets are too small to make a strudel for 6 people, we're going to have to 'weld' them together. To do this, first of all melt the remaining butter in a small saucepan, then take 1 sheet of filo pastry (remembering to keep the rest covered), lay it on one end of the baking sheet and brush it with melted butter. Then place another sheet beside it overlapping it by about 2 inches (5 cm), then brush that with melted butter. Place a third sheet next to the second overlapping it again by 2 inches (5 cm).

Now sprinkle a quarter of the breadcrumb mixture all over the sheets and then place 2 more sheets of filo, this time horizontally, buttering the first one with melted butter and welding the other one with a 2-inch (5-cm) join. Brush that layer as before with melted butter and repeat the sprinkling of breadcrumbs. Then place the next 3 sheets as you did the first 3, again brushing with butter and sprinkling with crumbs. Then place the final 2 sheets horizontally and brush with butter.

After that place half the cheese and vegetable mixture all the way along the filo, sprinkle the cubes of Gorgonzola on top of that, then finish off with the rest of the mixture on top. Now just pat it together firmly with your hands. Take the edge of the pastry that is nearest to you, bring it up over the filling, then flip the whole lot over as if you were making a giant sausage roll. Neatly push in the vegetables, before tucking the pastry ends underneath. Now brush the entire surface with the remaining butter, scatter the rest of the crumb mixture over the top and bake in the oven for 25–30 minutes or until it has turned a nice golden brown colour.

To serve the strudel, cut off the ends (they are great for the bird table but not for your guests) and cut the strudel into slices, giving each person one pickled pear.

Spiced Pickled Pears
6 hard pears (Conference or similar variety)
4 oz (110 g) soft brown sugar
12 fl oz (330 ml) cider vinegar
1 tablespoon balsamic vinegar
1 tablespoon whole mixed peppercorns
4 whole cloves
6 crushed juniper berries

You will also need a flameproof casserole approximately 10 inches (25.5 cm) in diameter, large enough to hold the pears.
Pre-heat the oven to gas mark 5, 375°F (190°C).

To pickle the pears, first peel the pears using a potato peeler, but be very careful to leave the stalks intact as they look much prettier. Place all the rest of the ingredients in a flameproof casserole, bring everything up to simmering point, stirring all the time to dissolve the sugar. Now carefully lower the pears into the hot liquid, laying them on their sides, then cover with a lid and transfer the pears to the oven for 30 minutes.

After that, remove the lid and carefully turn the pears over. Test with a skewer to see how they are cooking – they'll probably need another 30 minutes altogether, so cover with the lid and leave them in the oven till they feel tender when pierced with a skewer. Then remove them and allow them to cool in their liquid until needed. When serving, there's no need to reheat the pears as they taste much better cold.

(Italics in the original)

Appendix 3: Recipes for Chocolate Chestnut Pavé and Chantilly Cream

Extracts taken from Willan (1989, p. 425 and p. 70), with permission.

Chocolate Chestnut Pavé (p. 425)
Chestnut pavé is moulded in a block shape like the paving stones that once lined the streets of Paris. For serving, it is sliced thinly and topped with whipped cream.

Serves 8
3 lb/1.4 kg fresh chestnuts or $1\frac{1}{2}$ lb/750 g canned, unsweetened chestnuts, drained
1 vanilla pod or 1 tsp vanilla essence
$\frac{3}{4}$ lb/375 g semisweet chocolate, chopped
4 fl oz/125 ml water
6 oz/175 g butter
7 oz/200 g caster sugar
2 tbsp brandy

For serving: Chantilly cream

$9 \times 5 \times 3$ in/$23 \times 13 \times 7.5$ cm loaf tin
Piping bag and medium star tube

1. Lightly grease the loaf tin, line the base with greaseproof paper, and grease the paper. If using fresh chestnuts, peel them, and put them in a saucepan with the vanilla pod, if using. Add enough water to cover, cover the pan and simmer until the nuts are tender, 25–30 minutes. *Note* Canned nuts need not be cooked. Remove the vanilla pod and drain the nuts. Purée fresh or canned nuts in a food processor or work through a food mill.
2. Melt the chocolate in the 4 fl oz/125 ml water over low heat, stirring until smooth. Let it cool to tepid. Beat butter and sugar until soft and light. Stir

in the cooled chocolate and then the chestnut purée, brandy and vanilla essence, if using. Mix until smooth. Pack the mixture into the prepared tin, cover and chill at least 12 hours or up to a week.

3. To serve, unmould the *pavé* and discard the paper. Cut the *pavé* in thin slices with a knife dipped in hot water. Set the slices on individual plates and decorate with rosettes of Chantilly cream, using a piping bag and star tube. Top the rosettes with chocolate decorations and chill until ready to serve.

Chantilly Cream (p. 70)

Chantilly cream is whipped cream flavoured with sugar, and vanilla or brandy. It is used in bavarian creams and charlottes, as a simple filling for *vacherins* and other meringue desserts or for pastries such as cream horns or Chantilly swans. Chantilly cream may also accompany fresh and poached fruits. It is often piped in decorative rosettes and patterns using a star piping tube. When piping, always whip the cream until just stiff and use a large tube. The cream will be worked further when forced through the tube and may separate if it is already too stiff. Work quickly, as the heat of your hand on the piping bag encourages separation.

For every 8 fl oz/250 ml cream, allow 1–2 tbsp granulated or icing sugar and $\frac{1}{2}$ tsp vanilla or 1 tsp brandy. Whip the cream until it starts to thicken, add sugar and flavourings and continue whisking until the cream stiffens again, about 1 minute. If you like, to lighten the cream further, fold in stiffly whisked egg white, allowing 1 egg white for every 8 fl oz/250 ml of cream.

Note. Cream that has been lightened with egg white is less stable, and must be used within two hours.

Notes from the present author:
- As usual, it is not prudent to use uncooked egg white in recipes, unless you are fully satisfied with all the health and safety aspects involved.
- Cross-referencing page numbers to other recipes in Willan's book has been omitted, to avoid confusion.

Appendix 4: Costings for Dinner Party (13.11.99)

Pumpkin Soup

Stock

$\frac{1}{2}$ Bottle wine		1.40	
$\frac{1}{2}$ Bottle spring water		0.35	
1 carrot		0.02	
1 onion		0.06	
Thyme		0.15	
Celery		0.15	
	Total	2.13	2.13

Pumpkin (costed at $\frac{1}{2}$ total price)		2.00	
Leeks		0.25	
Turnips		0.35	
Onion		0.06	
Cream		0.39	
	Total	5.18	5.18

Bread rolls		0.89	
Margarine		0.52	
	Total	1.41	1.41

Savoury Strudel

Leeks		1.29	
Celery (8 oz)		0.80	
Bramley & Cox apples		0.40	
Mozzarella cheese		1.19	
Spring onions		0.55	
Walnuts		0.85	
Parsley pot		0.79	
Filo pastry		1.25	
Gorgonzola cheese		1.59	
4 oz butter		0.45	
Sundries (bread, garlic)		0.50	
	Total	9.66	9.66

Herb & Lettuce salad leaves			1.79

Spiced Pickled Pears

Conference pears		0.70	
Cider vinegar		1.09	
Sugar (approx.)		0.25	
Sundries (berries, peppercorns, etc)		0.50	
	Total	2.54	2.54

Chocolate Chestnut Pavé

Chocolate		2.30	
Chestnut purée		2.50	
Butter		0.70	
Sugar		0.30	
Sundries (brandy)		0.50	
	Total	6.30	6.30

Chantilly Cream

Cream		0.73	
Sundries		0.50	
	Total	1.23	1.23

Cheese Board

Regional (Nettle & Beamish)		7.00	
Brie		2.29	
Crackers (approx)		1.00	
	Total	10.29	10.29

Sundry Items

Mineral water (approx)		1.80	
Coffee (approx)		0.60	
Napkins		1.49	
	Total	3.89	3.89

Grand Total (excluding wine)	42.29
Cost per head for 8 diners	5.29

Approximate costs in English pounds (most of the items were purchased in a supermarket in Sunderland, England, November 1999).

Bibliography

Abelson, R.P. (1973) 'The structure of belief systems', in R.C. Shank and K.M. Colby (eds), *Computer Models of Thought and Language*. San Francisco: Freeman.

Abelson, R.P. (1975) 'Concepts for representing mundane reality in plans', in D.G. Bobrow and A. Collins (eds), *Representation and Understanding: Studies in Cognitive Science*. London: Academic Press.

Abensur, N. (1996) *The New Crank's Recipe Book*. London: Weidenfeld & Nicolson.

Acton, E. (1845/1993) *Modern Cookery for Private Families*. Lewes: Southover Press.

Ajzen, I. (1991) 'The theory of planned behavior', *Organisational Behavior and Human Decision Processes*, 50, 1–33.

Ajzen, I. and Fishbein, M. (1980) *Understanding Attitudes and Predicting Social Behavior*. Englewood-Cliffs, NJ: Prentice-Hall.

Allport, G.W. (1962) 'The general and the unique in psychological science', *Journal of Personality*, 30, 405–22.

Anand, K.B. and Brobeck, J.R. (1951) 'Localization of a "feeding center" in the hypothalamus of the rat', *Proceedings of the Society for Experimental Biology and Medicine*, 77, 323–4.

Antaki, C. (ed.) (1988) *Analysing Everyday Explanation: A Casebook of Methods*. London: Sage.

Asher, N.S. and Asher, K.C. (1999) 'Qualitative methods for an outsider looking in: lesbian women and body image', in M. Kopala and L.A. Suzuki (eds), *Using Qualitative Methods in Psychology*. London: Sage.

Austin, J.L. (1962) *How To Do Things with Words*. Oxford: Oxford University Press.

Axelson, M.L. and Brinberg, D. (1989) *A Social-Psychological Perspective on Food-Related Behavior*. New York: Springer-Verlag.

Bales, R.F. (1950) *Interaction Process Analysis: A Method for the Study of Small Groups*. Cambridge, MA.: Addison-Wesley.

Bandura, A., Ross, D. and Ross, S.A. (1961) 'Transmission of aggression through imitation of aggressive models', *Journal of Abnormal and Social Psychology*, 63, 3, 575–82.

Bannister, D. and Fransella, F. (1971) *Inquiring Man: The Theory of Personal Constructs*. Harmondsworth: Penguin Books Ltd.

Barthes, R. (1973) *Mythologies* (trans. A. Lavers). London: Paladin.

Bartoshuk, L.M. and Beauchamp, G.K. (1994) 'Chemical senses', *Annual Review of Psychology*, 45, 419–49.

Baumeister, R.F. (1990) 'Suicide as escape from self', *Psychological Review*, 97, 90–113.

Bear, M.F., Connors, B.W. and Paradiso, M.A. (1996) *Neuroscience: Exploring the Brain*. Baltimore: Williams & Wilkins.

Beardsworth, A. and Keil, T. (1997) *Sociology on the Menu: An Invitation to the Study of Food and Society*. London: Routledge.

Beeton, I. (1861/1982) *Mrs Beeton's Book of Household Management*. London: Chancellor Press.

Billig, M. (1999) *Freudian Repression: Conversation Creating the Unconscious*. Cambridge: Cambridge University Press.

Birch, L.L. and Fisher, J.A. (1996) 'The role of experience in the development of children's eating behavior', in E.D. Capaldi (ed.), *Why We Eat What We Eat: The Psychology of Eating*. Washington DC: American Psychological Association.

Blanc, R. (1988) *Recipes from Le Manoir Aux Quat' Saisons*. London: Guild.

Booth, D.A. (1994) *Psychology of Nutrition*. London: Taylor & Francis.

Booth, D.A. (2000) 'The next twenty years: an editorial perspective', *Appetite*, 34, 1–3.

Bourdieu, P. (1984). (trans. R. Nice) *Distinction: A Social Critique of the Judgement of Taste*. London: Routledge.

Bowie, M. (1991) *Lacan*. London: Fontana Press.

BPS (1999) *The 1999 Annual Report*. Leicester: The British Psychological Society.

Bredahl, L. (1999) 'Consumers' cognitions with regard to genetically modified foods. Results of a qualitative study in four countries', *Appetite*, 33, 343–60.

Brentano, F. (1874/1995) *Psychology from an Empirical Standpoint*. (trans. A.C. Rancurello, D.B. Terrell and L.L. McAlister). London: Routledge.

Bruch, H. (1973) *Eating Disorders*. New York: Basic Books.

Bunster, E. and Meyer, R.K. (1933) 'An improved method of parabiosis', *Anatomical Record*, 57, 339–43.

Cannon, W.B. and Washburn, A.L. (1912) 'An explanation of hunger', *American Journal of Physiology*, 29, 441–54.

Carver, C.S. and Scheier, M.F. (1998) *On the Self-Regulation of Behavior*. Cambridge: Cambridge University Press.

Chaney, Lisa (1998) *Elizabeth David: A Biography*. London: Pan Books.

Charmaz, K. (1995) 'Grounded theory', in J.A. Smith, R. Harré, and L. Van Langenhove (eds), *Rethinking Methods in Psychology*. London: Sage.

Colman, A. (1987) *Facts, Fallacies and Frauds in Psychology*. London: Hutchinson.

Comuzzie, A.G. and Alison, D.B. (1998) 'The search for human genes', *Science*, 280, 1374–6.

Condor, S. (1997) 'And so say all of us? Some thoughts on "Experiential democratization" as an aim for critical social psychologists', in T. Ibáñez and L. Iñiguez (eds), *Critical Social Psychology*. London: Sage.

Conran, T. (1996) *The Kitchen Book: How to Plan, Design and Equip Your Kitchen*. London: Conran Octopus.

Cosmopolitan (2000) September issue. London: The National Magazine Co Ltd.

Coufopoulos, A.-M. and Stitt, S. (1997) 'Homeless and hungry: the evidence from Britain', in B.M. Kohler, E. Feichtinger, E. Barlösius and E. Dowler (eds), *Poverty and Food in Welfare Societies*. Berlin: Ed. Sigma.

Cracknell, H.L. and Kaufmann, R.J. (1999) *Practical Professional Cookery*, 3rd edn. London: Macmillan – now Palgrave.

David, E. (1986) *An Omelette and a Glass of Wine*. Harmondsworth: Penguin.

Davidson, A. (1999) *The Oxford Companion to Food*. Oxford: Oxford University Press.

Dirks, R. (1980) 'Social responses during severe food shortages and famine', *Current Anthropology*, 21, 21–44.

Dobson, B. (1997) 'The paradox of want amidst plenty: from food poverty to social exclusion?', in B.M. Kohler, E. Feichtinger, E. Barlösius and E. Dowler (eds), *Poverty and Food in Welfare Societies*. Berlin: Ed. Sigma.

Douglas, M. (1975) 'Deciphering a meal', *Daedalus*, 101, 61–81.

Dowler, E.A. (1997) 'Nutrition and poverty in contemporary Britain: consequences for individuals and society', in B.M. Kohler, E. Feichtinger, E. Barlösius and E. Dowler (eds), *Poverty and Food in Welfare Societies*. Berlin: Ed. Sigma.

Dowler, E.A. and Dobson, B.M. (1997) 'Symposium on "Nutrition and poverty in industrialized countries". Nutrition and poverty in Europe: an overview', *Proceedings of the Nutrition Society*, 56, 51–62.

Dragsted, C.A. and Mullenix, B. (1931) 'Experimental esophageal fistula', *Journal of Laboratory and Clinical Medicine*, 16, 591–3.

Drèze, J. and Sen, A. (1989) *Hunger and Public Action*. Oxford: Oxford University Press.

Duffy, V.B. and Bartoshuk, L.M. (1996) 'Sensory factors in feeding', in E.D. Capaldi (ed.), *Why We Eat What We Eat: The Psychology of Eating*. Washington DC: American Psychological Association.

Eastwood, M. (1997) *Principles of Human Nutrition*. London: Chapman & Hall.

Edwards, D. and Potter, J. (1992). *Discursive Psychology*. London: Sage.

Eibl-Eibesfeldt, I. (1970) *Ethology: The Biology of Behavior*. New York: Holt, Rinehart & Winston.

Einstein, M.A. and Hornstein, I. (1970) 'Food preferences of college students and nutritional implications', *Journal of Food Science*, 35, 429–35.

Elle (1954) Paris: Régis Press.

Elle (2000) September issue. London: Hachette-EMAP Magazines.

Elliot, R. (1988) *Vegetarian Cookery*. London: Octopus.

Escoffier, A. (1921/1979) *The Complete Guide to the Art of Modern Cookery: The First Translation into English in its Entirety of Le Guide Culinaire* (trans. H.L. Cracknell and R.J. Kaufman). Oxford: Heinemann Professional Publishing.

Etzioni, A. (1993) *The Spirit of Community*. New York: Touchstone.

Fairburn, C.G., Shafran, R. and Cooper, Z. (1999) 'A cognitive behavioural theory of anorexia nervosa', *Behaviour Research and Therapy*, 37, 1–13.

Fischler, C. (1980) 'Food habits, social change and the nature/culture dilemma', *Social Science Information*, 19, 937–53.

Fleming, D.G. (1969) 'Food intake studies in parabiotic rats', *Annals New York Academy of Sciences*, 157, 985–1003.

Foucault, M. (1972) *The Archeology of Knowledge and the Discourse on Language* (trans. A. Sheridan). New York: Pantheon Books.

Fox, B.A. and Cameron, A.G. (1961) *A Chemical Approach to Food and Nutrition*. London: University of London Press Ltd.

Freud, S. (1963/1973) (trans. J. Strachey) *Introductory Lectures on Psychoanalysis*. Harmondsworth: Penguin Books.

Fuller, J. and Renold, E. (1972) *The Chef's Compendium of Professional Recipes*, 2nd edn., Oxford: Heinemann Professional Publishing Ltd.

Garfinkel, H. (1967) *Studies in Ethnomethodology*. Englewood Cliffs: Prentice Hall.

Goffman, E. (1959) *The Presentation of Self in Everyday Life*. New York: Allen Lane.

Good Housekeeping (2000) September issue. London: Good Housekeeping Institute.

Goody, J. (1982) *Cooking, Cuisine and Class: A Study in Comparative Sociology*. Cambridge: Cambridge University Press.

Gregory, S. (1999) 'Gender roles and food in families', in L. McKie, S. Bowlby and S. Gregory, *Gender, Power and the Household*. London: Macmillan – now Palgrave.

Grieshaber, S. (1997) 'Mealtime rituals: power and resistance in the construction of mealtime rules', *International Journal of Sociology*, 48, 649–66.

Grigson, J. (1971) *Good Things*. London: Michael Joseph.

Grigson, J. (1977) *English Food*. Harmondsworth: Penguin.

Grigson, J. (1980) *Jane Grigson's Vegetable Book*. Harmondsworth: Penguin.

Grogan, S.C., Bell, R. and Conner, M. (1997) 'Eating sweet snacks; gender differences in attitudes and behaviour', *Appetite*, 28, 19–31.

Gura, T. (1998) 'Cell biology: uncoupling proteins provide new clue to obesity's causes'. *Science*, 280, 1369–70.

Halliday, M.A.K. (1961) 'Categories of the theory of grammar', *Word, Journal of the Linguistic Circle of New York*, 17, 241–92.

Harper, R., Land, D.G., Griffiths, N.M. and Bate-Smith, E.C. (1968) 'Odour qualities: a glossary of usage', *British Journal of Psychology*, 59, 231–52.

Harré, R. (1983) *Personal Being: A Theory for Individual Psychology*. Oxford: Blackwell.

Harré, R. and Secord, P.F. (1972) *The Explanation of Social Behaviour*. Oxford: Blackwell.

Hetherington, A.W. and Ranson, S.W. (1940) 'Hypathalamic lesions and adiposity in the rat', *Anatomical Record*, 78, 149–72.

Janowitz, H.D. and Grossman, M.I. (1949) 'Some factors affecting the food intake of normal dogs and dogs with esophagostomy and gastric fistula', *American Journal of Physiology*, 159, 143–8.

Kalat, J.W. (1998) *Biological Psychology*, 6th edn. Pacific Grove: Brooks/Cole.

Kearney, R. (1994) *Modern Movements in European Philosophy*, 2nd edn. Manchester: Manchester University Press.

Kelley, H.H. (1967) 'Attribution theory in social psychology', in D.L. Vind (ed.), *Nebraska Symposium on Motivation*. Lincoln: University of Nebraska Press.

Kirwan, B. and Ainsworth, L.K. (eds) (1992) *A Guide to Task Analysis*. London: Taylor & Francis.

Klein, M. (1981) *Love, Guilt and Reparation: And Other Works 1921–1945*. London: Hogarth Press.

Koocher, G.P. (1977) 'Bathroom behavior and human dignity', *Journal of Personality and Social Psychology*, 35, 120–1.

Kulbartz-Klatt, Y.J., Florin, I. and Pook, M. (1999) 'Bulimia nervosa: mood changes do have an impact on body width estimation', *British Journal of Clinical Psychology*, 38, 279–87.

Lacan, J. (1977) *Écrits*, trans. A. Sheridan. London: Tavistock.

Langenhove, L. van and Harré, R. (1999a) 'Introducing positioning theory', in R. Harré and L. van Langenhove (eds), *Positioning Theory: Moral Contexts of Intentional Action*. Oxford: Blackwell.

Langenhove, L. van and Harré, R. (1999b) 'The writing of science', in R. Harré and L. van Langenhove (eds), *Positioning Theory: Moral Contexts of Intentional Action*. Oxford: Blackwell.

Lawson, N. (1998) *How to Eat: The Pleasures and Principles of Good Food*. London: Chatto & Windus.

Lerner, M.J. (1980) *The Belief in a Just World: A Fundamental Delusion*. New York: Plenum.

Lévi-Strauss, C. (1966) (trans. P. Brooks) 'The culinary triangle', *Partisan Review*, 33, 586—95.

Lewin, K. (1936/1966) *Principles of Topological Psychology*, trans. F. Heider and G.M. Heider. New York: McGraw-Hill.

Lockyer, K. and Gordon, J. (1991) *Critical Path Analysis and Other Project Network Techniques*, 5th edn. London: Pitman Publishing.

Logue, A.W. (1991) *The Psychology of Eating and Drinking: An Introduction*, 2nd edn. New York: W.H. Freeman.

Lowe, C.F., Dowey, A. and Horne, P. (1998) 'Changing what children eat', in A. Murcott (ed.), *The Nation's Diet: The Social Science of Food Choice*. Harlow: Addison-Wesley Longman.

Lupton, D. (1996) *Food, the Body and the Self*. London: Sage.

Lyman, B. (1982) 'Menu item preferences and emotions', *School Food Service Research Review*, 6, 32–5.

Lyman, B. (1989) *A Psychology of Food: More Than a Matter of Taste*. New York: Van Nostrand Reinhold.

MAFF (1985) *Manual of Nutrition: Reference Book 342*. London: HMSO.

Malson, H. (1992) 'Anorexia nervosa: displacing universalities and replacing gender', in P. Nicolson and J. Ussher (eds), *The Psychology of Women's Health and Health Care*. London: Macmillan – now Palgrave.

Malson, H. (1998) *The Thin Woman: Feminism, Post-Structuralism and the Social Psychology of Anorexia Nervosa*. London: Routledge.

Mars, V. (1993) 'Parsimony amid plenty: views from Victorian didactic works on food for nursery children', in G. Mars and V. Mars (eds), *Food Culture and History. Volume 1*. London: The London Food Seminar.

Maslow, A.H. (1968) *Toward a Psychology of Being*, 2nd edn. New York: Van Nostrand Reinhold.

McDougall, W. (1933) *An Outline of Psychology*, 6th edn. London: Methuen.

McGee, H. (1984) *On Food and Cooking: The Science and Lore of the Kitchen*. London: Unwin Hyman.

Meiselman, H.L. and Waterman, D. (1978) 'Food preferences of enlisted personnel in the armed forces', *Journal of the American Dietetic Association*, 73, 621–9.

Mennell, S., Murcott, A. and van Otterloo, A.H. (1992) *The Sociology of Food: Eating, Diet and Culture*. London: Sage.

Mennella, J.A. and Beauchamp, G.K. (1996) 'The early development of human flavor preferences', in E.D. Capaldi (ed.), *Why We Eat What We Eat: The Psychology of Eating*. Washington DC: American Psychological Association.

Middlemist, R.D., Knowles, E.S. and Matter, C.F. (1976) 'Personal space invasions in the lavatory: suggestive evidence for arousal', *Journal of Personality and Social Psychology*, 33, 541—6.

Miller, G.A., Gallanter, E. and Pribram, K.H. (1960) *Plans and the Structure of Behaviour*. London: Holt, Rinehart & Winston.

Mitchell, J. (1982) 'Introduction – I', in J. Mitchell and J. Rose, *Feminine Sexuality: Jacques Lacan and the École Freudienne*. London: Macmillan – now Palgrave.

Mitchell, J. and Rose, J. (1982) (eds) *Feminine Sexuality: Jacques Lacan and the École Freudienne*. London: Macmillan – now Palgrave.

Murcott, A. (ed.) (1998) *The Nation's Diet: The Social Science of Food Choice*. Harlow: Addison Wesley Longman.

Murray, K.D. (1995) 'Narratology', in J.A. Smith, R. Harré, and L. Van Langenhove (eds), *Rethinking Psychology*. London: Sage.

Norris, C. (1996) *Reclaiming Truth: Contribution to a Critique of Cultural Relativism*. London: Lawrence & Wishart.

Oakley, A. (1972) *Sex, Gender and Society*. London: Temple Smith.

O'Farrell, M. (2000) 'I like my man in an apron', *Elle* (September UK edition) pp. 165–6. London: Hachette-EMAP Magazines.

Ogden, J. (1992) *Fat Chance! The Myth of Dieting Explained*. London: Routledge.

Orbach, S. (1988) *Fat is a Feminist Issue ... How to Lose Weight Permanently – Without Dieting*. London: Arrow.

Paisley, C., Lloyd, H., Sparks, P. and Mela, D.J. (1995) 'Consumer perceptions of dietary changes for reducing fat intake', *Nutrition Research*, 15, 1755–66.

Palmer, G. (1993) *The Politics of Breastfeeding*. London: HarperCollins.

Patten, M. (1972) *Perfect Cooking*. London: Octopus Books.

Pavlov, I.P. (1910) *The Work of the Digestive Glands*, 2nd edn (trans. W.H. Thompson). London: Charles Griffin & Co.

Pollio, H.R. Henley, T.B. and Thompson, C.J. (1997) *The Phenomenology of Everyday Life*. Cambridge: Cambridge University Press.

Potter, J. (1996) *Representing Reality: Discourse, Rhetoric and Social Construction*. London: Sage.

Potter, J. and Wetherell, M. (1987) *Discourse and Social Psychology: Beyond Attitudes and Behaviour*. London: Sage.

Prilleltensky, I. and Nelson, G. (1997) 'Community psychology: reclaiming social justice', in D. Fox and I. Prilleltensky, *Critical Psychology: An Introduction*. London: Sage.

Rachman, S. (1993) 'Obsessions, responsibility, and guilt', *Behaviour Research and Therapy*, 31, 149–54.

Rachman, S. (1997) 'A cognitive theory of obsessions', *Behaviour Research and Therapy*, 35, 793–802.

Rasmussen, K.M. (1992) 'The influence of maternal nutrition on lactation', *Annual Review of Nutrition*, 12, 103–17.

Rawls, J. (1972) *A Theory of Justice*. New York: Oxford University Press.

Reason, J.T. (1990) *Human Error*. Cambridge: Cambridge University Press.

Richards, A. (1939) *Land, Labour and Diet in Northern Rhodesia*. Oxford: Oxford University Press.

Ricoeur, P. (1981) (trans. J.B. Thompson) *Hermeneutics & the Human Sciences*. Cambridge: Cambridge University Press.

Ritzer, G. (1996) *The McDonaldization of Society: An Investigation into the Changing Character of Contemporary Social Life* (rev. edn). Thousand Oaks, CA: Pine Forge Press.

Rose, J. (1982) 'Introduction – II', in J. Mitchell and J. Rose, *Feminine Sexuality: Jacques Lacan and the École Freudienne*. London: Macmillan – now Palgrave.

Rothenbuhler, E.W. (1998) *Ritual Communication: From Everyday Conversation to Mediated Ceremony*. London: Sage.

Rotter, J.B. (1966) 'Generalised expectancies for internal versus external control of reinforcement', *Psychological Monographs*, 80, 1, 1–28.

Roustang, F. (1990) *The Lacanian Delusion* (trans. G. Sims). Oxford: Oxford University Press.

Roux, A. and Roux, M. (1983) *New Classic Cuisine*. London: QED Publishing.

Rowland, N.E., Li, B.-H. and Morien, A. (1996) 'The role of experience in the development of children's eating behavior', in E.D. Capaldi (ed.), *Why We Eat What We Eat: The Psychology of Eating*. Washington DC: American Psychological Association.

Rozin, E. (1983) *Ethnic Cuisine: The Flavor Principle Cookbook*. Lexington, MA: The Stephen Greene Press.

Rozin, P. (1996) 'Sociocultural influences on human food selection', in E.D. Capaldi (ed.), *Why We Eat What We Eat: The Psychology of Eating*. Washington DC: American Psychological Association.

Rycroft, C. (1970) 'Causes and meaning', in S.G.M. Lee and M. Herbert (eds), *Freud and Psychology*. Harmondsworth: Penguin.

Sachs, M., Buchanan, P., Broodfoot, M. and Greiner, T. (2000) 'Infant feeding and HIV study does not support the BMJ's conclusion', electronic letter to the *British Medical Journal*. Http://www.bmj.com/cgi/letters/320/7236/724

Sampson, E.E. (1989) 'The deconstruction of the self', in J. Shotter and K.J. Gergen (eds), *Texts of Identity*. London: Sage.

Saussure, F. de (1960) *Course in General Linguistics*. London: Peter Owen.

Schafe, G.E. and Bernstein, I.L. (1996) 'Taste aversion learning', in E.D. Capaldi (ed.), *Why We Eat What We Eat: The Psychology of Eating*. Washington DC: American Psychological Association.

Schifferstein, H.N.J. (1997) 'Perceptual and imaginary mixtures in chemosensation', *Journal of Experimental Psychology: Human Perception and Performance*, 23, 278–88.

Searle, J.R. (1969) *Speech Acts: An Essay in the Philosophy of Language*. Cambridge: Cambridge University Press.

Sen, A. (1981) *Poverty and Famines: An Essay on Entitlement and Deprivation*. Oxford: Oxford University Press.

Shafran, R. (1999) 'Obsessive compulsive disorder', *The Psychologist*, 12, 588–91. Leicester: The British Psychological Society.

Shafran, R., Bethany, A., Teachman, S.K. and Rachman, S. (1999) 'A cognitive distortion associated with eating disorders: thought-shape fusion', *British Journal of Clinical Psychology*, 38, 167–79.

Sherif, M. (1966) *Group Conflict and Cooperation*. London: Routledge & Kegan Paul.

Slater, N. (1992) *Real Fast Food*. Harmondsworth: Penguin.

Smith, D. (1995) *Delia Smith's Winter Collection*. London: BBC Books.

Smith, D. (1998) *Delia's How to Cook: Book One*. London: BBC Books.

Smith, J.A., Harré, R. and Van Langenhove, L. (eds) (1995a) *Rethinking Psychology*. London: Sage.

Smith, J.A., Harré, R. and Van Langenhove, L. (eds) (1995b) *Rethinking Methods in Psychology*. London: Sage.

Smith, J.A., Harré, R. and Van Langenhove, L. (1995c) 'Idiography and the case study', in J.A. Smith, R. Harré and L. Van Langenhove (eds), *Rethinking Psychology*. London: Sage.

Smith, J.L. (1996) 'Expectancy, value, and attitudinal semantics', *European Journal of Social Psychology*, 26, 501–6.

Smith, J.L. (1999) 'An agentic psychology model based on the paradigmatic repositioning of the theory of planned behaviour', *Theory & Psychology*, 9, 697–700.

Smith, J.L. (2000) *The Psychology of Action*. London: Macmillan – now Palgrave.

Smith, P.B. (1980) *Group Processes and Personal Change*. London: Harper & Row.

Spears, R. (1997) 'Introduction', in T. Ibáñez and L. Iñiguez, *Critical Social Psychology*. London: Sage.

Stainton Rogers, R., Stenner, P., Gleeson, K. and Stainton Rogers, W. (1995) *Social Psychology: A Critical Agenda*. Cambridge: Polity.

Stallberg-White, C. and Pliner, P. (1999) 'The effect of flavor principles on willingness to taste novel foods', *Appetite*, 33, 209–21.

Stephens, T.W., Basinski, M., Bristow, P.K., Bue-Walleskey, J.M., Burgett, S.G., Craft, L., Hale, J., Hoffmann, J., Hsiung, H.M., Driauclunas, A., MacKellar, W., Rosteck, P.R. Jr, Schoner, B., Smith, D., Tinsley, F.C., Zhang, X-Y. and Helman, M. (1995) 'The role of neuropeptide Y in the antiobesity action of the obese gene product', *Nature*, 377, 530–2.

Steptoe, A., Wardle, J., Lipsey, Z., Oliver, G., Pollard, T.M. and Davies, G.J. (1998) 'The effects of life stress on food choice', in A. Murcott (ed.), *The Nation's Diet: The Social Science of Food Choice*. Harlow: Addison-Wesley Longman.

Stewart, K. (1972/1980) *The Times Cookery Book*. London: Book Club Associates.

Stratton, P. and Bromley, K. (1999) 'Families' accounts of the causal processes in food choice', *Appetite*, 33, 89–108.

Stringer, P. (1990) 'Prefacing social psychology: a textbook example', in I. Parker and J. Shotter, *Deconstructing Social Psychology*. London: Routledge.

Sullivan, O. (2000) 'The division of domestic labour: twenty years of change?', *Sociology*, 34, 437–56.

Theunissen, M.J.M. and Kroeze, J.H.A. (1996) 'Mouth movements diminish taste adaptation, but rate of mouth movement does not affect adaptation', *Chemical Senses*, 21, 545–51.

Theunissen, M.J.M., Kroeze, J.H.A. and Schifferstein, H.J. (2000) 'Method of stimulation, mouth movements, concentration, and viscosity: effects on the degree of taste adaptation', *Perception & Psychophysics*, 62, 607–14.

Thomas, M.H., Horton, R.W., Lippincott, E.C. and Drabman, R.S. (1977) 'Desensitization to portrayals of real-life aggression as a function of exposure to television violence', *Journal of Personality and Social Psychology*, 35, 450–8.

Tovey, J. (1990) *Radio Times Step-by-Step All-Colour Cookbook*. London: BBC Books.

Turner, K., Turner, J. and Lynn, A.B. (1997) *The Pudding Club Book*. London: Headline.

Vandereycken, W. and Deth, R. van (1990) *From Fasting Saints to Anorexic Girls: The History of Self-Starvation*. London: Athlone Press.

Visser, J., Kroeze, J.H.A., Kamps, W.A. and Bijleveld, C.M.A. (2000) 'Testing taste sensitivity and aversion in very young children: development of a procedure', *Appetite*, 34, 169–76.

Visser, M. (1991) *The Rituals of Dinner: The Origins, Evolution, Eccentricities, and Meaning of Table Manners*. Harmondsworth: Penguin.

Walsh, B.T. and Devlin, M.J. (1998) 'Eating disorders: progress and problems', *Science*, 280, 1387–94.

Warde, A. (1997) *Consumption, Food and Taste: Culinary Antinomies and Commodity Culture*. London: Sage.

Warde, A. and Hetherington, K. (1994) 'English households and routine food practices: a research note', *The Sociological Review*, 42, 4, 758–78.

Warde, A. and Martens, L. (2000) *Eating Out: Social Differentiation, Consumption and Pleasure*. Cambridge: Cambridge University Press.

Waugh, P. (1984) *Metafiction: The Theory and Practice of Self-Conscious Fiction*. London: Methuen.

Whalley, J.I. (1701/1983) *The School of Manners*. London: Oregon Press.

Wiggins, S., Potter, J. and Wildsmith, A. (2001) 'Eating your words: discursive psychology and the reconstruction of eating practices', *Journal of Health Psychology*, 6, 5–15.

Willan, A. (1989) *Reader's Digest Complete Guide to Cookery*. London: Dorling Kindersley.

Winter, E. (1963) *And Not to Yield: An Autobiography*. New York: Harcourt Brace & World Inc.

Woods, S.C., Seeley, R.J., Porte Jr, D. and Schwartz, M.W. (1998) 'Signals that regulate food intake and energy homeostasis', *Science*, 280, 1378–83.

Woods, S.C., Schwartz, M.W., Baskin, D.G. and Seeley, R.J. (2000) 'Food intake and the regulation of body weight', *Annual Review of Psychology*, 51, 255–77.

Woodworth, R.S. and Schlosberg, H. (1954) *Experimental Psychology*. London: Methuen.

Wrigley, N. (1998) 'How British retailers have shaped food choice', in A. Murcott (ed.), *The Nation's Diet: The Social Science of Food Choice*. Harlow: Addison-Wesley Longman.

Name Index

Abelson, R.P.   75, 114
Abensur, N.   116
Acton, E.   187–8
Ainsworth, L.K.   90, 108
Ajzen, I.   2, 44, 114, 209
Alison, D.B.   101
Allport, G.W.   xvi, 197, 208, 209, 210
Anand, K.B.   52
Antaki. C.   15
Asher, K.C.   85
Asher, N.S.   85
Austin, J.L.   204
Axelson, M.L.   2, 14

Bales, R.F.   170
Bandura, A.   85
Bannister, D.   11
Barthes, R.   37–9, 46
Bartoshuk, L.M.   48, 54–5, 68
Basinski, M.   53
Baskin, D.G.   53, 98, 99, 101
Bate-Smith, E.C.   59
Baumeister, R.F.   159
Bear, M.F.   48, 55, 57
Beardsworth, A.   xi, 31
Beauchamp, G.K.   3, 48, 55
Beeton, I.   3, 4, 183, 188, 197
Bell, R.   209–11
Bethany, A.   97
Bijleveld, C.M.A.   207
Billig, M.   47
Birch, L.L.   9
Blanc, R.   190
Booth, D.A.   3, 6, 13, 194, 197
Bourdieu, P.   42–6, 188
Bowie, M.   78
Bredahl, L.   11
Brentano, F.   68

Brinberg, D.   2, 14
Bristow, P.K.   53
Brobek, J.R.   52
Bromley, K.   12, 198
Broodfoot, M.   4
Buchanan, P.   4
Bue-Walleskey, J.M.   53
Bunster, E.   51
Burgett, S.G.   53

Cameron, A.G.   4, 60, 176, 205
Cannon, W.B.   49
Carver, C.S.   96
Chaney, Lisa   141
Charmaz, K.   xvi
Colman, A.   75
Comuzzie, A.G.   101
Condor, S.   xvi, 148–9, 157, 163, 199
Conner, M.   209–11
Connors, B.W.   48, 55, 57
Conran, T.   181
Cooper, Z.   89, 94, 97–8
Coufopoulos, A-M.   21
Cracknell, H.L.   190
Craft, L.   53

David, E.   39
Davidson, A.   179
Davies, G.J.   12
Deth, R. van   75–6, 89
Devlin, M.J.   100
Dirks, R.   17
Dobson, B.M.   17–21
Douglas, M.   34–6, 40, 46
Dowey, A.   9–10, 198
Dowler, E.A.   17–9, 21
Drabman, R.S.   15
Dragstead, C.A.   50
Drèze, J.   14–6

Driauclunas, A.   53
Duffy, V.B.   54, 68

Eastwood, M.   4, 60, 62
Edwards, D.   212
Eibel-Eibesfeldt, I.   2, 197
Einstein, M.A.   10
Elliot, R.   118
Escoffier, A.   188–9
Etzioni, A.   20

Fairburn, C.G.   89, 94, 97–8
Fischler, C.   40
Fishbein, M.   209
Fisher, J.A.   9
Fleming, D.G.   51
Florin, I.   97
Foucault, M.   76
Fox, B.A.   4, 60, 176, 205
Fransella, F.   11
Freud, S.   28, 30
Fuller, J.   36

Gallanter, E.   89
Garfinkel, H.   35, 43, 153
Gleeson, K.   11, 174, 202, 209
Goffman, E.   xiv, 43, 110, 115, 130
Goody, J.   145
Gordon, J.   110, 140, 143–4
Gregory, S.   xi, xii
Greiner, T.   4
Grieshaber, S.   7–8
Griffiths, N.M.   59
Grigson, J.   xix, 188, 191
Grogan, S.C.   209–11
Grossman, M.I.   50
Gura, T.   100

Hale, J.   53
Halliday, M.A.K.   34, 36
Harper, R.   59
Harre, R.   xvi, xvii, 11, 109, 110,
   155, 197, 199, 204, 208
Helman, M.   53
Henley, T.B.   169, 170, 172
Hetherington, A.W.   52
Hetherington, K.   xi
Hoffmann, J.   53
Horne, P.   9–10, 198
Hornstein, I.   10

Horton, R.W.   15
Hsiung, H.M.   53

Janowitz, H.D.   50

Kalat, J.W.   53
Kamps, W.A.   207
Kaufmann, R.J.   190
Kearney, R.   200–1, 209
Keil, T.   xi, 31
Kelley, H.H.   15
Kirwan, B.   90, 108
Kline, M.   28, 46
Knowles, E.S.   164
Koocher, G.P.   164
Kroeze, J.H.A.   56–7, 207
Kulbartz-Klatt, Y.J.   97

Lacan, J.   80, 102
Land, D.G.   59
Langenhove, L. van   xvi, xvii, 194,
   197, 208
Lawson, N.   120, 141, 192
Lerner, M.J.   15
Lévi-Strauss, C.   32–4, 36
Lewin, K.   31, 207
Li, B-H.   xv
Lippincott, E.C.   15
Lipsey, Z.   12
Lloyd, H.   209–10
Lockyer, K.   110, 140, 143–4
Logue, A.W.   6, 13, 48–52, 75
Lowe, C.F.   9–10, 198
Lupton, D.   9, 89
Lyman, B.   6, 10, 12
Lynn, A.B.   37

MacKellar, W.   53
Malson, H.   74, 76–8, 81–2, 88,
   102–3, 194
Mars, V.   9
Martens, L.   xi, 107, 127, 141–2,
   147–8, 160, 199
Maslow, A.H.   19–20, 189, 198
Matter, C.F.   164
McDougall, W.   6
McGee, H.   48, 55–6, 58, 63–5, 70
Meiselman, H.L.   10
Mela, D.J.   209–10
Mennell, S.   13–4, 22, 37, 43
Mennella, J.A.   3

Meyer, R.K.   51
Middlemist, R.D.   164
Miller, G.A.   89
Mitchell, J.   79, 81
Morien, A.   xv
Mullenix, B.   50
Murcott, A.   13–4, 22, 37, 43, 194
Murray, K.D.   207

Nelson, G.   21
Norris, C.   78

Oakley, A.   xii, 197
O'Farrell, M.   176
Ogden, J.   103
Oliver, G.   12
Orbach, S.   84, 86–7, 102
Otterloo, A.H. van   13–4, 22, 37, 43

Paisley, C.   209–10
Palmer, G.   4–5
Paradiso, M.A.   48, 55, 57
Patten, M.   xiii, 36
Pavlov, I.P.   50
Pliner, P.   13
Pollard, T.M.   12
Pollio, H.R.   169, 170, 172
Pook, M.   97
Porte, D. Jr   54
Potter, J.   viii, 10, 13, 46, 74, 76,
    198, 202, 212
Pribram, K.H.   89
Prilleltensky, I.   21

Rachman, S.   97
Ranson, S.W.   52
Rasmusen, K.M.   4
Rawls, J.   20
Reason, J.T.   142
Renold, E.   36
Richards, A.   27
Ricoeur, P.   201, 204, 205
Ritzer, G.   41
Rose, J.   79
Ross, D.   85
Ross, S.A.   85
Rosteck, P.R. Jr   53
Rothenbuhler, E.W.   162
Rotter, J.B.   15, 198
Roustang, F.   79

Roux, A.   190–1
Roux, M.   190–1
Rowland, N.E.   xv
Rozin, E.   13
Rozin, P.   xiv
Rycroft, C.   31

Sachs, M.   4
Sampson, E.E.   158–9
Saussure, F. de   76, 78
Scheier, M.F.   96
Schifferstein, H.N.J.   56–7, 169
Schlosberg, H.   48, 54–9, 69, 168,
    170, 180
Schoner, B.   53
Schwartz, M.W.   53–4, 98, 99, 101
Searle, J.R.   204
Secord, P.F.   11, 109, 110, 155, 199
Seeley, R.J.   53–4, 98, 99, 101
Sen, A.   13–6, 198
Shafran, R.   89, 94, 97–8
Sherif, M.   16, 198
Slater, N.   192
Smith, D.   xix, 53, 67, 118
Smith, J.A.   xvi, xvii, 197, 208
Smith, J.L.   xvi, 2, 16, 90, 115, 210,
    212
Smith, P.B.   212
Sparks, P.   209–10
Spears, R.   xvi
Stainton Rogers, W.   11, 174, 202,
    209
Stalberg-White, C.   13
Stenner, P.   11, 174, 202, 209
Stephens, T.W.   53
Steptoe, A.   12
Stewart, K.   36
Stitt, S.   21
Stratton, P.   12, 198
Stringer, P.   174
Sullivan, O.   xi

Teachman, S.K.   97
Theunissen, M.J.M.   56–7
Thomas, M.H.   15
Thompson, C.J.   169, 170, 172
Tinsley, F.C.   53
Tovey, J.   120, 142, 190
Turner, J.   37
Turner, K.   37

Vandereycken, W.   75–6, 89
Visser, M.   7, 129, 144, 207

Walsh, B.T.   100
Warde, A.   xi, 40–2, 107, 127,
    141–2, 147–8, 160, 173–4, 181,
    183, 186, 199, 200
Wardle, J.   12
Washburn, A.L.   49
Waterman, D.   10
Waugh, P.   154
Wetherell, M.   74, 76

Whalley, J.I.   7, 8
Wiggins, S.   xviii, 10, 13, 46, 198, 212
Wildsmith, A.   xviii, 10, 13, 46, 198,
    212
Willan, A.   xix
Winter, E.   163
Woods, S.C.   53–4, 98, 99, 101
Woodworth, R.S.   48, 54–9, 69, 168
    170, 180
Wrigley, N.   40

Zhang, X-Y.   53

Subject Index

anorexia nervosa   xv, 74–6, 82–4, 102–4
audition   72

babies, feeding   2–6, 29
breast, good   28–30
bulimia nervosa   xv, 74, 102

capital
  cultural   43–6
  economic   43–6
cholecystokinin (CCK)   54, 99
class   37, 39, 42–6, 145, 187–8
cognitive deconstruction   159
cybernetics   89–90, 103–4

desensitisation   14
dieting   71, 74, 83, 90–8, 103, 177
digestion   60–2
dinner party, defined   107–8, 127
discourse, post-structuralist, Lacanian   76–82, 101–2
dramaturgy
  back-stage   134
  front   126

eating, grammar of   34–7
eating out, venues   147
ecclecticism   16
eggs   63–5, 66–71, 73
episode, definition   109
existentialism   20

famine   13–17
fatness   84–8, 102
fish and chips   35
float   143–4
food, preferences   9–13

frame-braking   154, 157

globalisation   41
grazing   40
Guy Fawkes   114

Heisenberg principle   70
hermeneutics   200–9
hierarchical task analysis   108–9
HIV virus   4, 180
homeostatic mechanisms   50–1, 98–9
hunger   49–54
hypothalamus   51–3

interdisciplinarity   194
intergroup conflict   16

just world, belief in   15

kitchen chemistry   63–5, 118

locus of control   15

manners, table   7–9
methodology
  discursive   10, 46, 192
  idiographic   xvi, 66–71, 173, 195, 208
  neomorphogenic   209–12
  nomothetic   xvii, 208, 210–11
  psychophysics   69
  qualitative coding   11–12

neo-tribalism   41
Neuropeptide Y   53, 71, 99–100

phenomenology   166–72, 208
photosynthesis   62

post-Fordism, 40–1
poverty and malnutrition   17–21
project network techniques   140–1,
   144
psychoanalysis   28–31
psychology
   community   20
   critical social   xvi, 148–9, 152, 163
   social   2

reflexivity   148
researcher-voyeur   149

satiety   53–4, 99
self-actualisation   19
self-control   89, 94, 103
self-presentation   43–6
semiology   37–40

sham-feeding   50
smell   57–9, 65, 67, 72
   adaptation   59, 168
   odour prism   57–8, 67
   olfactory epithelium   58
   rubber odour   59
Spotted Dick   36
stomach distention   49, 52
structuralism   31–7

task and critical path analysis   109
taste   54–7, 65, 72
   map   54–6
   sensitivity   56–7
thought–shape fusion   97
triangle
   culinary   31–4, 57–58
   kitchen   181